The Family: Change or Continuity?

ELLIOT, Faith Robertson. The family: change or continuity? Humanities, 1986. 235p bibl indexes 85-27072. 29.95 ISBN 0-391-03392-1; 15.00 pa ISBN 0-391-03393-X. HQ 518. CIP

Elliot's study reflects the macrolevel orientation of its author. Her purpose is to understand contemporary family structures of Western capitalist societies through the frameworks of Marxism, feminism, and functionalism. The data comes mostly from England and Wales, with some materials from elsewhere in Western Europe. The citations are heavily British, but with a sprinkling of pertinent authors in the American sociological tradition. The bibliography is authoritative and current. The subject index and charts are clear, readable, and helpful. Elliot's work is comparable to David A. Schultz's *The Changing Family: Its Function and Future* (3rd ed., 1982) in style, although the latter is not a macrolevel analysis. Elliot's strategy is to apply theoretical analysis to selected topics, supported by previous investigators or empirical data. Most American sociology of the family texts (e.g., Stephen R. Jorgensen's *Marriage and the Family: Development and Change*, 1986) follow a life-cycle perspective, organizing information around sociological concepts. A solid effort to synthesize an almost impossibly large topic. Upper-division undergraduates and above.—*Y. Peterson, Saint Xavier College*

The Family:
Change or Continuity?

Faith Robertson Elliot

HUMANITIES PRESS INTERNATIONAL, INC.
ATLANTIC HIGHLANDS, NJ

First published in 1986 in the United States of America by
Humanities Press International, Inc., Atlantic Highlands, NJ 07716

© Faith Robertson Elliot 1986

Library of Congress Cataloging in Publication Data

Elliot, Faith Robertson.
  The family—change or continuity?

  Bibliography: p.
  Includes indexes.
  I. Family. 2. Family—History—20th century.
I. Title.
HQ518.E43   1986   306.8′5   85-27072
ISBN 0-391-03392-1
ISBN 0−391-03393-X (pbk.)

Printed in Hong Kong

For my family

Contents

List of Tables and Figures

Tables

Figures

Acknowledgements

Robert Chester, Paul Close, Janet Finch, Chris Harris and David Morgan read first or early drafts of particular chapters of this book, while Stephen Edgell, John Selby and Nick Tilley read the penultimate draft of the whole. I am grateful to them all for their constructive, albeit sometimes critical, but always useful comments, for their time and encouragement. There are others who in different ways have also contributed to the production of this book and whom I wish to thank: Robert C. Elliot for stimulating my interest in current developments in family law; my colleagues in the Department of Applied Social Studies, Coventry (Lanchester) Polytechnic – in particular Ken Blakemore, Juliet Edmonds and Brian Ranson, and Robert Gingell in the Department of Legal Studies – who share my interest in the family and in gender for the discussions I have had with them in general or on particular chapters; my students for their interest in this project, in particular Derek Smith and Dave Richardson who commented on one chapter from a student viewpoint; the Polytechnic Library staff for their exceptional helpfulness, courtesy and efficiency; and Sue Page for the equability and skill with which she deciphered my nearly illegible handwriting, typed and retyped the early drafts and produced the final typescript.

FAITH ROBERTSON ELLIOT

The author and publishers wish to thank those who have kindly given permission for the use of copyright material in charts and tables, namely: *The British Journal of Sociology* and Routledge & Kegan Paul for Table 6.3; The Equal Opportunities Commission for Tables 4.3, 4.4 and 4.5; The Controller of Her Majesty's Stationery Office for Tables 4.1, 6.6 and 7.1 and for Figures 6.2 and 6.3; *Population Studies* for Table 6.4; The Registrar General for Tables 6.2 and 6.5; The Statistical Office of the European Communities for Figure 6.1.

1

Introduction

In many modern Western societies, the regulation of sexual and parental relationships has become the subject of vigorous and heated debate. On the one hand, traditional values define sexual relationships, procreation and child-care as properly taking place within a family unit based on lifelong marriage and women's mothering, and the naturalness, importance and moral superiority of 'the family' is asserted. On the other hand, there is pressure for the legitimation of different ways of ordering sexual and parental relationships – such as unmarried cohabitation and/or parenthood, same-sex pairings and multiple sexual relationships – and 'the family' is attacked as an 'oppressive and bankrupt' institution whose 'demise is both imminent and welcome' (Rossi, 1977, p.1). Traditional family ideologies assert that the family is basically the same everywhere, arises out of fundamental biological or societal processes, and is the arrangement that can best provide the stable, intimate relationships necessary to the care and support of children and adults. From this ideological stand, other ways of ordering sexual and parental relationships may be defined as pathological or deviant, and stigmatised. In contrast, alternative life-style ideologies insist on the variability and social nature of sexual and parental relationships and assert that the conventional family, together with women's mothering and men's breadwinning, are the outcome of specific cultural, economic and political processes. From this point of view, alternative arrangements are possible and their legitimation desirable.

Alternatives to 'the family' have been advocated in the past – in certain sections of nineteenth-century socialist and feminist thought, for example. However, contemporary anti-family movements have an exceptional vitality and spring from a wide range of 'causes'. They are part of a more general estrangement from the social order, an element in a counter-culture founded on visions of individual freedom and on beliefs in the viability and desirability of a social life ordered, not by prescribed rules, but by the mutual negotiation

1

of commitments. They also have specific impulses. One such impulse is a revolt by young people against traditional restrictions on sexual behaviour; another is women's protest against their imprisonment within the wife–mother role; a third is pressure for gay liberation; a fourth is the resurgence of Marxist thought and the development of a Marxist critique of 'the family' as an instrument of capitalist oppression; a fifth comes from the development by radical psychiatrists such as Laing and Cooper of a critique of the family as destructive of individuality. These anti-family forces have, in turn, evoked a strong reaction in favour of traditional values and well-organised pro-family groups have emerged on both sides of the Atlantic. The pro-family movement, like the anti-family movement, is an agglomeration of 'causes'; it arises from traditionalist fears about 'permissiveness' becoming 'decadence', from a male backlash against feminist demands, and from attempts by the political Right to resolve the problems of unemployment and rising welfare expenditure by sustaining ideas of the family as a unit of care.

These debates about appropriate ways of ordering sexual relationships, child-care and the roles of men and women are not simply private debates about personal values and codes of conduct. Reproduction and child-care are critical to the social group as a whole and are a matter of public concern and social regulation in every society. Moreover, the 'moral' debate interweaves with 'academic' debates about the origins of 'the family', the forms it takes in different social classes and societies, how and why it changes over time and the interests that particular arrangements serve.

This textbook is about these debates. The primary intent is to provide a dispassionate review of the major sociological accounts of change in the family. However, in the study of the family boundaries between sociological, psychological and political (including feminist) thought are not easily drawn and this book refers to the insights of writers in all these fields.

This introductory chapter is concerned with basics. It looks at the problem of defining the family and highlights the way in which definitions of 'the family' incorporate ideas of what the family ought to be. It also outlines, in very general terms, the way in which the study of the family is approached in two major schools of sociological thought – functionalism and Marxism – and in feminist thought.

Chapter 2 examines the question of the relative role of the biological and the social in shaping the familial. This nature-nurture debate, as it has sometimes been called, is examined in relation to the ubiquity (near universality) of the nuclear family unit, the dependence of the child and the sex-ascribed division of labour.

Chapter 3 considers accounts of the development of the conjugal family as the dominant family form in modern Western societies. It begins with a look at functionalist views of the relationship between urban-industrialisation and the emergence of the nuclear family as a relatively isolated unit concerned primarily with child-rearing and emotional supportiveness. Empirical accounts of change in extra-nuclear kin bonds and in the role of the family are then examined. This is followed by an outline of Marxist views of the relationship between the conjugal family and capitalism. The chapter concludes by examining the construction in religious thought of ideas of the family as a sentimental reality.

Chapter 4 considers relationships within the conjugal family. It looks first at empirical accounts of changes in marriage, parenthood and the roles of women and men, and then at theoretical explanations of gender divisions.

Chapter 5 counterposes traditional images of the conjugal family as a private arena of love and intimacy and present-day images of the conjugal family as supportive of capitalism, oppressive of individuality and oppressive of women. The significance of these ideas of 'the family' for legitimating change in conventional ways of ordering sexual and parental relationships is briefly sketched in.

Chapters 6 and 7 consider changes which are currently taking place in sexual and parental relationships. Chapter 6 considers the legitimation of divorce, the emergence of one-parent families and remarriage families and the restructuring of 'the family' which these developments entail. Chapter 7 explores the search for alternatives to the conjugal family. It provides a general sketch of alternative life-style movements, examines in detail cohabitation, same-sex pairings and group living and ends with an evaluation of the impact of the alternative life-style endeavour on conventional ways of ordering sexual and parental relationships.

A brief epilogue summarises these debates.

The issues discussed in this book have become matters of debate within the context of attempts to understand the structures of Western capitalist societies, and are in different ways and to different degrees relevant to all such societies. However, every society has its own history and for this reason the substantive material used relates to a particular society, Britain (or more specifically and accurately to England), as the birthplace of capitalism, though American theoretical material is also used and some American experiences are recounted by way of comparison and contrast. There are many topics to which limited reference is made; among them sexuality, fertility control and the medicalisation of childbirth, family violence, the family life of the aged, religious, ethnic and regional (and in particular Scottish and Welsh) variation and state regulation. The length and disparateness of this list of 'omissions' is, in itself, indicative of the formidable selection problem which must be confronted in writing a short textbook. Clearly, the scope for debate over inclusions and exclusions is considerable. The choices made here reflect in part the wealth or paucity of the sociological literature and in part the author's predominant concern with macrosocial trends.

1.1   WHAT IS THE FAMILY?

In modern Western societies 'the family' denotes a unit consisting of a husband and wife, and their children. This unit is widely thought of as a group based on marriage and biological parenthood, as sharing a common residence and as united by ties of affection, obligations of care and support and a sense of a common identity. This taken-for-granted conception of what the family *is* clearly reflects traditional beliefs as to the way in which sexual and parental relationships *ought* to be ordered. It also informed some early social science definitions of the family.

However, this way of delimiting the family is problematic. Ball (1974) points out that it conflates two logically distinct categories, 'the household' and 'the family'. The household, he says, is a spatial concept and refers to a group of persons (or a person) bound to a *place* whereas families are groups of persons bound together by ties of blood and marriage. They are thus analytically distinct categories. They are also empirically differentiated because, although families may form households, they do not necessarily or always do so. For example, children may live away from home if they are at boarding school. Conversely, unrelated people – for example, students – may live together and form households but they are not families. The family (a kin group) must therefore be differentiated from the household (a spatial group).

This distinction is critical to our understanding of the family. However, it does not resolve the definitional problem. This is because the range of blood relationships that are used to form familial ties varies considerably: at one extreme, the married couple and their dependent children may be encapsulated within a large-scale cohesive kin group based on descent from a common ancestor; at the other extreme, they may form a more or less independent unit and only a limited range of blood ties may be given social recognition. Moreover, sexual unions and marriage may not coincide, as in unmarried cohabitation. Biological parenthood and social parenthood may also not coincide, as in adoptive families.

So how do we define 'the family'? A recent text (Worsley, 1977, p. 168) asks, do we confine our definition to a group consisting of a legally married couple and their children or do we extend it to include groups such as adoptive families, foster families, cohabiting units and so on? Do we confine our definition of marriage to a union that has been formalised by a legal ceremony or do we extend it to include consensual sexual unions? If so, then at what point does an 'affair' become a 'marriage'? How do we deal with remarriage, same-sex pairings and group marriage? Similarly, do we confine our definition of parenthood to biological parenthood or extend it to include social parenthood such as that found in adoptive families? How do we deal with families who delegate child-care to paid persons, as in the Royal Family and in the Israeli kibbutzim? And how do we deal with residential child-care?

Some writers have sought to resolve these definitional problems by arguing that 'the family' is what a particular social group believes it to be. On this view, the attempt to define 'the family' in a specific way is misconceived because it obscures the diversity of family arrangements. Thus it has been argued that we are all engaged in 'defining "the family" by the ways in which we think and act in relation to those whom we label as family or non-family', that these definitions vary over time, between cultures and even within cultures, and that we should be wary of 'giving the idea of "the" family some fixed "thing-like" quality, thereby perhaps smuggling in some notion of a universal or unchanging family' (Worsley, 1977, pp. 169–70).

This approach to the problem of defining 'the family' is now generally accepted and the old concept of 'the family' has given way to a new concept, that of 'families'. Berger and Berger (1983, pp. 59–65) point out that this change in terminology recognises the empirical fact of diversity *and* reflects a shift in ideological positions.

It reflects, they say, the normative acceptance of diversity and a reluctance to accord any particular arrangement moral superiority as *the* family.

However, this change in terminology does not solve the definitional problem for it raises the question: What is it that is varying but is regarded as familial? Moreover, it leaves us with the problem of labelling and differentiating between the various arrangements that are regarded as familial. For example, we still have the problem of devising a classificatory scheme which will enable us to distinguish between the biological group of parents and their natural children, the adoptive family, the foster family and residential care.

However, although this problem remains unresolved in formal terms, distinctions are made in practice and some have become common currency in sociological discourse. The term 'nuclear family' is used to refer to a unit consisting of spouses and their dependent children. This term, Skolnick (1978, p. 43) notes, is sometimes used to refer to an observable group of people who live together and are set off from the rest of society in tangible ways, but it is also used in an abstract way to denote simply the recognition of bonds between parents and children. This abstract usage treats the form and content of this set of relationships as an empirical question. It does not imply that parents and children live together and act as a unit, or that relationships within nuclear families or between related nuclear families are the same in all societies or historical periods. The term 'the conjugal family' is then used to refer to a family system in which the nuclear family unit is more or less independent of kin and in which the main emphasis is on the marital relationship (Goode, 1963). The conjugal family may be contrasted with the 'extended family', a term used to denote 'any grouping, related by descent, marriage or adoption, that is broader than the nuclear family' (Bell and Vogel, 1968, p. 3.). Distinctions may also be drawn between extended families. One such distinction is that made by Litwak (1960a and 1960b) between the 'classical extended family' – a family system based on the geographical propinquity of related nuclear families, economic interdependence, the authority of extended family groupings over the nuclear family and stress on extra-nuclear kin relationships – and the 'modified extended family' – a loose set of kin relationships in which nuclear families, though geographically dispersed and autonomous, value and maintain extra-nuclear kin relationships. The term 'descent group' is used to refer to a social group based on common descent from a real or mythical ancestor (Abercrombie *et al.*, 1984). Such groups commonly constitute corporate groups in that their members act together and form political and economic units. Finally, as in everyday usage, units which do not consist of a married couple and their children are specifically labelled 'adoptive families', 'one-parent families', 'remarriage families', 'cohabiting units', 'lesbian families' and so on. Common to all these specifications of various types of families is a conception of 'the familial' as referring to social units based on biological reproduction and blood relationships (or simulated blood relationships, as in the adoptive family).

Some of the terms commonly used in the sociological literature in discussing the roles of women and men also need clarification. To begin with, it is now customary to distinguish between women and men as persons with specific biological characteristics and as persons to whom we have attributed specific social attributes. 'Sex' is used to refer to women and men as biologically-differentiated beings while 'gender' is used to refer to women and men as socially-differentiated beings. They may thus be seen as belonging to female/male sex categories and to feminine/masculine gender categories. (The debate which has given rise to this distinction is discussed in Chapter 2.) The phrase 'the sexual division of labour' is commonly used to refer to the ascription of different social tasks to women and men on the basis of sex. It refers in particular to the allocation of primary responsibility for mothering and related nurturant tasks to women, and of primary responsibility for economic activity and the defence of the society to men. This terminology may seem confusing, given the distinction between 'sex' and 'gender', so it must be emphasised that it denotes only that tasks are allocated on the basis of sex, not that women's mothering and men's breadwinning are biological characteristics. The phrase 'sexual relationship' is sometimes used to refer to relationships between men and women in general and sometimes to refer to specific relationships involving physical sexuality. This is confusing and to clarify matters we shall use the phrase 'sexual relationships' to refer only to relationships involving coition and associated activities, while general relationships between men and women will be referred to as 'gender relationships'. The term 'gender inequality' is used to refer to power and status differences between women and men. This concept is distinct from that of the sexual division of labour since it is, in principle, possible for women and men to perform specific tasks and to be equally rewarded, though in practice this rarely seems to happen. In addition, the term 'patriarchy' has come into common use. This term was in the past sometimes used to refer to a type of household in which older men dominate the whole household, including younger men, and it has sometimes been used in this way in feminist discourse. However, it is now more commonly used to refer to the power relationships through which men dominate women.

Finally, a note of caution must be sounded. Many of the terms which have been used to differentiate between family structures or between different aspects of the roles of women and men are, in fact, used in a variety of ways and we need always to be alert to these different usages. The foregoing definitions merely identify what appear to be common and sensible usages of these terms and the way in which they will be used in this text.

1.2   SOCIOLOGY AND THE FAMILY

Two important schools of sociological thought, functionalism and Marxism, provide radically opposed descriptions, explanations and evaluations of contemporary ways of ordering sexual and parental relationships. Functionalism emphasises the importance of the nuclear family to the stability and continuity of society and so meshes with traditional family values. This school of thought dominated the sociology of the family for a long time. However, it has been subjected to extensive criticism and now commands little support, while Marxist perspectives have come to the fore. This trend parallels similar developments in other fields of sociology, but in family sociology it derived a particular impetus from the growth of feminism and from the attempts of Marxist-feminists to reveal the blindness of traditional Marxist thought to the differential positions of women and men in society and to expand Marxist thought in ways that would remedy this 'defect'. Feminism has also produced a specific and distinctive 'radical-feminist' account of the family and of relationships between women and men. Unlike functionalism, Marxist and feminist perspectives challenge the existing social order and advance interpretations of the social world which legitimate demands for change.

Each of these schools of thought has a distinct unity and identity. Nevertheless, there are substantial differences within each approach as well as some similarities between them. Moreover, because they focus on different aspects of the social world and ask different questions, functionalism, Marxism and feminism are in some respects complementary. They are not, of course, the only approaches to the study of the social world, but they are the perspectives in which the most extensive analyses of the social structure of the family and of its changing relationship to other social institutions are to be found. They are therefore the perspectives on which we concentrate, though some phenomenological accounts of the family (those of Berger and Kellner and Laing) are examined in Chapter 5.

This section provides thumbnail sketches of functionalist, Marxist and feminist approaches to the study of the family. It simplifies what are complex theories, glosses over similarities between, and differences within, each of them and highlights their distinctive features so as to provide a basic introduction to the more substantial analyses of later chapters.

Functionalist theories are founded on conceptions of societies as systems of interrelated and interdependent parts and of the parts as having an in-built tendency to adapt to each other so that the society as a whole is in a state of equilibrium or balance. Moreover, the various parts of the society are seen as performing functions (having effects) which contribute to the maintenance, integration and continuity of the whole. This means that social arrangements tend to be accounted for in terms of the functions which they are presumed to serve. It also means that there is an overall emphasis on social integration – that is, on the way in which different parts of the system fit together. Furthermore, change in any one part of the system is seen as leading to change in other parts of the system. Functionalist theorists tend to regard change as slow and evolutionary, and as arising out of processes such as urbanisation and industrialisation which have a momentum of their own. Thus, from the functionalist perspective modern society is an 'urban-industrial society' and its institutions are congruent with urban-industrialisation.

Given this general orientation, functionalist analyses of the family focus on the relationship between the family and other social institutions, seek to establish the way in which change in any part of the society affects the family and to identify the functions which the family performs. There are different approaches to the identification of functions performed by the family and rather different sets of functions have been identified (see Morgan, 1975, for an excellent discussion of various approaches) but, broadly speaking, the nuclear family and the sexual division of labour are seen as arrangements which meet certain basic societal needs, namely the need for the regulation of sexual behaviour and procreation, for child-care and for the socialisation of children into the values of the society. In other words, functionalism tends to treat the nuclear family and women's mothering as performing functions necessary to the survival of the society. These arrangements are in general regarded as universal but they are also depicted as changing in ways that fit with change in other parts of the society so as to meet specific social needs. For example, the nuclear family is very generally seen as having been submerged in wider kin groupings in pre-modern societies, but as becoming relatively independent of other kin in urban-industrial societies (see Chapter 3). Functionalist theory thus asserts that there are constants as well as variants in family structures. It also tends to presume that the family, as we know it, is functioning in ways that maintain the overall stability and integration of the society. There is, says Morgan (1975, p. 59), an overall emphasis on harmony and equilibrium and a strong presupposition that 'functional' equals 'highly important' in functionalist accounts of the family.

Marxist theory, a large, diverse and complex body of social and political thought founded on the theories of Karl Marx (1818–83) provides a radical alternative to functionalism. Marx's conception of the social world is based on the simple observation that human beings must produce food and material objects in order to survive. Productive activity is therefore, Marx argued, central to the ordering of society. He maintained that the forces and relations of production form a base for all other aspects of the social order (the family, education, political and legal institutions, systems of knowledge, belief and value systems and so on). Marx in that way drew a distinction between base (constituted of the forces and relations of production) and superstructure (the other elements of the social order) and maintained that the character of the superstructure is congruent with the character of the base. Marx further contended that the crucial feature in the social organisation of production is the division of society into two opposing classes on the basis of ownership or non-ownership of the means of production. Thus, in writing of capitalist society, Marx described a fundamental class division between a capitalist class who owned the means of industrial production and a non-property-owning proletariat who, having nothing but their labour power (capacity to work), perforce sold this to the capitalist in return for a wage. Moreover, Marx maintained that ownership of the means of production brings not only wealth but also political power; he thus saw the property-owning classes as dominant and the non-owning classes as subordinate and oppressed. However, Marx also believed that social relations are historically specific and subject to change. In his view, humankind's capacity to produce is constantly developing as technology expands. Developments in the forces of production give rise to contradictions (tensions) in the social order and to change in the social relations of production. At certain moments in time, class conflicts erupt and, ultimately, the existing relations of production are swept away and a new social order based on a new mode of production comes into being. Thus, for Marx class conflict is endemic in the social order and change comes about, not through a gradual evolutionary process, but as a result of conflict between opposing forces.

Marx's treatment of the family is not entirely consistent with his central arguments and is fragmentary. McDonough and Harrison (1978) say that Marx seems to have viewed the family as a natural institution for the propagation of the human species and as lying outside the relations of production. As a consequence, he treated the family as peripheral to, and of marginal interest in the analysis of, social life. Marx's collaborator, Engels, developed an elaborate but problematic evolutionary account of the origins of the monogamous nuclear family (see Section 3.3). Thereafter, the family was more or less neglected in Marxist thought and it is only in recent years that significant Marxist accounts of the family have been developed.

Broadly speaking, Marxist accounts of the family take as their starting-point the premise that 'the family is ultimately dependent upon the dominant mode of production for its existence and form' (Seccombe, 1974, p. 5), and emphasise the impact of dominant class interests on family structure and functioning. However, Marxist thought is elaborated in diverse ways. In some strands of Marxism the superstructure is said to be determined by the base in a fairly direct way. In line with this approach, ways of ordering sexual and parental relationships (like other aspects of the superstructure) may be seen as shaped by the material conditions and interests of the dominant class. This understanding of Marxism has led to economic reductionism and to somewhat static structural analyses in which capitalism is depicted as requiring and producing a certain family form which sustains the capitalist mode of production. For example, some writers have seen the modern family as reproducing a labour force for capitalism, socialising children into values which maintain the capitalist system and providing a refuge from, and counterbalance to, the oppressions of the workplace (see Section 3.3). On the other hand, some elaborations of Marxist thought posit only a general correspondence between base and superstructure and allow for the relative autonomy of social institutions. They may seek to show how capitalism developed out of, and acted upon, pre-existing social forms or they may emphasise class struggles, contradictions within the social order and pressures for change. Thus some Marxist writers (for example, Barrett, 1980, whom we discuss in Section 4.2) suggest that family forms, though transformed by the development of the capitalist mode of production, bear the imprint of their pre-capitalist pasts, and others (for example, Humphries, 1977, to be dealt with in Section 3.3) have shown that family forms are shaped by the class struggle and may reflect the interests of the working class.

In mainstream functionalist and Marxist accounts of the social world 'man' is the reference point, the 'norm' against which all else is measured. *Feminist theories* seek to redress this balance. They take 'woman' as their starting-point to which all else is to be related, assert women's subordination to men and seek to describe and explain the world from woman's position of subordination (Spender, 1985). Marxist-feminists take as their question the relation of women to the economic system. They explain women's subordination to men in terms of their position in the relations of production and utilise and expand Marxist theory to argue that capitalism uses women for the tasks involved in reproducing the labour force (the rearing and socialisation of children and the servicing of men) and as a reserve army of labour. In contrast, radical-feminist thought takes as its question the relation of women to men, explains women's subordination in terms of that relation and emphasises men's power over women rather than capitalist domination. For radical-feminists, social relationships in all societies are based on male domination and gender divisions (not class divisions) constitute the basis of social life. This perspective leads to a view of modern society as patriarchal and of the family as shaped by patriarchal imperatives. More specifically, the sexual division of labour is seen as securing personal domestic services for men and the family is seen as socialising girls and boys into their sex-designated roles and thereby reproducing the patriarchal order. From this point of view, the family is an institution that oppresses women. Pressures for change are seen as stemming from women's struggle to establish a social order based on gender equality.

Functionalist, Marxist and feminist approaches to the family are in certain respects similar. They each see social institutions as inter-related and the family as consonant with and in some measure adapted to other social institutions. Moreover, in each approach, the family is seen as playing a critical role in biological reproduction and in social reproduction (that is, in maintaining, replenishing and transmitting social values and structures from generation to generation). However, as the foregoing account has shown, functionalist, Marxist and feminist approaches to the family have different starting-points, focus on different aspects of the social world and provide different kinds of explanations of the relationship between the family and other social institutions. Functionalist approaches to the 'modern' family take as their starting-point the notion of society as an integrated whole and as their frame of reference urban–industrial society, and see the family as serving fundamental societal needs. Marxist models take as their starting-point the notion of society as class divided and as their frame of reference capitalism, and see the family as structured by capitalist imperatives. Radical-feminist theories take as their starting-point gender divisions, and as their frame of reference partriarchy, and see the family as the primary site of patriarchal power. Thus, functionalist models see the family as reproducing members of society and values which are generally shared; Marxist models see the family as reproducing a labour force for capitalism and capitalist values and relations, while radical-feminism sees the family as reproducing a patriarchal social order. Marxist models highlight class conflict and exploitation, radical-feminist models highlight gender conflict and exploitation. By contrast, functionalist models see co-operation and consensus rather than conflict and oppression as inherent in the system and highlight the positive aspects of family living.

The different accounts which functionalism, Marxism and feminism provide of the relationship between the family and society are more or less supportive of change in that relationship. Functionalism, with its positive evaluation of the family as important and valuable, its stigmatisation of alternatives and its emphasis on stability and the maintenance of the social order, provides support for traditional family values. Conversely, Marxist and feminist theories provide a critical analysis of the family and society and so lend support to demands for change.

2

Family Structures: Biological or Social?

The role played by human biology in the social organisation of sexual and parental relationships is a central issue in contemporary family debates. Though the arguments are diverse, three broad positions may be identified.

The first and most traditional position insists on the fundamental importance of biology. It asserts that the nuclear family and the sexual division of labour arise almost naturally and universally out of the conditions of human reproduction. This mode of explanation assumes that biology limits the variability of family patterns, that some familial behaviours are instinctive and unlearned, and that there is continuity between the behaviour and characteristics of animals, primates and human beings. This argument is advanced in the biological and psychological sciences, is found in various forms in functionalist sociology, and is commonly used to 'back up' traditional beliefs in the naturalness and moral superiority of the nuclear family.

The second position denies biology a role in the organisation of sexual and parental relationships and insists that the nuclear family and the roles of women and men are socially constructed. This mode of explanation suggests that family patterns are shaped by economic, political and ideological processes. It assumes that human nature is pliable and social arrangements variable, that the behaviour of humans and animals is discontinuous, and that family roles are learned. This position is espoused in the main strands of feminist thought and in Marxist theory. It is commonly used to 'back up' beliefs in the cultural relativity of moral values and the desirability of legitimating alternatives to the nuclear family.

The third set of arguments suggests that, while there is variability in the needs of the child and in parental and sexual relationships, there are also basic continuities so that both biological and social factors must be taken into account. This argument suggests that our task is to chart the limits of the biological and the social and to determine how they interrelate.

These arguments are explored in this chapter in relation to the ubiquity of the nuclear family, the needs of the child and the roles of women and men.

2.1   THE NUCLEAR FAMILY

Many early accounts of the organisation of sexual and parental relationships stress the existence of certain biological imperatives, namely the necessity of procreation to the survival of the species, the lengthy physical and psychological dependence of the child and the need for security in sexual relationships. They also assume that these imperatives merge to produce a biological group, the nuclear family. For example, Linton's (1949) account of the nuclear family posits a permanent heterosexual relationship resting on innate physical and psychological needs. For Linton these are: (i) the constant sexual activity and dominance of the male which operates to enable men to keep particular women for themselves and to prevent these women from bestowing their favours elsewhere; (ii) a basic need for security in personal relationships and for congenial companionship, and (iii) the dependence of the child which necessitates permanent matings so as to ensure male assistance for the mother in caring for offspring. Linton suggests that this family unit differs little from similar units among other primates. In an often-cited account, Murdock (1968) claims, on the basis of a cross-cultural examination of 250 societies, that the nuclear family is a 'universal human grouping'. The nuclear family, says Murdock, may form an autonomous unit or it may be embedded in larger kinship groups. There may be sexual licence and there may be polygamous families formed by the marriage of one man to two or more women or one woman to two or more men. But whatever 'larger family forms' exist, the nuclear family always constitutes a unit apart from the remainder of the community. Its universality, says Murdock, is explained by its utility in performing tasks necessary to the survival of the species and to social continuity, namely the regulation of sexual relationships, reproduction, the socialisation of children and economic co-operation between the sexes. Murdock further argues that, though each of these activities could be performed by other institutions, their fusion within a single institution, the nuclear family, means that the performance of each task is reinforced and improved by the performance of the other tasks. The ordering of sexual relationships, reproduction, child-rearing and the economic support of family members are, says Murdock, closely interrelated tasks; they are therefore best performed if fused within a single institution.

Standing in opposition to the foregoing thesis is the argument that ways of ordering sexual and parental relationships are variable and socially structured. This position rests in the first place on the theoretical argument that reproduction, socialisation and the regulation of relationships between the sexes, though necessary to social life, are not necessarily and inevitably fused within the nuclear family. Harris (1969), for example, maintains that infancy necessitates child-care but that child-care can in principle be undertaken by adults who are not the genetic parents of the child. Harris further argues that the father is a weak link in the biological group since his role in procreation is limited and there is no biological need for him to wait around for nine months for the birth of his child. Therefore, Harris continues, the existence of the nuclear family as a group depends on a *social* arrangement – marriage – whereby the genetic father is bound to the mother for her help and support.

This line of argument suggests that mate relationships are separable from parental relationships and sees the nuclear family as the outcome of social processes rather than of biological imperatives. It is reinforced by empirical arguments which seek to show that the nuclear family is not in fact a universal family form. This claim is most usually supported by pointing to various arrangements in which the biological father is absent from the household and plays little part in child-rearing.

The most commonly cited type of 'father-absence' is an arrangement in which the mother's male kin assume many aspects of the father role. Where this happens, the biological father is only marginally involved in the life of his own children but may be social father to his sister's children. The Nayar, a warrior caste found in south-west India, provides an extreme example of this pattern. According to the reconstruction in Gough (1968) of traditional Nayar patterns, Nayar girls before they reached puberty were ceremonially paired with a man from a lineage which had ritual links with their own lineage. The pairing carried no obligation other than that the bride perform appropriate rituals for her husband on his death, and the couple were not required to have further contact with each other. However, the bride was accorded adult status and now had the right to receive 'lovers'. In general, Nayar women had a small but not a fixed number of lovers or 'visiting husbands' and could, in addition, receive casual visitors. Children belonged to the mother's lineage and their guardianship, care and economic support was the concern of the matrilineal kinsfolk. Biological paternity was often uncertain, but as a child whose father was of an inappropriate caste could not be admitted into his mother's lineage, it was essential that a man of the appropriate caste acknowledge paternity by paying the midwife's fee. Beyond this, biological paternity was of little social significance. Thus, according to Gough, individual Nayar men did not have significant rights in their particular 'wives' or children and the nuclear family was not institutionalised.

A second 'variation' from the biological family group is that in which the biological father is absent from the family group and the mother secures another man as her lover/husband and as father to her children. The child may then have two 'fathers' – the mother's current lover/husband and its biological father. This pattern arises where lifelong monogamy is replaced by serial mating (a succession of sexual partners). It is increasingly found in contemporary Western societies as a result of trends towards divorce and remarriage (see Chapter 6) and cohabitation (see Chapter 7).

Serial mating also creates female-headed households, that is, situations in which women spend periods of their lives between mates and without effective male support in caring for children. This maternal dyad, or matrifocal unit as it is sometimes called, is also commonly cited as evidence of the non-universality of the biological family group. In contemporary Western societies marital breakup frequently results in female-headed households but the father is expected to support his child even though he is no longer attached to the mother (see Chapter 6). However, in low-income black communities in the West Indies and the United States, marriage is not institutionalised and many women have transient relationships with a number of men. The resultant children are the woman's responsibility. The mother-child unit may go through stages when there is a man attached to it and when it is effectively a nuclear family but most women, with the assistance of female kin, are both mothers and fathers to their children for much of their lives.

In all the 'departures' from the nuclear family so far discussed, biological motherhood remains firmly fused with social motherhood. However, instances in which the biological mother is missing from the family can also be cited. Contemporary patterns of marriage, divorce and remarriage produce father–child units as well as mother–child units and remarriage families with stepmothers as well as remarriage families with stepfathers (see Chapter 6). In foster families and adoptive families the biological mother as well as the biological father are replaced by social parents. In the Israeli kibbutzim children live separately from their parents in *bet yeladim* (children's houses) for much of the time, are cared for and socialised by nurses and teachers and are supported economically by the community (Spiro, 1968). Child-care is thus separated not only from the sexual partnership but also from biological motherhood and is extensively delegated to professional child-carers.

As is evident from the foregoing review, much of the argument as to the biological or social origins of the nuclear family revolves round the empirical question of its universality or non-universality. Moreover, the evidence of exceptions to the nuclear family which exponents of the social nature of the family argument have presented is sometimes regarded as ending the debate. Nevertheless, there are further issues to be raised and these point to a less dogmatic conclusion.

First, exponents of biological arguments can claim that there is variation in nature. Second, disagreement over what constitutes the nuclear family means that the same arrangement may be seen both as constituting a nuclear family and as a breach of the nuclear family principle, depending on the definition used. For example, the kibbutz has been seen as departing from the nuclear family because parents and children do not share a common residence, the relationship of spouses is not characterised by mutual economic support and child-care is in the hands of professional child-rearers. However, it has also been seen as having nuclear families because parents and children form distinct units based on psychological identifications with each other (Spiro, 1968). Third, it is clear that the nuclear family is a very common social form. It is found either as an autonomous unit or as part of a larger kinship structure in widely varied social and economic contexts – in simple hunting and gathering societies, in agrarian societies and in industrial societies. We have therefore to explain why procreation and basic child-care are so generally located in the nuclear family and in such diverse situations.

Harris (1969), though he does not believe the nuclear family to be a biological inevitability, suggests that it is difficult to avoid having something like the family if humankind is to reproduce itself. Harris emphasises that men and women must everywhere procreate and care for children if life is to continue. He also argues that the need which children appear to have for stable, warm relationships with adults (see next section) rules out arrangements based on impersonal relationships and presumes particularistic relationships. The biological parents, says Harris, are the obvious, though not the inevitable, candidates for this child-care task. Further, Harris claims that as child-rearing requires economic co-operation between the sexes and the co-residence of rearers and children, it would be absurd not to use as rearers people having a sexual relationship with one another. We should thus end up with a group like the family but without biological parenthood were parents not used as rearers.

This line of argument suggests that there are biological realities which, though not determining, constrain us in working out effective social arrangements and commonly lead to the formation of nuclear family units. However, to say this is not to say very much about family organisation. As later chapters will make clear, relationships within the nuclear family – between spouses, between parents and children, and between siblings – are elaborated in many and varying ways. Further, the nuclear family may exist as an independent unit or as part of a larger kinship group. Furthermore, relationships between the nuclear family and other social institutions are complex and diverse. All these elements of family life are clearly 'social' and must be explained in social terms.

2.2   THE NEEDS OF THE CHILD

We found in the previous section that explanations of the ubiquity of the nuclear family rely heavily on the argument that the child has a basic physiological need for stable, intimate relationships. This latter thesis is the concern of this section.

The 'children-need-stable-relationships' argument owes much to Bowlby's (1953) account of the consequences of 'maternal deprivation' for personality development. Bowlby argues that a 'warm, intimate and continuous relationship' between mother (or mother-substitute) and child is essential to healthy personality development and that physical, intellectual and emotional development are impaired where the child is without such a relationship. Bowlby based this thesis on his own and other studies of children reared in institutional environments. These studies seemed to show that children who experience residential care and/or a succession of carers and who as a result have been deprived of stable and close relationships with a major mother-figure are unable to receive or give love, are compelled to adopt a career of destructive anti-social relationships and in extreme cases become psychopathic personalities.

In a later development of his thesis, Bowlby (1969) seeks to show how and why children are adversely affected by maternal deprivation. He argues that the human infant is predisposed by a number of instinctual response systems to form a particular attachment to its primary carer, who will normally be its mother. This tie develops in a regular way and is usually well-established by the time the infant is one year old. If it is disrupted, the child experiences anxiety while prolonged separation from, or total loss of, the mother impairs the child's ability to form stable relationships, and has a variety of long-lasting detrimental consequences. Bowlby maintains that the various instinctive responses which lead to attachment to the mother or primary carer – crying, gazing, grasping and smiling, for example – have a bio-evolutionary origin; they are responses which enhance the infant's chance of survival by increasing closeness to the mother and protection from predators.

The Bowlby thesis is opposed by the argument that the importance of the mother–child bond – and therefore the consequences of maternal deprivation – is mediated by the socio-economic environment. This argument states that where, as in present-day Western societies, primary child-care is located in an isolated nuclear family unit and revolves round the mother–child bond, the child's primary attachments are to the mother. However, attachments to persons other than the mother or multiple relationships will, it is argued, develop where the environment provides opportunities for such attachments. This argument is supported by a longitudinal study (Schaffer and Emerson, 1964) of sixty infants in their first eighteen months. This study found that some babies developed a tie with more than one other person and that even where the attachment object was one person the bond was not restricted to the infant's mother. The sole bond of a few infants was with their father or grandparent. Further, data from other cultures seem to suggest that where child-rearing is shared with others multiple relationships develop. Fox (1977) found that in the Israeli kibbutzim, where child-rearing is shared between parents and professional child-rearers, mothers and child-carers are interchangeable attachment figures. Moreover, Bettelheim (1969) found little evidence of mental illness, high anxiety states and delinquency among kibbutz children. Oakley (1976) maintains that in Samoa, where children are reared in households of between fifteen and twenty people and are cared for by many adults, children learn not to care for one person greatly and separation from the mother does not mean the loss of a fundamental relationship. Maternal deprivation, says Oakley, is a syndrome of a culture oriented around the mother–child bond which in turn occurs where primary child-care is located in an isolated nuclear family unit. Wortis (1974) makes a similar argument. Wortis says that Bowlby's theory of attachment behaviour assumes that the natural mother is present and that the infant is biologically structured to adapt to it. This neglects the wide range of socio-cultural environments in which children are in fact reared. It also idealises the Western situation: it obscures the ambivalence of many mothers towards their children and the limited experiences and relationships available to children in many nuclear family units.

Arguments for the social construction of childhood have been advanced from another and more general angle. Some scholars claim that the incompetence and dependence of the child and our beliefs in its psychological vulnerability are peculiarly modern and Western and that much that we think of as 'childish nature' is the product of our special treatment of the child rather than the cause of it. Thus Ariès (1962) has argued that in the Middle Ages infant-care and child-care were focussed on physical well-being, children were exposed to the realities of the adult world from an early age and little value was placed on ties of affection between parents and children. Ariès maintains that images of the special and fragile nature of childhood emerged only between the fifteenth and seventeenth centuries. He also claims that it was during this period that childhood became a prolonged period of dependence separated from the world of adults and perceived as having special needs. Childhood, Ariès's argument suggests, is a social invention (see pp. 70–1 for further elaboration).

The experimental and anthropological evidence presented by opponents of the Bowlby thesis strongly suggests that it does not matter *to the child* whether its rearers are its biological parents or some other person. The child can, it seems, form bonds with persons other than the biological parents and can form multiple bonds. The evidence also strongly suggests that beliefs in the importance of the mother–child relationship and the fragility and dependence of the child are peculiarly Western and peculiarly modern. However, the Bowlby argument has not been entirely vanquished: there are counter-considerations which suggest that the needs of the child and commitments to biological parenthood are not entirely social but are the outcome of the complex interaction of biological and social processes. Three considerations point in this direction.

First, it is not clear that adults can respond in a particularistic way to any child. Bowlby (1969) contends that a substitute mother's responses to an infant may be less strong and less consistently elicited than those of a natural mother. He explains this in terms of the hormonal changes occurring during pregnancy, childbirth and lactation which, he says, increase the natural mother's maternal capacity and lay a basis for continued mothering behaviour. This evidence is however inconclusive and may be countered by evidence which shows that infants activate care-taking behaviour in virgin females and in men as well as in parturient females (Chodorow, 1978).

Second, and more importantly, the central plank of the maternal deprivation thesis – the notion that the infant and young child need warm, intimate and stable relationships so that bonds with others may be formed and healthy psychological development take place – has not been overturned. A considerable body of research (reviewed by Rutter, 1981) provides general support for Bowlby's contention that a multiplicity of carers and/or a succession of carers have deleterious consequences for children. This suggests that children, though they can form multiple bonds and though their main bond need not be with their mother nor even with their primary carer, have difficulty in forming secure bonds when they have a great number of carers. One recent review of the literature (Smith, 1980) suggests that this is because carers who do not have constant contact with the children in their care have difficulty in understanding and predicting their behaviour and thus fail to achieve a mutually-rewarding relationship with them. It has also been pointed out by Ainsworth (1965) that the maternal deprivation thesis is not undermined by accounts of the viability of the collective child-rearing structures of the kibbutzim and of small-scale horticultural societies. In her view, the evidence does not show that a major mother-figure is missing from such structures or that care is discontinuous and unstable. She suggests that there is in these structures a partial dispersal of child-care responsibility among a few adults among whom there is a high degree of continuity, and parents are potentially available as central foci of identification. Ainsworth also contends that the partial dispersal of child-care is compatible with the maternal deprivation thesis since the latter is an argument for a major mother-figure and for continuous intimate relationships, not for an exclusive mother–child relationship.

Third, the now considerable evidence of the 'failure' of child-rearing arrangements having multiple and/or changing care-takers indicates that the child is 'best off' when reared in primary (small, affectionate, face-to-face) groups. This raises the question: 'What are the primary groups available to us for child-care?' Harris (1969) suggests, as we noted in the last section, that the nuclear family is the most readily available primary group. Moreover, Harris and Firth *et al.* (1969) advance arguments that point to the particular suitability of the nuclear family to the child-care task. Harris says that the social recognition of biological relationships presents us not simply with familial relationships but with particular people as our family. Unlike the ties of friendship, neighbourhood, workplace and class, the ties of blood are unique to the individual. Firth *et al.* (1969) emphasise that blood relationships, if socially recognised, are presented to us at birth and so have a pre-established built-in character. These arguments suggest that blood ties are uniquely suited to the task of constituting particularistic (personal, non-substitutable) relationships. They also suggest that biological and social factors combine to produce a social commitment to biological parenthood.

Some caveats must however be added. First, all indicators of child development contain implicit value judgements as to what constitutes 'normal' or 'successful' development. Second, the suitability of the nuclear family to the child-care task does not mean that the nuclear family automatically or naturally comes into being. Conversely, it cannot be assumed that the *effect* of the nuclear family – its suitability for child-rearing – is the *cause* of its existence. Third, a commitment to biological parenthood does not necessarily mean that child-rearing will be located exclusively in the nuclear family. Throughout history parents have been assisted, sometimes to a very considerable extent, by varying categories of other people – by kin and older children, by wet-nurses, child-minders, nannies and governesses and, in modern times, by day-nurseries and playgroups as well as by the school and a vast array of health and social services. Thus, the content of parental roles has varied considerably. Finally, the ubiquity of the nuclear family as a child-rearing unit does not mean that it is unproblematic. As later chapters make clear, tensions, contradictions and dilemmas permeate the modern version of the nuclear family.

2.3 THE SEXUAL DIVISION OF LABOUR

Finally, we come to the question of the sexual division of labour – that is, to the allocation of primary responsibility for child-rearing and general caring activities to women, and for economic provision and the defence of the society to men – and to associated images of women as nurturant and dependent and of men as go-getting, aggressive and independent.

Most biologically based accounts of these arrangements revolve round the notion that the roles of men and women in human reproduction give rise to 'natural predispositions' which, though they may be modified by culture, are a basic influence on behaviour. Thus women's child-rearing and presumed nurturant capacity are explained in terms of their role as bearers of children while men's breadwinning, together with their domination of the economic, political and military arenas, are explained negatively in terms of their minimal role in reproduction and/or positively in terms of their presumed greater physical strength and aggressiveness. Rationales as to why the different reproductive roles of men and women should give rise to a sexual division of labour may be sought in bio-evolutionary processes believed to be favourable to species survival and in sex differences in hormonal functioning.

The bio-evolutionary argument was first advanced in the late nineteenth century by social Darwinian theorists such as Bagehot and Spencer and is now being reformulated in various ways by a school of thought known as socio-biology. Rossi (1977) utilises this perspective to argue that women have a natural capacity for parenting and that men do not. She argues that, because more than 90 per cent of human history was lived in hunting and gathering societies and because our 'most recent genes' derive from this longest period of human history, the adaptations and selection processes that were then essential to species survival are built into our genetic heritage. According to Rossi, reproductive success in these societies went to males equipped with the skill for big-game hunting and group defence and to females capable of two conjoint activities: bearing and rearing their young, and hunting small game and gathering food within the restricted geographical range compatible with infant-care and child-care. Female activities involved manual dexterity, physical and emotional endurance and persistence, while male activities involved body stature, shoulder strength and visual sharpness. These adaptations equipped men and women with different physiological propensities which shape the ease with which they learn different skills. Thus, Rossi argues, men as a group are less apt than women at infant handling and food preparation.

Tiger and Fox (1971) use a similar argument to explain the dominance, aggressiveness and competitive bonding which they assume to be common features of male behaviour and which, in their view, underpin men's occupation of positions of power. Human beings, they argue, are 'programmed' or equipped with genetically-based predispositions which were evolved by our primate ancestors and which reflect successful adaptations to a hunting and gathering way of life. 'Nothing worth noting' they say 'has happened in our evolutionary history since we left off hunting and took to the fields and the towns. . . .; we are still man the hunter' (Tiger and Fox, 1971, p. 21), and are in some degree genetically programmed to that way of life. In hunting and gathering societies, males hunted and were responsible for the protection of the band and for alliances or combat with other bands. Consequently, say Tiger and Fox, men are programmed for aggressive activity and for competitive bonding and come to monopolise positions of power – in modern industrial societies as well as in primitive hunting societies. Women, on the other hand, are seen by Tiger and Fox as programmed for reproduction and nurturant activity; they believe that nature intended mother and child to be together and that a close emotional mother–child bond is a biologically-based predisposition for both.

Differences between men and women in hormonal functioning have also been used to explain women's mothering and men's occupancy of dominant positions. Two prongs of this many-pronged thesis are of particular interest to us. First, it is argued that the 'female hormones' associated with pregnancy, childbirth and lactation stimulate in parturient females caring responses to the newborn infant and so provide a physiological basis for mothering (which men lack). Second, it is argued that the sex hormones which affect the development of reproductive organs also affect the brain during pre-natal development so as to produce behavioural and psychological differences between men and women; for example, the male hormone, testosterone, is said to be associated with aggressiveness and to inhibit nurturant behaviour. These arguments are made in various ways and may be advanced on their own or in conjunction with a bio-evolutionary argument (as in the work of Rossi). They are largely based on studies of persons with hormonal abnormalities and on animal experiments (which, for example, have observed the effects of priming female rats with male hormones, and of priming male and virgin non-parturient female rats with the hormones associated with pregnancy and childbirth). Detailed accounts of many of these studies and of the debates that surround them may be found in Archer and Lloyd (1982).

Except in their cruder versions, these bio-evolutionary and hormonal functioning arguments do not assert that biology totally determines sex-roles. They assert only that men and women have certain natural predispositions on which a social superstructure is constructed. For example, Rossi (1977) says only that women and men have different *propensities for learning* particular skills and that compensatory training could fit men for child-care, while Tiger and Fox (1971) say that predispositions are modified by culture. Gender roles are thus seen as varying around a common biological core and as similar between cultures only at a broad level of generality.

Standing in opposition to these biological arguments is the argument that the roles of men and women are variable and that this variability points to their social construction. It is then also argued that men and women are socialised into, and learn the roles prescribed for them by, their culture. From this perspective, femininity and masculinity are not universally and naturally given but are constructed within specific cultural settings.

One of the earliest and most frequently cited accounts of variability in the roles of women and men is Mead's (1935) study of three neighbouring New Guinea tribes. Mead suggests that social roles may be undifferentiated by sex or may reverse the stereotypes found in modern Western societies. She reports that among the Arapesh both sexes demonstrate traits that we define as 'feminine'. Self-assertion and competitiveness are disapproved of, and nurturance approved of, in men as well as women. Among the Mundugamor, on the other hand, both sexes are aggressive and ruthless and enmity permeates all social relationships, including the mother-child relationship. The Tchambuli reverse many of our accepted role patterns: the women are aggressive and impersonal in their orientations, the men emotionally dependent; the women work in the fields, trade and manage the affairs of the society, the men look after the domestic sphere, adorn themselves and gossip.

Oakley (1976) provides a relatively recent account of cultural variability in the roles of men and women. She suggests that men's and women's roles are minimally differentiated in some societies. For example, among the Mbuti Pygmies, a hunting and gathering society found in the Congo Rain Forests, both sexes share responsibility for child-care and both sexes hunt. She further claims that in some societies – for example among the people of the Indonesian island, Alor – mothers engage in productive work that takes them away from the home base, while the father, older children or other women perform child-care functions. Furthermore, there is, says Oakley, extensive evidence from various cultures of women's involvement in heavy manual work – in lumbering, land clearance, building and construction, agriculture and mining. In Oakley's view, this proves that work demanding physical strength need not be a male preserve. Similarly, Oakley points to women's involvement in the armed forces of China, of the USSR, Cuba and Israel as evidence that combat, like physical work, is not necessarily a male preserve. Differences in the roles of men and women, in Oakley's view, are socially, not biologically, determined and 'sex' must be distinguished from 'gender' (see p. 7 for the definition of these terms).

The argument that men's and women's roles are culturally prescribed presumes that men and women, far from instinctively acting in ways that are 'natural' to them, are socialised from birth onwards into adopting culturally-prescribed behaviour, personality traits and roles. Moreover, a massive body of social psychological research (see Archer and Lloyd, 1982, or Lott, 1981, for recent reviews), has shown that children – and adults – are constantly presented with particular models of femininity and masculinity and that their conformity with these models is expected and encouraged. The literature suggests that in Western societies this happens in three ways. First, children are gender-labelled. They are designated female or male at birth, given a sex-appropriate name and sex-typed clothing and have sex-appropriate appellations applied to them. They are told that they are girls 'just like mummy' or boys 'just like daddy', that 'girls do this' and 'boys do that', that they are 'good girls' or 'bad boys'. Sex-appropriate physical attributes and temperament are ascribed at a very early stage and even in infants the same behaviour may be interpreted in different ways depending on their sex. Second, children's activities and interests are channelled in the directions thought appropriate to their sex. The research literature emphasises that they are given sex-differentiated toys and games, presented with stereotyped images of femininity and masculinity in books and television programmes and trained in sex-appropriate skills. Third, behaviour thought to be sex-appropriate or inappropriate is rewarded and punished by parents, teachers, and other children. Lott (1981) says that ultimately sex-inappropriate behaviour may be 'punished' by being labelled 'maladjusted' or 'deviant'. She suggests that aggression, which in boys is seen as 'normal', in girls may be referred to child-guidance clinics. Similarly boys, but not girls, who display passivity and emotionality may be referred to child-guidance clinics.

Some explanations of gender divisions take both the biological and the social into account. This approach seeks to remedy the 'defects' which, it is argued, are found in 'hard' or 'pure' versions of both the biological and the social-construction arguments.

The biological argument is based on the assumption that men and women have certain natural predispositions which are important influences on their social roles. However, critics of this position maintain that the existence of such natural predispositions has not been demonstrated. Chodorow (1978) says that the bio-evolutionary hypothesis that aptitudes adaptive or necessary for group survival in hunting and gathering societies have become genetically embedded is difficult to substantiate given the complexity of our genetic make-up. Chodorow also claims that the hormonal functioning argument is based on data which is at best inconclusive. In her view, studies of people with hormonal abnormalities do not adequately test the thesis, since we do not know whether such people were treated in the same way as 'normal' people, and accounts of hormonal functioning among animals may not be valid for humans. It has also been argued that there is so little continuity between infant-care and all the manifold tasks connected with the care of older children that it is hard to see how a biological capacity to rear infants (assuming this exists) could extend to all child-care tasks. Similarly, Sayers (1982) points out that the attempt to explain men's position in the public world in terms of male aggression means that we must equate game-hunting in early human societies with wage-earning in modern societies and dominance behaviour among primates with modern status-seeking. Moreover, the whole biological argument seems to ignore the fact that women, although they have primary responsibility for child-care, may also undertake a very wide range of productive activities (as will be shown in Chapter 4). These arguments suggest that it is difficult to sustain an argument based on the determining influence of natural predispositions.

Yet it is also difficult to sustain arguments which assume the infinite malleability of sex-roles. This is so for two reasons. In the first place such arguments obscure (often, as in the work of Mead and Oakley, through selective interpretation of the data) the fact that there is in all societies a sex-ascribed division of labour and that this division of labour, however variable, seems to have at its core women's mothering and caring and men's greater participation not only in economic production but also in dangerous and life-threatening activities (Friedl, 1975; Sanday, 1981). This degree of continuity in the roles of women and men is not adequately accounted for in many of the social-construction arguments.

In the second place, the 'social-construction-of-the-roles-of-men-and-women' argument tends to assume that boys and girls develop a masculine or feminine persona through their ready assimilation and internalisation of the attitudes and behaviours which are prescribed for them by their culture. However, there are arguments which suggest that masculinity and femininity cannot simply be learned. Chodorow (1978) points out that women's mothering is not simply a set of behaviours, but participation in an interpersonal, diffuse, affective relationship. It is, she says, pre-eminently a psychological role which requires certain relational capacities and cannot be taught simply by giving a girl dolls and telling her she ought to mother. A woman, says Chodorow, cannot provide adequate mothering unless she has a sense of self as maternal. Moreover, some writers (see, for example, Morgan, 1975) insist that children are not the passive recipients of socialisation but themselves initiate action and elicit responses from their carers. Both these arguments suggest that we need a theory which allows for processes internal to the child and for the child's active collaboration in socialisation. The work of Kohlberg (1966) and of Chodorow (1978) points to two different kinds of processes which may be at work. Kohlberg suggests that the child has the cognitive ability to understand that he or she is a boy or girl and actively selects and participates in sex-designated activities on the basis of that understanding. Chodorow, on the other hand, roots the development of gender identity in the fact that mothers experience their infant daughters as extensions of themselves but their sons as male opposites and as separate from themselves. Consequently, girls experience themselves as involved in an attachment characterised by fusion of the self in another and develop a capacity for empathising with others and for nurturance but boys experience themselves as separate from the mother – and from the father since he is relatively absent from the child-rearing process – and so come to suppress relational capacities and needs. Chodorow thus maintains that women's mothering includes the capacities for its own reproduction: it reproduces in women psychological self-definitions and capacities appropriate to mothering but curtails these capacities and self-definitions in men. Neither of these theorists suggest that there is a natural, biologically-given femininity or masculinity, but they do suggest that we are directed by inner processes and make sense of our cultural environment in terms of these processes. To Kohlberg we are pre-eminently cognitive beings and gender identity develops on the basis of the child's early self-categorisation of himself or herself as a boy or girl. For Chodorow, we are pre-eminently psychological beings and gender identity develops on the basis of the different psychological relationship which girls and boys have with their mothers because they are of the same or opposite sex.

It seems therefore that neither a 'hard' biological argument nor a 'hard' social-structuring-of-sex-roles argument can be sustained. This leads to the argument that the biological and the social must be seen as interacting to shape gender divisions. This thesis has as its basis the notion that biology sets limits to sex-role variability, and this can be argued in a number of ways. Archer and Lloyd (1982) say that biological sex differences seem to ensure that there will be social differences between men and women but that the content of these differences is socially determined. Rossi (1977) points out that women's physical experiences – menstruation and menopause, pregnancy, childbirth and lactation – are specific to women and, *whether or not women choose to have children*, they have a biological experience and a biological potential that are different from men's. In Rossi's view, to deny that the reproductive and endocrine systems which underlie child-bearing are significant to female psychology and to the organisation of family life is to deny a central fact in human species survival and women's critical role therein. The work of yet another writer (Sacks, 1974) suggests that women's child-bearing means that their labour power is different from that of men. All these arguments suggest that men and women are different biological beings and will therefore have different social experiences.

However, the interaction-of-the-biological-and-social argument also asserts that although women's child-bearing has consequences for their social position, the nature of these consequences depends on the social environment – on the availability of birth control, on the way in which childhood and mothering is elaborated, on the kind of labour force that the economy requires, and on the social meanings which are given to male/female biology. Furthermore, though differences in the social tasks and personae of men and women may be influenced by biology, equality is clearly a social and political concept and differences in the power and status of men and women can only arise from the differential way in which their roles are evaluated and rewarded. Though women perform different social tasks from men, they could have equal social standing with men if their tasks were equally valued and rewarded.

2.4   SUMMARY

The preceding discussion of the debates surrounding the origins of the nuclear family and the sex-ascribed division of labour suggests that neither a 'hard' social-construction-of-the-family argument nor a 'hard' biological argument can be sustained. Social-construction arguments neither take account of nor explain the presence of the nuclear family and the sex-ascribed division of labour in widely varying economic, political and cultural situations. On the other hand biology, though it may be pressed into service to explain the ubiquity of the nuclear family form and of women's mothering, clearly tells us very little about family life. A simple biological model cannot take account of the meanings we give to sexuality, procreation, biological parenthood, childhood and biological differences between the sexes. It tells us little about the content of either marital or parental roles or of relationships between the nuclear family and extra-nuclear kinspeople. Nor can it tell us much about relationships between the nuclear family and other political, economic and cultural institutions.

Thus, as the preceding sections have indicated, some writers suggest that family forms must be seen as structured by biological as well as by ideological, economic and political forces. This mode of explanation suggests that the dependence of the child and the fact that women, not men, bear children do have consequences for social life but that the nature of these consequences is mediated by the economic, political and ideological context in which they occur. From this point of view, the social science task involves charting the limits of, and the interrelation between, the biological and the social.

3

The Development of the Modern Family

This chapter examines one of the central concerns of family sociology: the characterisation of the form and role of the modern Western family and of its relationship to the wider society. The most notable of early accounts, that of Talcott Parsons, is outlined in Section 3.1. Parsons, as we shall see, characterises the modern family as a structurally isolated nuclear unit which cherishes husband-wife and parent-child bonds and has as its main 'functions' socialisation and the stabilisation of adult personality. He also depicts women as responsible for the family's emotional well-being and men as responsible for its economic well-being. Writing from a functionalist perspective, Parsons sees this family unit as serving the 'needs' of technologically-advanced industrial urban economies.

Parsons' account of the modern family is a functionalist version of a whole stream of traditional theorising in which urban-industrialisation is associated with major changes in family form and functioning. However, this 'traditional' view of the nature and direction of family change has been radically rethought over the past twenty years in the light of historical and sociological research, while Marxist and feminist theorists have provided us with new models of the relationship between the modern family and the wider society. The latter sections of this chapter explore some of the issues which this 'new' family sociology raises. The issue of what changes have taken place in kinship structures and in the role of the family is examined in relation to England in Section 3.2. Section 3.3 examines some Marxist accounts of the relationship between the family and the wider society. Section 3.4 looks at the construction of the nuclear family as 'a sentimental reality' in the religious thought of the seventeenth to nineteenth centuries and considers the impact of religious ideas on the family. Consideration of two further critical issues, the changing role of women and men within the family and competing images of the modern family as 'haven' and 'prison', are postponed to Chapters 4 and 5 respectively.

3.1   A FUNCTIONALIST APPROACH: THE WORK OF TALCOTT PARSONS

Talcott Parsons is the most notable of the early family theorists and, although few people now agree with much that he wrote, he remains a commanding figure in the sociology of the modern family. This is partly because he presents us with a coherent and carefully elaborated theory and partly because the issues he raises are important and have remained central themes in the sociology of the family.

Though writing with particular reference to the American middle-class family, Parsons (see especially Parsons, 1949, 1955 and 1964) sought to provide a general theory of the family and its relationship to the wider society. He points to (i) the lessening importance of the family as an economic, political and welfare institution and its increasing importance as an arrangement for socialising and raising children and for the psychological support of adults; (ii) the disintegration of large kin groups and the intensification of relationships within the nuclear family; and (iii) the association of women with the private world of the family and of men with the political and economic world. From Parsons' functionalist perspective, these changes in family structure and activities represent its adaptation to change in other parts of the society. In his view, the modern family is particularly well suited to an industrial economy in that it facilitates labour mobility, socialises children and provides a source of emotional support for adults in an otherwise competitive, rootless and impersonal society.

Parsons' Thesis

Parsons' argument has as its starting-point the characterisation of traditional societies as societies in which large-scale kinship units dominated the social structure and performed religious, political, educational and economic 'functions'. He draws particular attention to the fusion of work and family. He also claims that obligations to the kin group were paramount and that affective inclinations within the nuclear family were checked so that the interests of the group should not be threatened.

Parsons then argues that as societies evolved, economic, political, religious and cultural institutions emerged as units independent of kinship structures and took over many of the family's functions.

The modern family, says Parsons, does not engage in economic production, is not a significant unit in the political power system and is not a major direct agency of social integration. However, it performs two vitally important functions, namely the socialisation of children and the provision of psychological support for adults. Parsons thus maintains that the family's 'loss' of functions does not mean that it has become an unimportant or enfeebled institution. In his view, the family has shed functions performed 'directly on behalf of society' but has come to specialise in functions performed on 'behalf of personality', and remains important. He sees change in family tasks as part of an evolutionary process of structural-differentiation in which the family, hitherto a 'multi-functional' unit (that is, an institution serving many social needs) has become 'functionally-specific' (that is, an institution specialising in the performance of particular activities).

Parsons goes on to argue that the transition to modernity also entailed the break-up of kin groups and the emergence of a family system in which nuclear family members are released from wider kin obligations and obligations between spouses are emphasised. Parsons maintains that an isolated nuclear family system has emerged since (i) production is no longer co-ordinated by kin groups and (ii) the imperatives and values of an industrial economy are incompatible with the maintenance of wide-ranging family obligations and loyalties. Modern occupations, Parsons says, are highly specialised, require a highly trained and competent labour force, and function best if effectiveness and efficiency, rather than personal loyalty, are the criteria by which people are judged and contracts made. They therefore give rise to 'universalistic' and 'achievement' values – that is, to values which emphasise impartiality and individual achievement, and consequently the use of merit and ability as criteria for selecting people for occupational positions. Further, modern occupations demand that individuals acquire skills and move about the country in accordance with the needs of the labour market and so give rise to social and geographical mobility. Familial values, says Parsons, are the opposite of these universalistic values. They are 'particularistic' in that they are based on obligations and loyalties to particular persons (family members) and could, for example, require employers to make appointments on the basis of family loyalties or bind workers to the social status and geographic area of their kin group. Consequently, cohesive kin groups which establish a wide range of kin obligations are incompatible with the values and demands of the economic system. By contrast, a family system based on the independence of the nuclear family unit limits family obligations. Moreover, because the husband–father is the only member of the nuclear family who is fully committed to the occupation system (the children being immature and the wife occupied in rearing them) there is, Parsons asserts, little likelihood that nuclear family loyalties will clash with the demands of the economic system. Parsons therefore concludes that the isolation of the nuclear family is an adaptive response to a technologically-advanced industrial economy and typical of modern societies.

Parsons characterises the modern family as a structurally isolated nuclear unit. It is his contention that although nuclear family members sometimes retain relationships with other kin, such relationships have no structural basis and are attenuated. The nuclear family in modern societies, says Parsons, is economically independent of other kin, forms a separate household unit and is bound neither to the mother's nor to the father's family of origin by clearly defined descent rules. Obligations to kin are limited, but nuclear family members are at the same time deprived of kin support and become singularly dependent on each other. Bonds between spouses and between parents and children are thus intensified and the marital bond becomes the 'structural keystone' of the modern family. It is also Parsons' contention that this family unit is primarily a child-rearing and affective unit and is linked to productive activities only through the breadwinning occupational role of the husband–father. Finally, it is Parsons' belief that this family system serves the 'needs' of mature industrial economies. On the one hand, it enables the economic system to operate unhampered by wide-ranging familistic obligations; on the other hand, it ensures that in a mobile, individualistic and impersonal world adults and children have a stable, if limited, set of affective relationships. This argument suggests that the modern family system serves the 'needs' of the economic system because it allows appointments to be based on suitability for the job and contracts on cost-effectiveness, young executives to move about the country unhampered by obligations to aging relatives, and working-class children to aspire to professional status unhampered by values which emphasise kin solidarity. It also implies that the modern family system serves individual needs because it provides a stable, primary group within which children may be socialised and spouses may find in each other and in parenthood personality-stabilising psychological satisfactions.

Parsons' account of the development of the modern family derives from the characterisation by sociology's founding fathers of the transition from the 'traditional' societies of the past to modernity. Moreover, somewhat similar accounts of the nature and direction of change in the family are to be found in the work of most early sociologists of the family. Thus the transition from corporate kin group to isolated nuclear family which Parsons depicts closely resembles both Le Play's (1935) contrast between the patriarchal family of pastoral and early agricultural societies and the individualistic family of modern (nineteenth-century) urban-indus-trial populations, and Linton's (1949) contrast between the consanguine family of small-scale societies and the conjugal family of modern America. It also resembles the distinction made by Burgess *et al.* (1963) between the traditional institutional family and the modern companionship family. Though they differ in their substantive emphases and theoretical orientations, all these writers emphasise, on the one hand, the shrinkage of kin groups, family functions and patriarchal authority and, on the other hand, the emergence of a relatively autonomous nuclear family based on the mutual affection and intimate association of husband and wife and parents and children and having as its goal the achievement of personal happiness.

Parsons Challenged

Parsons' account of family change – and the whole body of 'traditional' family sociology of which it is the leading example – has come under considerable fire. Three major issues are considered here: (i) his account of the nature, direction and timing of change; (ii) his conceptualisation of the modern Western family as an 'isolated nuclear family'; and (iii) his conception of a 'fit' between the isolated nuclear family and technologically-advanced industrial economies. (His treatment of gender divisions has also been vigor-ously attacked. This issue is dealt with in detail in Chapter 4.)

(i)   The nature, direction and timing of change

At the heart of Parsons' account of family change lies the idea that there is a specific modern urban-industrial family and that this family is distinctively different from the pre-modern, pre-industrial family. However, cross-cultural research has pointed to variations in family patterns and values between industrial societies. Moreover, historical research in Britain, the USA, Japan and elsewhere suggests that in any given society present-day family patterns and values are continuous with the patterns and values of its past. For example, it has been shown that family life in sixteenth and seventeenth century England, as in modern England, was based on individualistic values and the independence of the nuclear family (see Section 3.2). There is also evidence to suggest that the limited kinship priorities of modern Anglo-Saxon America are similar to the kinship priorities of seventeenth-century New England (Gordon, 1972) while the contrasting collectivistic values and strong kinship bonds of the modern Japanese family have been shown to be continuous with traditional Japanese family values and patterns. The general conclusion to be drawn from this evidence is that family patterns vary between industrial societies in ways that reflect their own specific pasts. To put this somewhat differently, it is now widely argued that we can neither identify a specific modern industrial family nor see the family as simply acted upon by urban-industrialisation, but must see modern family patterns as shaped, at least in part, by their own past. Some writers (notably Goode, 1963; Macfarlane, 1978; Laslett, 1983) go further and suggest that patterns of industrialisation may have been shaped by the family patterns and values which existed prior to industrialisation or that both industrialisation and family structures may have been shaped by some third factor, such as the force of ideas (see pp. 59–60 and Section 3.4).

These problems in Parsons' characterisation of the nature and direction of change stem from a fundamental methodological weakness in his sociology. Parsons' conception of the contemporary Western conjugal family as evolving out of multi-functional corporate kin groups is based on (i) the assumption that the corporate kin group which anthropologists have found in some small-scale societies is typical of 'traditional' societies; and (ii) the assumption that the 'isolated nuclear family' meets the requirements of a technologically-advanced occupational system and is characteristic of modern industrial economies. However, Parsons' critics (see, for example, Harris, 1983; Morgan, 1975) maintain that this mode of analysis fails to take account of the wide array of circumstances and experiences that fall under the labels 'pre-industrial' and 'industrial'.

Pre-industrial societies, it is argued, are very different in economic and political organisation. Consequently, industrialisation has different starting-points. Moreover, it does not everywhere follow the same pattern, is not a fixed process, and may be subject to socialist as well as capitalist modes of organisation. Historical analyses which seek to examine the processes of change within particular societies are therefore needed. Parsons, as Harris (1983) notes, depicts societal development in terms of a polar opposition between ancient societies dominated by kinship and modern societies dominated by market relations. This leads to global and misleading cross-cultural generalisations, not to an account of change in specific historical contexts.

(ii)   Parsons' conceptualisation of the modern Western family

Parsons' characterisation of the modern Western family as an isolated nuclear family *seems* to imply the reduction of family relationships to a nuclear core of parents and children. This notion has been much criticised on empirical grounds for there is now considerable evidence of the maintenance of extra-nuclear kin relations in Western societies (see Section 3.2). There is also a theoretical reason for believing that family structures cannot be reduced to a nuclear core. 'At a minimum' says Goode (1963, p. 70) 'the members of each unit are tied to other units through a common member of a given nuclear family'. For example, a brother has continued social relations with his sister, and thereby with his brother-in-law and nephews.

Parsons' conception of the isolated nuclear family has been defended (for example, by Harris, 1983) on the grounds that he uses this term to refer only to the structural weakness of bonds between related families – that is, to the absence of normative and economic bases for the regular formation of kin groupings wider than the nuclear family. This usage, it may be argued, presumes the absence of extended family groups but does not preclude the maintenance in an informal way of psychologically significant relationships. Nevertheless, the term 'isolated nuclear family' is ambiguous, has been much misunderstood and does not readily encompass the wide variety of kin relationships which are found in modern societies (see Section 3.2 for a more detailed discussion). Moreover, it does not capture the essence of the family pattern it denotes for it emphasises what does not form its structural basis (extra-nuclear kin bonds), rather than what does (the marital bond). 'The conjugal family', the term used by Goode (1963) – who presents an analysis of present-day family structures which is very similar to that presented by Parsons – avoids these difficulties. It is therefore used in this text.

(iii)   The fit between the 'isolated nuclear family' and the industrial economy

Parsons' conception of the modern family as congruent with the industrial economy depends critically on his characterisation of the latter but this has been challenged. His assumption that an industrial economy requires social and geographical mobility of its labour force is critical to his argument. It has, however, been pointed out that social and geographical mobility are not peculiar to industrial societies and were not uncommon in pre-industrial Europe (Goode, 1963). Conversely, it has been argued that modern industrial economies do not require social and geographical mobility of all sectors of the labour force. Geographical immobility appears to be characteristic of traditional working-class communities, for example (see Section 3.2), and the transmission of class privilege and advantage from one generation to another is emphasised in nearly all studies of social mobility (see, for example, Goldthorpe, 1980).

More fundamentally, Parsons' account of the 'fit' between the isolated nuclear family and the industrial economy assumes, says Harris (1983, p. 60), that the values and practice of economic individualism are inevitably associated with industrial development. Harris comments: 'That historically there has been that association is indisputable. Its necessity, however, is nowhere demonstrated in Parsons' work: it is uncritically assumed.' Again, Parsons sees modern Western societies as urban-industrial societies. However, Marxist writers see modern societies as capitalist and feminist writers see them as capitalist and/or patriarchal. For Parsons, the society is a functioning whole held together by shared values, and class and gender differences are not incorporated in any systematic way into his analysis. By contrast, his Marxist critics locate the family in a world that is class-divided and capitalist-dominated, while his feminist critics locate the family in a world that is sex-divided and male-dominated. Finally, Parsons' belief in the eufunctionality of the family for its members has been challenged.

Parsons' analysis obscures, it has been argued, the tensions and strains which in reality permeate the conjugal family and which are destructive. Pressures for change in the family therefore go unrecognised and unexplained.

All these criticisms derive from views of the social order which are fundamentally opposed to the view held by Parsons. These alternative Marxist and feminist views of the world are examined in full in Sections 3.3 and 4.2, while ideas of the destructive nature of the conjugal family are examined in Chapter 5.

3.2   EMPIRICAL ACCOUNTS

The issue of the nature, direction and timing of change in the form and role of the family is explored in this section in the light of recent historical and sociological research and in relation to the English experience. Two questions are addressed. First, have kin groups wider than the nuclear family given way to an isolated nuclear family system and, if so, at what point in time did change occur? Second, has the family ceased to be a multi-functional unit and become a unit for child-rearing and for intimate, personal relationships only and, if so, at what point in time did change occur?

In examining these issues, three kinds of difficulties confront us. The first stems from the partial and inadequate nature of much of the data. Evidence of pre-industrial and early industrial family patterns may be derived from demographic data on marriages, births, deaths and household composition, and from literary, ecclesiastical and legal records. However, these data are fragmentary and may relate only to particular socio-economic or regional groups. Moreover, data for periods earlier than the sixteenth century are extremely fragmentary and the nature of our earliest family structures is shrouded in obscurity. Sociological studies provide evidence of present-day family patterns, but they are also limited to particular groups and are not always readily comparable. The second difficulty is the confusion which arises from the different (and often simplistic) ways in which the extended family is defined, and Parsons' concept of the structural isolation of the nuclear family interpreted. Much of the disagreement and debate over the nature and direction of change has in fact arisen from confusion and ambiguity in the use of terms. The third difficulty is the problem of identifying the timing of shifts in family patterns. This arises partly because of the fragmentary nature of the data but also because there is considerable regional and socio-economic variation in the adoption of new trends. All these methodological problems mean that accounts of change in the structure and role of the family are tentative.

Nevertheless we turn to our first question. Have large kin groups been replaced by structurally isolated nuclear family units?

Kinship in Decline?

Parsons' account (see pp. 36–8) of the disintegration of large kin groups is a functionalist version of an old-established theme in the sociology of the modern family. This theme first appeared in embryonic form in the characterisation by sociology's founding fathers of the social changes accompanying urban-industrialisation, reappeared in various guises in the writings of functionalist and other early family sociologists, and is implicit in some Marxist and feminist literature. However, recent historical and sociological research challenges the assumption that kin groups wider than the nuclear family were characteristic of all pre-industrial societies. It also provides extensive evidence of the vitality of extra-nuclear kin relationships in modern Western societies and of the diverse ways in which they are mediated by class interests.

This debate is examined in relation to the English experience. We look at studies of kinship in (i) the pre-industrial period, and (ii) the industrial period.

(i) The pre-industrial period

The assumption that kin groupings wider than the nuclear family were common in pre-industrial England was first seriously attacked by Laslett. Using data derived from listings of the inhabitants of 100 communities, Laslett and his associates in the Cambridge Group for the History of Population and Social Structure (see especially Laslett, 1972, 1977 and 1983) have established that in sixteenth-century and seventeenth-century England the nuclear family typically constituted a separate household unit. Only about 10 per cent of households contained extra-nuclear kin and mean household size seems to have been about 4.75 persons. Laslett maintains that young people set up independent households when they married. He also suggests that family members were often dispersed by geographical mobility since it was common practice for children to leave home to go into service or become apprentices. Furthermore, he suggests that because of the high rate of mortality few young men and women were likely to have had both parents alive when they themselves married. Finally, Laslett claims that provision by kin for the old was probably no more extensive in the seventeenth century than it is in the twentieth century.

Laslett's account of pre-industrial kinship patterns relies heavily on data on household composition. This does not by itself provide an adequate basis for asserting – as he tends to do – the independence of the nuclear family in pre-industrial England since related families may be bound together by complex social rules and economic dependences even though they do not live in the same household. However, his work is complemented and extended by Macfarlane's (1978) account of the origins of English individualism. Macfarlane claims that, as far back as the available historical evidence makes it possible for us to go, family life was organised on individualistic rather than collectivistic principles. He bases his argument on land law, testamentary practice and the existence of an intense market in land and shows that even in the thirteenth century English social life was characterised by the individual ownership of land and primogeniture (inheritance by the first son) as opposed to a peasant family system based on collective rights in land. He suggests that even in prosperous families children left home at an early age to go into service, subsequently acquiring farms on their own account and establishing themselves as independent units. Finally, he emphasises that social as well as geographical mobility were high. Thus Macfarlane's data, like Laslett's, point to the nuclearity of the family in pre-industrial England.

Not all the evidence suggests that the nuclear family was as independent of kin as Laslett and Macfarlane imply. Accounts of upper-strata life suggest that at this level lineage was a basis for social honour and identity and a means of mobilising support in economic and political life (Stone, 1977). Among the middle ranks kin seem to have been sometimes used to secure political and economic advancement (Houlbrooke, 1984). These data suggest that in some groups at least kin ties were used to further life-goals and were an important feature of social organisation. However, none of these data points to the existence of clearly-defined kin groups wider than the nuclear family. It is clear that descent was traced bilaterally – that is through both the mother and father. As a result each new generation possessed a unique range of kin, and kinship groupings lacked clear structural persistence over time. Relatedly, kinship terminology made no clear distinction between maternal and paternal kin and terms for kin beyond the nuclear family and the nuclear families of origin of parents and spouses were vague (Wrightson, 1981). Further, the circle of effective kin seems generally to have been very flexible, varying according to economic circumstances, geographical and social mobility, ease of communication and personal preference (Houlbrooke, 1984; Wrightson, 1981). These data relate for the most part to the sixteenth and seventeenth centuries. However, there is nothing to suggest that there were marked differences between the sixteenth century and earlier periods. Laslett (1983) claims that there is scattered evidence of nuclear family households in the Middle Ages and Lancaster's study (1958) of kinship terminology suggests that extra-nuclear kin bonds were not clearly delimited even in the Anglo-Saxon period.

These findings have provided the basis for two important propositions about the nature and direction of change in the form of the family. First, they show that family patterns in pre-industrial England were closer to present-day patterns than was once thought. In the past as in the present, nuclear families formed independent households and economic units and the principles of family organisation were individualistic. 'There is a sense' says Laslett (1983, p. 559) 'in which the end was present at the very beginning.' The second proposition to be advanced is that the English experience was unique. For Macfarlane, individualism was quintessentially an English experience. For Laslett, English household and marriage patterns were similar to those of north-western Europe but this 'Western pattern' was different from that of southern and eastern Europe where co-residence and early marriage were more common. The family patterns of southern and eastern Europe are seen by Litwak (1965) as exemplifying the classical extended family (that is, as an example of a family system which emphasises extra-nuclear kin relations and involves co-residence, economic co-operation between kin and the authority of the kin group over the nuclear family). We may also note that this classical extended family, as well as 'the Western pattern', differed from the large, cohesive descent groups which anthropologists have found in some small-scale societies (and which Parsons seems to have had in mind in his account of the evolution of the modern conjugal family).

(ii)   The industrial period

A substantial body of research findings suggests that in industrial, as in pre-industrial, England, related families do not regularly form clearly-bounded, integrated kin *groups*. Nevertheless, the data suggest that extra-nuclear kin *relationships* are maintained and are important. The evidence also suggests that the range and strength of kin ties and the way in which they are used vary as between the 'traditional' and 'affluent' working class and the 'traditional' and 'new' middle class. We look first at studies of kin relationships in the industrial working classes, then at studies of kin relationships in the professional middle classes and conclude the section with a discussion of the implications of their findings for Parsons' theoretical assumptions.

Anderson's (1971) study of nineteenth-century Lancashire suggests that in the working class industrialisation and urban migration frequently led to a clustering together of kin in the new urban areas. Using data from the 1851 census, Anderson shows that in mid-nineteenth century Preston 23 per cent of households contained kin other than the nuclear family and neighbourhoods contained clusters of kin. He also shows that kin were an important source of aid in 'critical life situations'. For example, aging parents, who lived with and were supported by their married children, provided a child-minding service which allowed the mother to work. Orphans found homes with relatives and, in an age of child-labour, contributed to the household's income. Newcomers to the city found accommodation with kin and in return contributed to their rent. Labour was recruited and jobs obtained through family connections. Anderson's work shows that at the onset of industrialisation kinship networks facilitated geographical mobility by providing a base for newcomers to the city and served as an insurance policy against hardship and crisis in a society in which wages were low, unemployment periodic, death rates high and widowhood common.

A series of neighbourhood studies conducted in the 1950s show that locality-based, close-knit networks of related families existed, even at this advanced stage of industrialisation, in old-established, low-income working-class communities. Young and Willmott's (1957) study of the London Borough of Bethnal Green provides us with a particularly vivid account of kin relationships in such a community. Young and Willmott found that in the Bethnal Green of the 1950s related families lived in close proximity to each other: 68 per cent of the married men and 75 per cent of the married women in their general sample lived within three miles of their parents; 53 per cent of relatives other than parents of couples in a small sub-sample of married couples lived in Bethnal Green or in adjacent boroughs. Young and Willmott also found that kin formed loosely-bounded, loosely-integrated networks based on emotional attachment, sociability, the sharing of domestic tasks and mutual aid. They show that kin networks were used to obtain housing and employment, acted as a bridge between the individual and the local community by increasing contact with other people, and provided links with local history. At the same time Young and Willmott show that the working-class kinship network was neither wide nor deep in that it embraced three generations only – the young couple, their families of origin and their children – and did not extend beyond first cousins. Further, it was partial in that some kin had moved away and so were not part of the locality-based group. Furthermore, it was mobilised by women and its basis was the assistance, support and companionship which young married women derived from their mothers and other female kin in child-rearing. The mother was the pivotal figure of the kinship network, her home the focal point of family gatherings and gossip, and her relationship with her daughter its central relationship.

Working-class kinship networks developed, say Young and Willmott (1957 and 1973), as a response to a situation in which poverty was intense and extensive and the welfare state not yet established. Like Anderson, they claim that the maintenance of kin bonds was an insurance policy against crises and hardship. Their work also suggests that geographical and social immobility were associated with poverty and a disadvantaged class position and tended to keep families together. Furthermore, Young and Willmott maintain that extra-nuclear kin relationships were particularly important to women since the brunt of family poverty – large families, the care of old people, the need to make ends meet in unemployment – was borne by women. However, they suggest that as conditions improved working-class families began to go their various and separate ways. They point out that, with the development of state housing, nuclear families were rehoused as independent units and were thus separated from other kin. They also point out that increasing affluence and greater security of employment, together with the establishment of the welfare state, reduced the need for kin-provided services. They further suggest that as material resources grew families sometimes sought to improve their status position by investing all their resources in a 'home' which would advertise their new-found affluence and became consumer-oriented rather than kin-oriented. Young and Willmott argue that as a result of these processes locality-based kinship networks have largely been replaced by relatively isolated and privatised, companionate and home-centred conjugal family units.

Broad support for this argument comes from studies of new council house estates (Young and Willmott, 1957; Mogey, 1956) and from a study of manual workers in Luton (Goldthorpe *et al.*, 1969). In the localities covered by these studies, working-class families were not typically surrounded by kin, neighbourhood bonds had weakened and the nuclear family had withdrawn into itself. These studies also show that, although relatives were visited and kin valued, kin interaction was less intense and less extensive than in long-established working-class communities. Visiting had become a formal weekend affair requiring 'dressing-up' and 'best behaviour', not the informal 'popping in' for 'a cuppa' that had been characteristic of Bethnal Green. Kin ties are retained, but the working-class family is now, these studies suggest, child-centred and home-centred rather than kin-oriented, and the husband–wife bond has replaced the mother–daughter bond as its central relationship.

There are broadly similar variations between the family structures of the 'traditional' and the 'new' middle classes, though for somewhat different reasons. Bell (1968) suggests that for traditional middle-class groups – independent professionals, small shopkeepers and owners of small-scale industries – economic advancement depends on the expansion of their concern and, therefore, on a local reputation and clientele. These categories of middle-class people, whom following Watson (1964) he calls 'burgesses', are tied economically and socially to a particular locality, and may have kin living near them and working with them. However, Bell points out, middle-class people increasingly work, not in local opportunity structures, but in large-scale organisations and for them advancement depends on 'spiralism', the readiness to move between branches of the organisation (or between organisations) so as to achieve promotion. They are therefore typically geographically mobile and kin are widely dispersed. Bell also shows that middle-class people may be upwardly mobile and may therefore be separated from kin by status differences. However, he finds that, despite geographical separation and status differences, ties – particularly with parents – persist. Contact over considerable distances is maintained by weekend visiting and telephone calls. Ceremonial occasions such as christenings bring various branches of the family together. Financial aid can be – and is – provided, regardless of distance, and may, Bell says, be of considerable importance in helping young couples to equip themselves with middle-class status props. Bell's findings are broadly corroborated by a number of other studies of middle-class life (see in particular Firth, Hubert and Forge, 1969). However, a careful reading of these studies suggests that, as in the new working-class, kin relationships are fragile. This is clearly brought out by Hubert (1965) in her account of the kin relationships of a sample of North London middle-class families. She shows that these families maintain contact with close kin regardless of distance but that frequency of contact decreases with distance. She also shows that relationships were limited in range. Only a small proportion of secondary kin were seen. Contact with these kin was intermittent and generally took place in terms of personal preference. Furthermore, kin ties impinged upon only a small part of the individual's life and took place in the context of values which emphasised independence and autonomy. There was no expectation that kin would or should provide help in getting jobs or accommodation and married women were not dependent on, and did not expect to be dependent on, their mothers or sisters for day-to-day services, emotional support or companionship. Hubert says that the positive evaluation of independence gives people the freedom to choose where they want to live and to go where their work takes them. In her view, the geographical separation of middle-class families is not an accidental concomitant of professional life, but is influenced by the fact that values stress the independence of the nuclear family.

To summarise

A substantial body of evidence suggests that within the industrial period families have experienced different degrees of geographical and social mobility and that this is associated with variation in family form. In stable social groups, locality-based, close-knit kin networks may develop and social life may be organised around kin and community, but where families are geographically and socially mobile, kin interaction may be intermittent, unco-ordinated and selective. Large parts of the lives of family members are free from kin observation and control and family life may be more sharply focussed on the nuclear family. However, the evidence also shows that kin relationships, though attenuated, are not destroyed and may even constitute a resource in adapting to mobility (as among the early industrial working-classes) or in maintaining status (as among the spiralling middle-classes). It seems that there has been no progressive and unilinear disintegration of extra-nuclear kin bonds but rather fluctuating and subtle shifts of emphasis.

Very similar findings have been produced for the USA and some scholars believe that Parsons' account of the isolation of the nuclear family in modern Western societies has been invalidated by the sheer weight of the evidence against him. With a finality rare in sociological research, the American researchers Sussman and Burchinal (1969, p. 147) declare that understanding of the family as a functioning social system is possible '*only by rejection of the isolated nuclear family concept*'. Another American writer, Litwak (1960a and b), says that the characteristic family unit of industrial society is not the 'isolated nuclear family' but the 'modified extended family'. Litwak sees the modified extended family as differing from the 'classical extended family' in that related families are geographically dispersed and economically independent, *and* as differing from the isolated nuclear family of Parsonian theory in that it is a network of kin wider than the nuclear family which provides affective relationships and in which significant services are exchanged.

However, these scholars seem to have interpreted Parsons' concept of the isolated nuclear family too literally. Writing in his own defence,

Parsons (1971, pp. 53–4) says that accounts of extra-nuclear kin relationships complement rather than contradict his thesis. He says that kin bonds will indeed be found in modern societies since 'the very psychological importance for the individual of the nuclear family in which he was born and brought up' means that there will be social relationships between members of nuclear families. Nevertheless, he contends, these relationships do not form 'firmly structured units of the social system' in the way that clans or lineages do: they do not give rise to productive or political units, are subordinated to obligations to spouse and children and have 'a marked optional quality'. The nuclear family is thus structurally isolated. In thus amplifying and defending his position, Parsons seems to be claiming that what he is arguing is that related families do not regularly form clearly-bounded, integrated kinship *groups* and to argue this is not to argue that family members do not maintain *relationships* of some kind with some kin. It is to argue only that such relationships are based on personal preference, not on structural principles.

This defence suggests that the difference between Parsons' 'structurally isolated nuclear family' and Litwak's 'modified extended family' is one of emphasis rather than of contradiction and that much of the controversy stems from ambiguity in, and misunderstanding of, terms. Further, though he believes that there is a progressive trend towards the isolation of the nuclear family, Parsons recognises as exceptions to his model the family patterns of the upper classes, the urban poor and rural communities. Furthermore, it could be argued that the empirical findings support Parsons' (as compared with Litwak's) greater emphasis on the attenuation of kin bonds for they suggest that kin networks are increasingly limited in range and in their impact on the life of the individual. Some studies have emphasised the loneliness and isolation which family members, and in particular wives, experience (see, for example, Young and Willmott, 1957).

However, these 'defences' do not get Parsons 'off the hook'. The evidence under review points to some *systematic* class and gender variations in extra-nuclear kin relations. Parsons provides us with no means of explaining these variations. Moreover, the evidence shows that kin relationships are not merely of psychological significance but serve individual and class interests and have economic value. As we have seen, middle-class life-styles are maintained by channelling aid from the parental to the younger generation, while working-class family bonds protect the individual from the uncertainties of capitalism and engender class solidarity (see also p. 68). It has also been shown that kin connections among 'top' decision-makers are common and constitute a mechanism for channelling information and mobilising resources (Lupton and Wilson, 1959). Moreover, it has been argued that extended family networks may facilitate economic development. For example, Grieco (1982) argues that kin-based recruitment strategies provide the employer with a cheap method of obtaining labour, an efficient screening mechanism and a means of employee-control. The upper-class use of kin connections for channelling information and mobilising resources may be seen as contributing to the efficiency of the enterprise, while working-class reliance on kin networks in the early industrial period has been seen as relieving the industrialist and the state of the need to provide for the relief of poverty. Finally, the evidence (particularly in Young and Willmott, 1957) points to the differential importance of kin bonds to women and men. These findings point to the need for a theory which systematically incorporates class and gender variations in the range and strength of extra-nuclear kin relationships and in the uses to which they are put. This Parsons does not provide.

The Changing Role of the Family

Sociologists of all persuasions point, as Parsons does, to the separation of productive activity from the family, to the 'take-over' by the state and other public institutions of welfare and related activities (such as education, health and the care of the aged) and to the structuring of the family as a private realm of intimacy and emotionality in opposition to the impersonal world of the economic and the political. These changes were described by Parsons (see pp. 35–6) in terms of the structural differentiation and specialisation of the family, but are now more commonly described in terms of the division of social life into public and private spheres and the association of the political and economic with the former and the family with the latter.

However, historical enquiry suggests that this characterisation of change in the scope and range of the family's activities is oversimplified. In the Western world the family's role in the pre-industrial period would seem to have been less considerable than is sometimes suggested. Conversely, it has been argued that in modern Western societies the family is neither entirely absent from the public world nor entirely in control of the private world.

This debate will be examined in relation to the English experience by looking at data on the family's changing role in (i) productive activity; (ii) welfare and related activities, and (iii) child-rearing and affective relations.

(i) The separation of productive activity from the family

Long-established accounts of the social changes accompanying urban-industrialisation suggest that, prior to the development of factory production in the eighteenth century, most goods and services were produced and consumed within the family unit. The family group, it is argued, was a work group, and productive activities were fused with reproductive activities and regulated by familial values. Industrialisation is then presented as involving the loss to the family group of ownership and control of the means of production, the removal of the father and other earners from the home for most of the day, the conversion of productive labour, which had hitherto been an integral part of family life, into a separate external activity, and the emergence of a social order dominated by economic values. This general and long-established picture of the transition from family production to factory production has not been rejected, but is qualified in three important ways in the 'new' family sociology.

First, historical research suggests that images of the family as a self-sufficient economic unit do not entirely accord with the realities of agrarian and craft production in pre-industrial England. Middleton (1979) shows that in the Middle Ages 'the holding', not the family, was the locus of economic obligation and the cornerstone of property relations. Its labour force normally included non-family members permanently in residence in the household and was sometimes extended by casual labour and by service contracts. Conversely, family members hired themselves out as day-labourers or went into service in the more prosperous families. The family was thus by no means a self-sufficient unit of production even in the Middle Ages. Moreover, in the sixteenth and seventeenth centuries wage labour formed an increasingly important part of the agrarian economy. Harris (1983, pp. 122–3) reminds us that in the sixteenth and seventeenth centuries agricultural holdings were increasingly consolidated and smallholding families displaced, thus creating both a demand for wage labour (by the enlarged estates) and a need to sell labour (by the displaced). In other words a substantial proportion of people worked outside the family and for a wage before industrialisation.

Second, the sixteenth and seventeenth centuries witnessed, in addition to the increase in wage labour in agricultural production, the growth of a merchant class, the early stages of capitalistic endeavour and the emergence of rural industries (proto-industrialisation as it has been called). Historians suggest that these processes created a role for the family in the economy which was transitional between that found in the Middle Ages and that found in the industrial period. Drawing on historical research, Harris (1983, Chaps. 6 and 7) says that, whereas the medieval family had been a self-regulating property-owning and productive unit, families engaged in proto-industrial activity depended on merchants for their raw materials and for markets for their goods. They were effectively employed by the merchants and in the course of time a new class of cottage workers who were entirely dependent on this type of employment for their livelihood came into being. This proto-industrial family sold its labour resources to outside employers, but it sold its labour as a unit and not in individualised packets as the industrial family was to do. It was thus transitional between the family as a property-owning unit of production and the family as a unit of labour supply.

Third, it is generally argued that industrialisation did not leave the family without an economic role. Some writers emphasise that the separation of production from the household took place over a long time and is not absolute even now: family businesses continue to exist; married women not only undertake paid home-work (for example, as typists) but are also routinely incorporated into the productive process through their contribution to their husband's job (see p. 89); and families provide from within themselves many of the services they need, as the growth of do-it-yourself-activity indicates. The importance of the family as a unit of consumption, as evidenced by family-targeted advertising, has also been stressed. Most writers also suggest that the family is important in maintaining a labour supply in that it socialises children into accepting paid work as a normal part of the (male) adult role, furnishes psychological support in meeting the rigours of the occupational world and constitutes married women as a reservoir of cheap labour. (For the Marxist version of this argument, see pp. 63–5). All these arguments suggest that the economic role of the family has changed but has not been eliminated.

(ii) The 'loss' of welfare and social control activities

The modern period has seen the development and expansion of state and private institutions for education, health, the care of the aged and the incapacitated, leisure, social control and other governmental activities. However, interpretations of these developments as a 'loss of functions' for the family are now generally said to be over-simplifications.

In the first place, some writers suggest that beliefs in the multi-purpose family of the past are poorly founded. Fletcher (1973), writing with particular reference to workers in agriculture and domestic industry in the eighteenth century, argues that poverty and unremitting toil meant that most families had neither the material resources nor the time to attend to the welfare, educational, recreational and other needs of their members. Many of the so-called functions of the family were therefore either performed in a rudimentary way or neglected. Moreover, conceptions of the multi-purpose family obscure the existence of institutional spheres other than the family. Perhaps the most important of these was the Church which performed a political as well as a religious 'function', was responsible for educating those who would assume high position in political and religious spheres and established, in a somewhat haphazard way, foundling hospitals and other caring institutions.

In the second place, some writers argue that the modern family is not without 'service' functions. For example, studies of educational performance show that early learning and play experience within the family provide children with the stimulation and motivation necessary to success in the formal education system (Douglas, 1964; Jackson and Marsden, 1962). Health-care studies show that ante-natal and post-natal clinics and health-visiting services provide particular services and guidance for parents but that the day-to-day surveillance of children's health remains with parents. Similarly, it has been shown that state provision for the aged and incapacitated is based on the assumption that the family (for which read women-in-the-family) should play a part in their care (Finch and Groves, 1983). Such data have been used to argue that the modern family complements public institutions in the provision of education, health-care and so on (see, for example, Litwak, 1965).

(iii) Child-rearing and affective relations

Central to Parsons' account of the family in modern society is his emphasis on its new and particular importance as a child-rearing and affective unit. He claims that in the kinship-dominated societies of the past, mate-selection was subordinated to the interests of, and controlled by, the kin group and the affective inclinations of spouses were checked by obligations to the group. He further claims that the erosion of kin groups left nuclear family members without external sources of support and consequently heightened the import- ance of marriage as a source of emotional support and compan- ionship and sharpened the responsibility of parents for child-rearing. He supports his argument by pointing to the increasing emphasis in our culture on romantic love, the personal affinity of spouses and the importance of 'good' heterosexual relationships.

This loving-conjugal-family thesis appears in one form or another in most pre-1965 accounts of the development of the modern family (see Chapter 5 for further elaboration). Moreover, it is complemented and supported by some historical research. The French historian, Ariès (1962), claims that the Middle Ages had no concept of childhood. Ariès maintains that images of the special and fragile nature of childhood and the celebration of affective ties between parents and children began to emerge only between the fifteenth and seventeenth centuries (see also pp. 70–1). Stone (1977), using data which largely relate to the upper classes, claims that at the beginning of the sixteenth century the nuclear family was enmeshed in kin and community obligations and had no emotional significance. Marriage, says Stone, was a means of extending influence, and procreation a means of perpetuating the family line and transmitting property. Stone characterises relationships between spouses and between parents and children as distant. He stresses male authoritar- ianism, emphasises that marriages were arranged, and claims that children were wet-nursed and swaddled in infancy and treated with indifference. He then goes on to depict an uneven and fluctuating movement away from this 'emotionless family' to what he calls 'affective individualism', that is to a family life-style characterised by affective bonds, a strong sense of individual autonomy and of the right to personal freedom in the pursuit of happiness, an emphasis on privacy, and the celebration of the sexual aspects of love. In Stone's view strong affective attachments between spouses and between parents and children emerged as a feature of family life only with the declining importance of kinship and lineage in the late sixteenth and early seventeenth centuries and became established only in the eighteenth century.

There are two important but very different challenges to these accounts of the modern conjugal family as a private realm of love and intimacy. First, it is now vigorously argued that the loving conjugal family is not in fact a late arrival on the historical stage but existed as an ideal and in practice well before the close of the Middle Ages. Macfarlane (1979) points out that Stone's argument fails to take account of the long-standing individualism of English life, ignores contrary evidence of conjugal and parental affection, and generalises from limited and ambiguous evidence and from continental data. Mount (1982) uses letters, poetry and ecclesiastical records to provide evidence of parental and marital affection for the medieval and Anglo-Saxon periods as well as the sixteenth and seventeenth centuries. He shows that love was not necessarily absent from even the most profitable of marriages and was an element in the validation of child-betrothal and of informal marriages. Mount also argues that accounts of indifferent mothers misinterpret the historical evidence. He says that swaddling, wet-nursing and the abandonment of children are not evidence of a lack of maternal affection: swaddling was believed to be good for the infant, wet-nursing was necessary in the absence of germ-free bottled milk and the abandonment of children to foundling hospitals was the result of destitution. Mount maintains that a family life based on choice, affection and the protection of individual autonomy are neither a novelty nor the product of unique historical forces but is the way most people have always preferred to live. Pollock (1983), Sarsby (1983) and Houlbrooke (1984) are other authors who have recently emphasised the long-standing existence of married love and parental affection as ideals and in practice.

A different kind of challenge comes from writers who believe that the modern conjugal family is neither all encompassing of the personal nor entirely autonomous and private. Litwak (1965) points out that in modern society the family is not exclusively responsible for nurture. Child-care is shared with playgroups and welfare clinics, the therapeutic professions and mutual support groups (such as Alcoholics Anonymous or Gingerbread) share in the provision of psychological support, while neighbourhood groups and associations ranging from working men's clubs, Women's Institutes, Church groups and sports clubs to street gangs provide extra-familial sources of companionship. Litwak's argument suggests that nurturant activities are shared between the family and a range of other institutions. More radically, some writers have pointed to the systematic intervention of the state in family life. Lasch (1977) maintains that the capitalist state has invaded the family through its welfare apparatus, asserted control over child-rearing and other activities once left to its members and destroyed paternal authority. The same argument is made from a feminist viewpoint by Ehrenreich and English (1978) and by Wilson (1977). Ehrenreich and English say that an army of 'experts' (gynaecologists, paediatricians, child psychologists, psychoanalysts, sociologists and home economists) have defined child-rearing in ways that fuse male interests with the requirements of industrial capitalism, and have degraded women's age-old skills. Wilson seeks to show that the welfare state, as it is constructed in Britain, amounts to 'no less than the state organisation of domestic life' (Wilson, 1977, p. 9). In her view, the welfare state sustains the nuclear family as a unit of care (for example, by promoting community care rather than residential care and by limiting day-nurseries), uses health visitors and social workers among other strategies to maintain 'appropriate' standards of child-care, and reinforces notions of men as breadwinners and women as child-carers. Donzelot (1980) presents the same kind of argument but, unlike Lasch and the feminist writers we have cited, he refuses to see the family as an instrument of either capitalist or patriarchal interests. He argues that social reformers, psychoanalysts, social workers, educators and the medical and legal professions have, on the basis of their professional knowledge and interpretations of the social world and through an elaborate structure of counselling, advice and supervision by statutory and voluntary agencies, established the family as an educative centre for the care, disciplining and training of its members. He seeks to show that this construction of the family as an educative centre was accomplished by enlisting the co-operation of family members – in particular of the mother who was used as an agent of moralisation. It is also his contention that the middle classes and the working classes attained domesticity by separate routes and that working-class domesticity was not imposed by the middle class. Nevertheless, like Lasch, Ehrenreich and English and Wilson, Donzelot shows that state action has subverted the ideological division between the 'public' and the 'private'. In effect all these writers are saying that family life has a public dimension.

Two propositions as to the nature and direction of change in the role of the family may be drawn from the foregoing data and arguments. First, there can be no doubt that the shift from a system of household-production based on familial relationships to a system of factory production based on a contract between capital and labour and subject to market conditions represented a fundamental change in the role of the family in society. Second, nevertheless, old ideas of the family as gradually shedding a wide range of economic, political and welfare activities to become, in modern times, a private arena of intimate relationships based on procreation, child-care and sexual love must be modified. The historical evidence suggests that even in medieval England family groups neither produced from within themselves everything they needed to satisfy their wants nor met all their welfare needs. It also suggests that supposedly modern ideals of individualism and of conjugal love and parental affection were present in pre-modern times. Conversely, some scholars now suggest that ideas of the modern family as a private world of nurturant relationships that stands in opposition to the harsh realities of the public world obscure, on the one hand, the continuing economic importance of the family and, on the other hand, the invasion of the family by public agencies which seek to regulate its child-care activities.

Summary

The data and arguments reviewed in this section point to continuity as well as change in the form and role of the family. All the available evidence suggests that throughout our recorded history the nuclear family has had its being within the context of a fluid and shifting network of extra-nuclear kin relationships; there is no evidence of a progressive disintegration of corporate kin groups, though there have been subtle and fluctuating shifts of emphasis in the strength, range and use made of kin relationships. Again, it seems that some separation of social life into public and private spheres (or, to use the functionalist jargon, differentiation of functions) existed even in medieval England and, conversely, in the modern period the boundaries between public and private appear not to be as sharply drawn as was once thought. Finally, the weight of recent evidence suggests that the emotional significance of the modern family is not distinctively modern but is continuous with its past.

If, as these data suggest, many elements of the 'modern industrial family' – its nuclearity, its individualism, its emphasis on affective relationships – existed as far back as the available historical evidence goes, then neither urban-industrialisation nor the capitalist organisation of production constituted a watershed in family arrangements. These findings thus pave the way for the argument that the modern family is continuous with and shaped by its own past. Some writers have gone further and suggest that the impetus to the capitalist organisation of production and industrialisation may have been fuelled by pre-existing family structures and values. Thus Macfarlane (1978) invites us to infer that the individualistic tendencies of English life (see p. 44) not only pre-dated industrialisation but explain the earlier appearance in England than in continental Europe of trends towards wage labour, capitalistic endeavour and industrial activity. This argument runs counter to arguments which see the modern conjugal family as the outcome of economic imperatives whether they come in a functionalist guise (such as that advanced by Parsons) or in Marxist guises (such as those considered in the next section).

A caveat, however, must be added. Traditional accounts of the development of the modern conjugal family recognise change in the relationship of the nuclear family to extra-nuclear kin and in its role in society, but assume the ubiquity of the nuclear family form. Moreover, as we have already noted, Parsons believes the modern conjugal family to be well adapted to the functions that it must perform and, although he allows for marginal adjustments to resolve particular problems, he clearly believes in its continuing existence and viability. The revisionist theories we have so far discussed also assume the ubiquity of nuclear family form – and of much more besides. They are valuable as a corrective to older ideals of urban-industrialisation as constituting a watershed in familial arrangements. However, they are subject to the criticism that, like

Parsonian theorising, they obscure not only past departures from the nuclear family form (for example, the prevalence of unmarried parenthood and the desertion of wives) but also the contradictions and tensions which permeate conjugal family life in the present and which constitute pressures for the legitimation of alternatives. These pressures for change are dealt with in Chapters 5–7.

3.3   MARXIST APPROACHES

The Marxist tradition presents us with an account of the modern Western family and its relationship to the wider society which is radically different from that found in the functionalist tradition and yet has certain similarities with it. At the substantive level, Marxist analyses, like functionalist analyses, assume the structural isolation of the nuclear family from kin and the intensification of nuclear family relationships. They also emphasise the structural separation of the modern family from other institutional spheres and conceive of the family as concerned primarily with procreation and child-rearing and the provision of psychological support for the individual. Moreover, Marxist analyses, like functionalist analyses, see change in the family as related to change in the economy and posit a close degree of 'fit' between the modern conjugal family and the present economic order. However, where functionalist accounts of the modern Western family take as their frame of reference 'industrial society' or 'modern society' and as their starting-point the notion of society as a functioning whole, Marxist accounts take as their starting-point the division of society into antagonistic classes whose resources, interests and power to influence the course of events are determined by their position in the relations of production. Thus Parsons sees the family's role in producing and rearing children and stabilising adult personality as contributing to the stability and continuity of 'the modern industrial order', but Marxist writers tend to describe these same activities as reproducing an 'oppressive capitalist system'.

In the first part of this section, the work of Friedrich Engels, whose provocative book, *The Origin of the Family, Private Property and the State* (first published in 1884), has profoundly influenced Marxist analyses, is examined. Some contemporary Marxist theories are examined in the second part of the section.

Engels

Engels' account of the development of the modern Western family contains ambiguities but his central argument is based on the Marxist premise that all social life is shaped by the forces and relations of production. On the basis of this premise, he argues that the development of private property was a critical factor in the emergence of monogamous marriage and the modern nuclear family.

Engels contends that during the early stages of history the means of production were communally owned, sexual relationships were promiscuous and domestic life was communistic. The family as such did not exist. Engels believed that as some men began to appropriate surplus wealth for themselves, the private ownership of property came into being and, with it, the development of social institutions for the protection of property. In his view, monogamous marriage was one such institution and was evolved by men as a mechanism for ordering the relations of human reproduction so that they could be sure that they were in fact the fathers of their prospective heirs.

Engels' account of the subsequent development of the family is sketchy, but he seems to have seen the family in feudal society as a unit of production which worked the land within a set of feudal property relationships and he conceives of capitalist industrialisation as acting upon this unit and destroying it. As he (and Marx) saw it, a capitalist class had appropriated the means of production and turned family members into wage labourers, and was creating working and living conditions which made family life almost impossible. At the same time, the bourgeois family was, in Engels' view, a form of prostitution in that it rested on a marriage relationship in which the husband provided the wife with her means of subsistence in return for her sexual fidelity and the reproduction of legitimate heirs.

Engels' work represents one of the earliest attempts to understand the nuclear family not as eternal and natural but as a changing social institution. Moreover, his work is notable for its devastating critique of the monogamous nuclear family as an arrangement through which men control women's sexuality. However, there is general agreement that his attempt to show that the monogamous nuclear family is intimately connected with particular economic arrangements does not 'work'. In the first place, his claim that the nuclear family emerged only with the rise of privately-owned, heritable property cannot be sustained for modern anthropological research has shown that the nuclear family existed in very early hunting and gathering societies. In the second place, his account of the subsequent development of the family is sketchy and of dubious historical validity (Morgan, 1975, pp. 136–40). Third, socialist revolutions have not led to the abolition of the family nor even to any significant change in its form. Finally, his thesis is not generally regarded as helpful in understanding the persistence of the monogamous nuclear family under capitalism. Barrett (1980, pp. 221–2) suggests that in this respect it contains two serious difficulties: (i) it does not explain why the family is now deeply entrenched in the proletariat since working-class men have no property to transmit and inheritance is not an issue for them; (ii) it does not explain the importance of the family to the bourgeoisie themselves since the reproduction of capital does not depend on established paternity; indeed the inheritor's legitimacy or otherwise is irrelevant to capital accumulation.

Contemporary Accounts

In much contemporary Marxist thought, the development and persistence of the conjugal family under capitalism is explained in terms of its utility in reproducing the capitalist system. The New Left of the post-war period emphasised the *ideological* importance of the family for capitalism. These writers (whose views are summarised by Middleton, 1974) present the family as propagating values which are supportive of the capitalist system and as inhibiting a working-class challenge to the capitalist order. They argue that the family socialises children into capitalist ideology and prepares them to accept their place in the class structure, provides an emotionally-supportive retreat for the alienated worker and so dissipates the frustrations of the workplace, and impedes working-class solidarity by privatising the household and generating financial commitments which discourage militant activity.

This thesis was extended in the early 1970s by the argument that the conjugal family is of *economic* as well as of ideological importance for capitalism. Seccombe (1974), in an important contribution to the debate, insists that our consciousness of the family as the opposite of, and separate from, the economy is an illusion. The family, he says, 'has functional aspects of both base and superstructure' (Seccombe, p. 16): it is a dual-faceted institution that both maintains the material world through the reproduction of labour power and the consumption of goods, and sustains the coherence of the social world through the reproduction of the relations of production. In elaborating this thesis, Seccombe argues that the family is of economic importance within capitalism in that it reproduces labour power (that is, the capacity to work). This, says Seccombe, is a twofold process involving the generational reproduction of human beings and the daily sustenance of workers. Generational reproduction (procreation and child-care) ensures that there are future generations of workers, daily sustenance ensures the physical and emotional fitness of today's workers. Further, the family acts as a unit of consumption. Here Seccombe argues that the worker's wage provides the means for purchasing goods for family consumption and these goods are transformed into a form suitable for the physical and psychological maintenance of the family by the labour of the housewife. He further argues that capitalism seeks to maximise family consumption so as to expand the market for its products. Finally, Seccombe maintains that the family is of ideological importance in that it reproduces the relations of production. In Seccombe's view, the primary socialisation of children within the family ensures acceptance of the attitudes and values required for life in a capitalist world and produces people who accept their place in class relations and are willing participants in the social order.

Amplifications of, and modifications to, the argument for the importance of the family as a unit for the reproduction of the capitalist system are manifold. Some writers (for example, Gardiner, 1976) emphasise the cost effectiveness of the conjugal family in reproducing labour power. This argument (as interpreted by Harris, 1983, p. 185) is based on the assumption that unpaid domestic labour (that is, the labour of the housewife) lowers the minimum cost of labour to the advantage of capital since workers would have to buy in domestic and child-care services if the family did not exist, thereby adding to their living costs and raising wage levels. Other writers (for example, Rushton, 1979) have suggested that the family as well as securing for capital unpaid domestic labour secures also a reserve army of labour in that housewives can be drawn upon in periods of high demand for labour and, when no longer needed, can return to the world of the family without appearing in unemployment statistics. Feminist writers have emphasised and drawn attention to women's particular position as unpaid domestic labourers and as a reserve army of labour and identified the implications for their social standing in relation to men (see also pp. 103–6). Finally, some writers have drawn attention to the relationship between the state and the family under capitalism. It has been suggested that the state has acted to ensure that the family performs its role in reproducing the capitalist system effectively. The introduction in the nineteenth century of legislation to restrict women's employment so as to protect their health and child-bearing capacity and to give them sufficient time for their role in the reproduction of labour power is cited as an example of this kind of state action (see p. 79). It has also been argued that the state complements the family in the reproduction of labour power in that it has taken over activities (for example, education and health care) which the family could not effectively perform. In Marxist terminology, the reproduction of the labour force has been partly socialised (in functionalist terminology, the family has lost some of its functions).

The Critics

Marxist accounts of the family take place within a theoretical framework which presupposes class antagonisms, the oppressiveness of capitalism and the permeation of our society by a variety of contradictions or tensions which constitute pressures for change. Nevertheless, the thesis that the family is a key institution for the reproduction of capitalism has frequently been criticised for sliding into a kind of functionalism (see especially Barrett, 1980; Harris, 1983; Morgan, 1979). It is argued that this Marxist formulation sees the modern family as maintaining and reproducing the 'oppressive capitalist order' – in much the same unproblematic way that Parsonian functionalism sees it as contributing to the stability and continuity of the generally beneficent 'modern industrial order'. Consequently, it obscures the effect which pre-existing family structures as well as present-day class and gender conflicts may have on the development and functioning of the family. The particular criticisms levelled against this Marxist thesis are very similar to the criticisms directed against Parsonian functionalism. Discussion has revolved round four sets of issues.

First, the existence of a specifically 'capitalist family' has been questioned in much the same way as the existence of a particular 'industrial family' has been questioned. It has been argued that family patterns in capitalist societies are continuous with and shaped by their pre-capitalist past. The historical evidence reviewed earlier for England (Section 3.2) is used to support this position as are cross-cultural comparisons (between England and Japan, for example) which point to differences between capitalist societies. It has also been argued that there are broad similarities between capitalist family patterns and the family patterns of self-styled socialist societies though Marxist formulations would lead us to expect marked differences. In 'socialist' as in capitalist society industrial labour has been separated from domestic labour and the conjugal family is the major family form. In 'socialist' as in capitalist societies the family reproduces and services the labour force and perpetuates societal values – but in the socialist instance the family is reproducing labour for a socialist mode of production and reproducing socialist rather than capitalist values.

Second and relatedly, the attempt to argue a functional relationship between the conjugal family and the capitalist mode of production takes for granted the existence of such a family form as the dominant type within capitalist societies. Some commentators (for example, Worsley, 1977) have suggested that this style of analysis, like functionalist analyses, obscures variation in family forms and plays down experimentation in alternatives. They have argued that the existence of minority arrangements – one-parent households, single persons living alone or with other single people, childless couples, unmarried couples – indicates that there is room for manoeuvre *within* the capitalist system.

Third, the utility of the conjugal family to capitalism has been questioned. Barrett (1980) says that we have not yet been presented with the kind of analysis that demonstrates that the family is either entirely necessary to capitalism or the most effective mechanism for reproducing labour power. She suggests that the cost of reproducing labour power through a privatised household system is not *prima facie* as low as it could be when compared with a system where migrant workers live in barracks and the cost of their reproduction is borne in the hinterland. Curtis (1980) makes a related point. He says that the profit which can be reaped from employing a male adult worker and paying him a family wage is less than that which can be reaped where each family member works for an individual wage. For 'necessary labour' – that is, that part of the worker's labour which produces a wage and provides for himself and his dependants – expands as the number of his dependants increases while 'surplus labour' – that is, that part of his labour which creates a value which is appropriated by the capitalist class – contracts accordingly. In short, the larger the number of workers relative to dependants the larger the sphere of surplus labour. Consequently, the incorporation of domestic work and child-care into 'capitalist industry proper' and the transformation of housewives into wage-workers would be 'most congenial' to capital.

Finally, the attempt to argue a functional relationship between the family and the requirements of capitalism confronts the problem of working-class support for the conjugal family. This is usually explained by arguing that 'the family' has been imposed on the working classes by the capitalist classes and that working-class support for the family is a form of 'false consciousness' – a lack of awareness of their 'true' interests. This 'ideological impregnation' argument has been challenged. Donzelot (1980, p. 52) suggests that to assert that support for the family from individuals who are not members of the ruling class is the result of 'ideological impregnation comes down to saying, in less delicate language, that these individuals are imbeciles and amounts to a not-too-skilful masking of an interpretative weakness'. Morgan (1979) takes a somewhat different line. He points to evidence of the existence of oppositional values and attitudes in traditional working-class communities – of well-established notions of 'them' and 'us', for example – and argues that the deep-rooted existence of such subversive notions implies not merely patterns of opposition, but patterns which are maintained and reproduced within the working-class culture by the family. His argument implies that different sets of values are reproduced by families in different class positions and that these values, far from being pre-given in terms of capitalist imperatives, are the outcome of, and/or may sustain, class conflict.

Some Marxist writers have attempted to avoid a functionalist–Marxist analysis and its problems. There are two ways of doing this. One is to see family forms under capitalism as the result of the interaction of the development of the capitalist mode of production with pre-existent family forms. This means that capitalist forces and relations of production, though seen as powerful, are not expected to explain every feature of life in capitalist society. This approach is best developed in attempts to 'marry' Marxist and radical-feminist perspectives on gender divisions and will be explored in the next chapter.

The second way of avoiding a functionalist–Marxism is to counterpose working-class struggle and ruling-class efforts to satisfy the needs of capital and to see working-class support for the conjugal family, not as predetermined by capitalist needs, but as the outcome of class struggle. This is what Humphries (1977) does. In a notable paper, Humphries counters the functionalism of the family-meets-the-needs-of-capitalism thesis with the argument that working-class support for the family is an important reason for its survival. Focussing on the nineteenth century, she argues that within the context of developing capitalism, extended kin networks provided a mechanism through which the working class supported its non-labouring members (the old, ill, orphaned), avoided the degradation of the workhouse, and developed the cohesion and solidarity necessary to class struggle. Humphries maintains that 'in a capitalist environment the working class has certain well-defined reasons for defending the family'. This leads to the conclusion that attempts to explain the persistence of the family in terms of the 'functional prerequisites of capitalism' neglect the role of the class struggle.

3.4   IDEATION AND THE CONJUGAL FAMILY

Standing in opposition to functionalist as well as Marxist attempts to locate the origins of the conjugal family in economic change is the argument that in the sixteenth and seventeenth centuries Protestantism fostered ideas, values and beliefs which were instrumental in bringing the modern conjugal family into being. This argument is based on the view that ideational currents develop in terms of their own logic and operate independently of, but in conjunction with, material conditions to sustain or effect change in social arrangements. We look at this argument as it has been developed by Goode (1963), by some feminist researchers and by Ariès (1962).

Goode (1963) sees the conjugal family as characteristic of industrial society and as fitting the needs of industrial economic systems in much the same way as Parsons does. However, he believes that disharmonies between the family and the industrial system together with variations in family patterns indicate that the industrial system does not entirely determine family structure and ideology. He further argues that industrialisation cannot come into being unless the social structure is being transformed in some way. 'Machines' he observes 'do not make social structures; people with specific social patterns make machines' (Goode, 1963, p. 374). With these observations, Goode clears the way for suggesting that ideas are a causal factor in the development of the conjugal family.

He begins this argument by identifying the distinguishing features of the ideology of the conjugal family. This ideology, he says, encourages love and asserts the rights of the individual over obligations to the group. It gives individuals the right to choose their spouse, place of residence and kin obligations and to change their family if they find their family lives unpleasant. Goode then argues that this ideology was derived from a set of more general radical principles, which asserted the equality of individuals as against class, caste or sex barriers and celebrated freedom and individual rights. These individualistic principles were rooted in ascetic Protestantism (Puritanism). Goode reminds us that ascetic Protestantism has been shown to have played a part in capitalist industrialisation, and he uses this argument to suggest that it may have played a part in the development of a conjugal family ideology which provides freedoms and new alternatives as against the rigidities and controls of traditional systems.

Where Goode emphasises the affinity between Puritan ideals and the individualism of the conjugal family system, the feminist researchers, George (1973) and Hamilton (1978), emphasise the affinity between Puritan ideals and the affectivity of the conjugal family. These writers argue that toleration of ungodliness in daily life, which had coexisted comfortably with the medieval Catholic doctrine of salvation through the Church, was totally incompatible with the Protestant doctrine of salvation through a godly life. Puritanism was, they say, committed to the creation of a truly Christian society in which 'the godly would reveal in their every moment of existence the living word of the Lord' (George, 1973, p. 164). They show, through a careful survey of sermons, pamphlets, treatises and other historical documents, that Puritanism exalted the family as having an important role to play in the creation of the godly society. It defined early socialisation as important in bringing the individual to God and invested marriage with the emotional content necessary to produce faithful husbands and stable non-adulterous marriages. Love was seen as purifying sexuality within marriage, 'domesticall virtues' were praised, mutual affection, trust and fidelity extolled and marriage defined as a partnership based upon common labour and love. This argument is extended by Hall (1979) who claims that at the onset of industrialisation the Puritan view of the family was echoed and reinforced by the Evangelical Movement. Hall says that the Evangelicals, like the Puritans, sought to reform manners and morals and defined the family as central to that reformation.

All these writers see religious conceptions of the family as being in part a response to the development of productive forces and in part an ideological form that must be understood in terms of its own logic. The Puritan preachers, says George, were not mouthpieces for capitalist entrepreneurs; they found the ruthless acquisitiveness of capitalism as hateful as the vulgar, rollicking, profane popular culture of the medieval period. But the religious vision of the spiritualised family meshed with a half-formed bourgeois notion of the family as a private retreat in which one could be loved, served and comforted by some dim, non-competitive half-self. Hamilton claims that Puritan ideals gave a family unit stripped of productive activity a *raison d'être* by making it the centre of morality. Similarly, Hall states that the Puritans and later the Evangelicals lived through periods of rapid social change and shared a need to build a protected space in a hostile world. The home provided a haven, an arena which could be controlled and which was, with the expansion of capitalist relations of production in the late eighteenth century, increasingly independent of what went on in the outside world. The emergence of a particular kind of home was thus directly related to the expansion of productive forces, 'but the way that home was realised, lived in and experienced within the middle ranks was crucially mediated by Evangelicalism' (Hall, 1979, p. 29).

Ariès (1962), in his account of the social construction of childhood, also links the development of the modern family to religious belief and practice. Ariès maintains that childhood as a distinctive phase of life did not exist in the Middle Ages and began to emerge only between the fifteenth and seventeenth centuries. He links this to the growing influence of Christianity on life and manners, the 'positive moralisation' of society and the development of a new concern for the moral and spiritual well-being of the child. Children, says Ariès, came to be seen as the fragile and innocent creatures of God, persons not yet ready for life, who must be carefully nurtured so that they might walk in godly ways.

Ariès goes on to argue that the family changed as the concept of childhood developed. He states that in the Middle Ages the infant's uncertain hold of life together with early apprenticeship precluded the development of particular attachments to particular children. Parents cared about children less for themselves than for their contribution to the common task and the family was a social reality that ensured the transmission of property and name. Moreover, life was lived in public, and the house was not a private place, but public space, a place in which friends, relatives, clients, protégés, servants, met and talked. But with the development of concern for the child's moral welfare, the family was, says Ariès, redefined as responsible for moulding souls and bodies. Parents began to watch more closely over their children, to desire that they stay nearer them, to avoid placing them with wet-nurses and apprenticing them to other families. A new value was placed on affection between parents and children and the family became a sentimental reality. This in turn led to the gradual establishment in the eighteenth century of the family as a private arena. The consciousness of the family as a sentimental reality presumed, says Ariès, a zone of physical and moral intimacy and so, beginning in the middle classes, families began to organise themselves as units apart from the community in homes designed for privacy.

These arguments are problematic. Some historians claim, as we have seen, that individualism as well as strong conjugal and parental affection existed both as ideals and in practice well before the close of the Middle Ages. Moreover, it has recently been argued that Protestant teaching concerning the family was not different in essentials from Roman Catholic teaching: both before and after the Reformation, marital and parental bonds were cherished, says Houlbrooke (1984). (See also Davies, 1981.) Furthermore, the actual impact of religious views of the family on behaviour is nowhere clearly documented. However, these accounts of the affinity between the Puritan ethic and conjugal family ideals are important. They show conclusively that individualistic and affective family ideals were not brought into being by industrialisation but flourished in sixteenth-century and seventeenth-century England and so coexisted with the early phases of capitalist entrepreneurial endeavour. It is also probable that individualistic orientations and affective family ideals pre-dated Puritanism. However, to assert this is not to negate the importance of Puritanism; the considerable emphasis which Puritan thought placed on the family as a moral and sentimental reality must have played an important part in refurbishing old ideals and sustaining them. Finally, these arguments, by emphasising familial ideals and their affinity with religious thought, give explanatory power to ideational currents. Family ideals are related to more general bodies of thought, and ideas are seen, not as the somewhat mechanical reflection of the interests of a dominant class, but as developing in terms of their own logic and as having internal validity.

4

Marriage, Parenthood and Gender Divisions

In this chapter we shift from considering arguments surrounding the development of the conjugal family as a relatively isolated and functionally specific unit to considering arguments surrounding relationships within the conjugal family. Here our primary concern is marriage and parenthood, and debates about the roles of men and women – which have so far only been hinted at – are brought on to the centre of the stage. Changes in marriage, parenthood and the sexual division of labour are discussed in the first part of the chapter. Theoretical accounts of gender divisions are discussed in Section 4.2.

4.1 THE NATURE AND DIRECTION OF CHANGE

We found in the previous chapter that present-day research suggests that differences between the industrial and pre-industrial periods in the form and role of the family are less marked than was once supposed. This also seems to be true of marriage, parenthood and the roles of women and men. In the Western world, the scope of women's participation in various productive activities inside and outside the family and men's participation in certain child-care and domestic activities have varied over time and between societies, as has the nature of the child-care task. There have also been some changes in women's formal legal rights and standing as citizens. However, as far back as the available historical evidence goes, child-rearing and domestic labour have been primarily feminine tasks. Changes in marriage, parenthood and the roles of men and women in the wider society have been variations in detail around this fundamental.

Studies of change in the family roles of men and women will be examined in relation to England and in terms of three broad periods:

the pre-industrial, early industrial and late industrial (post-Second World War). It should, however, be borne in mind that these periods are not discrete and that within any period there are class, regional, religious and ethnic variations. It must also be borne in mind that the historical data is often partial and inadequate. In addition, gender relationships are many-layered, and at any one time there may be change in some aspects of gender relations but not in others, or change may be in contradictory directions. Some accounts of change have in fact been distorted by the use of limited or biassed indicators or by a tendency to conflate task-differentiation with inequality. In the discussion that follows an attempt is made to give a balanced account of the history of marriage and gender relationships by keeping task-differentiation and gender inequality separate, and by covering many aspects of both.

The Pre-Industrial Period: The Economic Partnership of Husband and Wife

In the predominantly household-based system of production found in pre-industrial England, domestic labour was not readily separable from productive labour. Family members (wives as well as husbands, children as well as parents) constituted a work group. Among smallholders and in crafts and trades, wives worked with their husbands and, among the nobility, they supported their husbands in the management of their estates (Hamilton, 1978, Chap. 2; Houlbrooke, 1984, Chap. 5). Wives thus contributed to their own maintenance and engaged in a wide range of productive activity. Child-care was rudimentary. Children were themselves involved in the productive activities of the family from an early age and the care of younger children was frequently left to older girls. However, the historical data suggest that, despite the familial nature of production and the rudimentary nature of child-care, gender divisions existed in the pre-industrial period.

Middleton's careful (1979) analysis of the historical materials for the medieval period suggests that there were, during this period, three sources of task differentiation. First, Middleton notes that housework and child-care were women's work. From poetic descriptions, admonitory tracts, proverbial sayings and contemporary illustrations, he says, we learn that it was women who kept house, cleaned, cooked, made clothes and looked after the young and the sick.

Second, Middleton points out that not all labour was familial (see p. 53) and he shows that divisions between domestic and non-domestic labour existed where family members laboured for others. He finds that where the feudal lord extracted labour service (rather than money rents) from the peasant family, male labourers were sometimes insisted upon. Moreover, married women were sometimes exempted from labour services. This practice, says Middleton, seems to indicate a belief in the possibilities of conflict between a married woman's domestic duties and her potential contribution to surplus production, and gave precedence to her household responsibilities. Again, in cottager families, where the meagre livelihood provided by the smallholding was supplemented by wage labour, husbands hired themselves out on a regular basis, wives on a seasonal basis. In other words, there would appear to have been a distinct and separate housewife role and a male breadwinning role even though wives engaged in a wide range of productive activities: it was husbands, not wives, who added to the family's resources by regular paid work.

Occupational specialisation, Middleton suggests, was a third source of medieval gender divisions for, although women performed virtually all the tasks performed by men, certain occupations tended to become the province of one sex. In agriculture and in animal husbandry, ploughing, hedging, ditching, reaping, mowing, spaying and gelding were predominantly male tasks; planting, gathering straw, stubble and chaff, weeding, the care of poultry and the dairy were usually the responsibility of women. In full-time paid employment on the manorial estates gender divisions of the kind found in wage labour under capitalism existed. Middleton finds that there were fewer opportunities for gainful employment for women than for men and that most women were recruited to non-specific service positions, whereas adult males were usually employed in specialist roles.

Middleton's account of occupational specialisation in agriculture is complemented by accounts of sex-segregation in 'urban' crafts and trades. It has been shown that some 'urban' crafts and trades – for example, carpentry and millinery – were identified by sex. Others were carried on as family industries and in these men worked at the more skilled tasks, women at processing the raw materials and finishing the end product. Girls were rarely apprenticed and there were few mistress craftswomen.

In the transitional period between the disintegration of medieval society and the growth of factory production in the eighteenth century, two powerful new forces impinged upon gender relationships. First, the consolidation of farm holdings and the beginnings of capitalistic endeavour brought an increase in wage labour. Women seem to have been pushed into less skilled, less well-paid wage work (Houlbrooke, 1984). Second, as we found in Section 3.4, the period saw the birth of Protestantism and the fashioning of Puritan images of the family as 'an indispensable institution for the rearing and maintaining of the godly' (Hamilton, 1978, p. 94). Hamilton (1978) says that Puritanism invested the economic partnership of husband and wife with a spiritual and emotional content and defined women as guardians of the moral well-being of men and children as well as their husbands' helpmates. The codification of women as domestic beings, which had been implicit in medieval arrangements, was thus reinforced and expanded by Puritanism. However, production remained firmly based in the household during this transitional period and Middleton (1983) shows that married women continued to participate in productive activity and to contribute to their own and to their family's economic maintenance. They also now contributed to capital accumulation. Middleton writes:

> A hardworking and provident wife was an indispensable material asset to any budding entrepreneur. If prosperous yeomen employed several women servants as well, it was not so that their wives and daughters could enjoy more ease and leisure; it was rather because there was too much work for them to cope alone (Middleton, 1983, p. 21).

Finally, women's social standing seems to have differed from that of men in important respects. In the medieval period and in the sixteenth and seventeenth centuries male ownership and tenanting of land was a fundamental feature of the social order. In broad terms, married women participated in the management of estates and in agricultural production on the basis of their marriage relationship and as their husband's subordinates. Hartmann's (1976) account of 'urban' crafts and trades in the sixteenth and seventeenth centuries points to gender inequality in these spheres also. Hartmann suggests that within trades and crafts organised on a family basis, the status of master artisan was a male status, and in trades organised on the basis of sex, women's trades were weakly organised. Furthermore, it was as owners of land or as representatives of the Church that people exercised social and political power. The owners of land were men. The Church was represented by a male and celibate priesthood.

To summarise: the data for medieval and sixteenth-century and seventeenth-century England seem to suggest that, although women engaged in a wide range of productive activities in this period, domestic labour and child-care were women's work, there was occupational specialisation and public power was male power.

The Industrial Period: The Amplification of the Housewife–Mother Role

In the functionalist as well as the Marxist traditions it is presumed that industrialisation had decisive consequences for women's position in society. Thus both Seccombe (1974) and Parsons (1955), the former writing from a Marxist perspective, the latter from a functionalist perspective, see the separation of productive activity from family activity as sharpening the sexual division of labour (see Section 4.2). This view is expanded by Oakley (1976). Writing from a feminist viewpoint, Oakley claims that capitalist industrialisation created the modern role of housewife as the dominant feminine role, produced a sharply segregated marital relationship in which each spouse had separate interests, activities and responsibilities, and led to women's economic dependence. However, recent research emphasises continuity rather than change and points to ways in which gender divisions in the industrial period were built upon gender divisions which had existed in the pre-industrial periods.

The data will be examined in terms of (i) the exclusion of married women from productive activity outside the home; (ii) the segregation of the conjugal relationship, and (iii) changes in women's social standing relative to that of men.

(i) The exclusion of married women from productive activity outside the home

In 1851 only one in four married women was in paid employment. By 1901 the proportion of married women in paid employment had dwindled to one in ten (Land, 1980).

This withdrawal of married women from productive labour outside the home began in the expanding and prosperous middle classes. Wainwright (1978) suggests that in the middle classes the growth of surplus wealth meant that married women no longer had to fulfil managerial functions and so were replaced by paid (male) managers and clerks. But though confined to domesticity, the Victorian middle-class wife did not actually do housework. Oakley (1976) says that like the more prosperous in the pre-industrial period, she employed servants and her role as housewife and mother involved their supervision and responsibility for the moral welfare of the children. Further, as leisure became a symbol of affluence, the possession of a purely decorative wife became a symbol of wealth and success for men.

In the early stages of industrialisation working-class women and children as well as men worked in the mines, mills and factories. Sometimes whole families were employed in the same place. However, the extent to which women were employed outside the home varied between regions and industries (Rushton, 1979). Moreover, even in the early decades of the nineteenth century wives of skilled workers who commanded high wages did not generally participate in paid work and by the end of the nineteenth century to have a wife who did not work had assumed as symbolic a character for the self-respecting industrial worker as it had for the middle-class husband (Oakley, 1976).

A number of reasons for the exclusion of married women from productive labour outside the home have been identified. First, Hartmann (1976) suggests that women's disadvantaged position in pre-industrial production meant that they did not enter the industrial labour force as equal competitors with men. She points out that at the onset of industrialisation there was already a tradition of lower wages for women, women were working at less skilled tasks than men, and women's guilds were less well-organised than men's guilds. In Hartmann's view, women's disadvantaged position in the pre-industrial economy constituted the basis for a disadvantaged position in the industrial economy.

Second, the spatial separation of work and home and long hours of work were defined as making the continued participation of married women in productive labour problematic. Contemporary observers identified women's employment as leading to child neglect and juvenile depravity and complained lengthily about the fate of men married to employed females who had no home but the beer shop. They emphasised the consequences of brutalising work conditions for maternal, foetal and perinatal mortality and for congenital defects in children. The outcome of this perception of the consequences of married women's employment was a series of legislative measures prohibiting women's employment in mines and limiting their working hours in factories. Barrett and McIntosh (1980) say that this legislation increased the differentiation of men's from women's work and reduced their competitive position in the labour market.

Third, during the nineteenth and early twentieth centuries the child-rearing task grew enormously. Oakley (1976) points out that children's dependence on adults was increased and extended first by legislation prohibiting or restricting their employment, and then by the introduction in 1870 of legislation allowing compulsory education up to the age of 13 and by subsequent extensions of the school-leaving age. It has also been suggested that the establishment, at the turn of the century, of ante-natal and post-natal clinics, of a health-visiting service and of other health services aimed particularly at children defined and raised standards of child-care. Oakley suggests that these and related developments amplified motherhood and tied women more firmly to child-care.

Finally, some writers stress the importance of ideas and ideals in codifying women as domestic beings. Hall (1979) suggests that the idea of the family as an important arena of struggle against the sinfulness of the world and of women as responsible for the moral well-being of family members which Puritanism had promulgated in the sixteenth and seventeenth centuries was also vigorously promoted in the eighteenth and nineteenth centuries, this time by the Evangelical Movement. Hall says that the Evangelical ideal became part of the dominant culture by the 1840s and, because home and family were now separate from work, its effect was to confine women to the family.

So we find that by the end of the nineteenth century married women were located in the home and were identified with domesticity. Apart from brief upsurges in their employment during the First and Second World Wars, they continued to take little part in productive labour outside the home until the 1950s. This had as its consequence women's economic dependence on men which, in turn, entailed men's increased responsibility for the support of their families. The concept of the male breadwinner, implicit in medieval arrangements, became explicit at an early stage in industrialisation. It was enshrined in the Poor Laws (Hamilton, 1978) and wages were customarily set higher for men than for boys and women (Land, 1980). Further, the (male-dominated) trade union movement struggled to establish the idea of the 'hard-working man' responsible for the support of his family and claimed a 'family wage' on this basis (Barrett and McIntosh, 1980; Land, 1980). Furthermore, men came to be identified with their occupational role in much the same way as married women were identified with the housewife role.

However, the division between men as breadwinners and women as domestic beings was not impermeable. Land (1980) shows that male wages were not always adequate and that some households were without a male head. Married women, Land points out, earned money and contributed to the family's support by taking in lodgers or boarders, child-minding, taking in washing and going out cleaning. Women's domestic labour has itself been seen as important to production in that it maintains the labour force. This argument suggests that married women keep the present generation of workers fit for work by providing for the physical and emotional needs of their husbands. It further suggests that married women nurture the future generation of workers by providing physical care for children and socialising them into acceptance of a work role. (See pp. 103–6 for a fuller examination of this 'domestic labour debate'.) All these arguments suggest that married women, even when not directly involved in paid work outside the home, play an important part in productive activity.

(ii)   The segregation of the conjugal relationship

Folklore and the sociological literature tell us that in the early industrial period the identification of married women with domestic labour and of men with breadwinning was paralleled by a further segregation of activities and interests within the domestic domain. The conjugal relationship, it is suggested, was one in which husband and wife had distinct and separate responsibilities, activities, interests and friendships. This type of relationship is commonly referred to as a 'segregated conjugal role relationship'. (This term was introduced into the literature by Bott, 1957.)

The separation of interests and activities appears to have been at its sharpest among the urban poor. Mid-twentieth century studies of low-income, long-established working-class neighbourhoods (Dennis *et al.*, 1956; Mogey, 1956; Young and Willmott, 1957) show that the husband's role in the family ended with the handing-over to his wife of a part of his wages. The management of the home and children were almost entirely the wife's responsibility. Moreover, there seems to have been little expectation of companionship or emotional supportiveness between husband and wife: for men, meaningful activity was located in the activities they shared with other men, while wives turned to their mothers and female kin for emotional support, companionship and advice. These studies suggest that in the working classes the good husband was typically defined as the husband who keeps to his regular routine and gives his wife her 'wages' regularly, and the good wife as the wife who keeps the home clean and the children quiet.

Men were not, however, entirely absent from family life. Household tasks requiring physical strength and/or training in manual skills were very generally male-defined tasks. Authority and discipline and the initiation of adolescent boys into the adult male role seem also to have been defined as paternal responsibilities. Further, role-differentiation seems to have broken down in emergencies (Roberts, 1984), where women were in full-time employment (Roberts, 1984) or where men, because of illness or the vicissitudes of the labour market, were unable to perform their breadwinning role (Angell, 1936; Dennis *et al.*, 1956).

(iii) Changes in women's social standing

Women's formal political and civil standing changed in important ways during the nineteenth and early twentieth centuries. Sachs and Wilson (1978) say that at the onset of industrialisation women's formal status was in important respects the legacy of their position in medieval society and reflected understandings of the family as an institution concerned with the ownership and transmission of land and family name through the male line. Husband and wife constituted a single legal personality. Married women's ownership and control of property was limited, and parental authority was formally vested in the father. Moreover, there were formal barriers to women's participation in the public world. Women had no vote and could not hold public office. Their right to education was limited and they were barred from the professions.

These 'disabilities' were removed in the closing years of the nineteenth century and early years of the twentieth century. Legislative reform gave married women the legal right to the independent control and use of their own property and income. Further, husband and wife were placed on an equal footing in child-custody disputes and, given beliefs in the importance of maternal care, this effectively de-legitimised the claim of the father to child-custody in divorce proceedings. Women also gained the right to vote, to hold public office, to obtain higher education and to enter the professions. As a result of these changes, women's formal political and civil status was higher in the early years of the twentieth century than it had been at the onset of industrialisation. However, Sachs and Wilson (1978) say that women's material position was not greatly improved by these reforms. Women's domestication, they argue, rendered them economically dependent on men, narrowed their options and left them without political and economic power. This was not altered by reforms which enhanced their marital and parental rights and their status as citizens but left untouched their position (or lack of position) in productive labour outside the home.

The Post-Second World War Period: A More Symmetrical Division of Labour?

The early post-war period witnessed the emergence of expectations of the husband–father's active involvement in family life and women's return to productive labour. These trends were variously portrayed in the sociological literature of the 1950s and 1960s as leading to a 'partnership marriage' (Young and Willmott, 1957), 'a joint conjugal role relationship' (Bott, 1957), 'companionate' marriage (Goldthorpe *et al.*, 1969) and a 'symmetrical relationship' (Young and Willmott, 1973). Bott (1957) defined the joint conjugal relationship as a relationship characterised by the joint organisation of family activity (as evidenced by the extent to which husbands and wives plan the affairs of the family together and share child-rearing, household tasks, leisure and social relationships). Her account of marriage recognised the coexistence of segregated and joint conjugal roles, but implied a progressive trend towards 'jointness'. Similarly, Young and Willmott (1973) suggested that the segregated relationship which was characteristic of the nineteenth century had given place to a 'symmetrical relationship' in which marital roles, although not the same, are similar in terms of the contribution each partner makes to family life. They described as 'symmetrical' an arrangement in which husbands play a part in child-rearing and household management, though the main responsibility remains with wives, and wives play a part in the economic support of the family, though the main responsibility remains with husbands.

The writers of the 1950s and 1960s did not suggest that there had been any fundamental realignment of the sexual division of labour. They suggested only that its rigidity had softened. Further, their main emphasis was not on labour but on leisure and the psychological closeness of husband and wife and parents and children. They pointed to the attrition of male peer group activities and female kin networks and to the greater companionateness of family members within the home and in leisure, and linked this with the wider diffusion of 'the loving conjugal family' ideal. Their objects of study were usually working-class families. Moreover, they pointed to change in men's rather than in women's roles. The modern working-class husband and father was implicitly compared with the 'absentee husband', 'partner only of the bed' (phrases used by Young and Willmott, 1957) that earlier studies of the urban poor had revealed. With the urban poor as their point of comparison, the writers of the 1950s and 1960s believed that we were witnessing the fortunate conversion of the 'absentee husband' into the 'family man', a trend towards joint conjugal roles and improvements in women's status.

This image of marriage and parenthood was shattered in the late 1960s by the sudden eruption of modern feminism. The feminist studies of the 1970s suggest that men's involvement in domestic labour is limited, point out that women have entered a specifically female labour market and say that there has been no fundamental change in the relative status of women and men. Feminist researchers focus on labour rather than leisure and relate men's familial labour not to their past performance but to women's present labour. From this standpoint, they find that joint conjugal roles are a myth. Furthermore, they see continued sex-role differentiation as indicating the continued subordination of women in marriage and in the wider society.

The debate will be examined in detail in terms of (i) the expansion of men's familial roles; (ii) women's re-involvement in productive activity outside the home; (iii) male/female power, and (iv) the effects of recession. (Useful discussions of the concepts and indicators used in this debate are to be found in Edgell 1980, Chaps. 2 and 5 and Harris, 1983, Chap. 12.)

(i)   The expansion of men's familial roles

Men's participation in family life was amply recorded in studies of the 1950s and 1960s. In the 1950s, Young and Willmott (1957) observed with surprise that modern young East End fathers wheel prams up Bethnal Green Road on Saturday mornings, take their daughters rowing and play with their sons on the putting green. They also demonstrated men's participation in household tasks and suggested that do-it-yourself home-improvement activities had become a significant and meaningful part of male leisure (Young and Willmott, 1957; Willmott and Young, 1960). Zweig (1961) reported similar changes in the life-style of affluent factory workers. He writes:

> Fathers of babies often push the pram, give them baths, see them to bed; fathers of toddlers often read them stories, play with them, take them for a walk at weekends; fathers of school-children often go to the school for progress reports and supervise their homework; fathers of adolescents try to apprentice them or find them suitable jobs (Zweig, 1961, p. 20).

Like Willmott and Young, Zweig also claimed that men now seek their 'pleasures and comforts' at home. Affluent workers, Zweig says, use their new-found resources to make their homes comfortable and to acquire consumer durables for family leisure. Television, he says, keeps men at home and provides family entertainment and 'the car' becomes a means to family outings. Yet further evidence of men's involvement in the intimate routines of family life came from various community studies (Mogey, 1956; Rosser and Harris, 1965), the affluent worker studies of Goldthorpe and his colleagues (1969) and two longitudinal studies of child-rearing (the Newsons' Nottingham study, 1963, and The National Child Development Study, 1976). Moreover, various changes in the public world pointed to the amplification of the husband–father role. Hospitals began to make arrangements for fathers to be present at the births of their children, pressures towards the institutionalisation of paternity leave developed and the idea that fathers, as well as mothers, can be child-carers began to be advanced in divorce and child-custody proceedings.

However, the feminist and feminist-influenced research of the 1970s and 1980s suggests that only a minority of husbands actually give the kind of help that conjugal role jointness implies (see, for example, Edgell, 1980; Marsden, 1982; Martin and Roberts, 1984; Oakley, 1974). This research has shown that men's participation in housework and child-care is low where wives are not in paid employment, that it may increase where they are in paid work or where husbands are unemployed, but that even in these circumstances primary responsibility for the home and children typically falls to women. Men's involvement in child-care seems to be greater than their involvement in housework, but is nevertheless limited to its pleasant side. 'Fathers' Oakley (1974, pp. 154–5) finds 'are there to play with children... The father is expected to take the children off the mother's hands occasionally at weekends, to be generally interested in their well-being and to take over in times of crisis'. The 'unpleasant' side of child-rearing – the nitty-gritty of nappy-changing and washing – is the mother's responsibility.

A number of recent studies (Cohen, 1977; Edgell, 1980; Elliot, 1978 and 1979; Finch, 1983; Pahl and Pahl, 1971) suggest that the limited amplification of 'the family man' role is the corollary of the continued definition of the husband–father as 'the family breadwinner' and of the way in which the present structuring of work roles limits the time and energy available for his familial involvement. Elliot (1982) points to three ways in which the male work role constrains the husband–father's participation in family life. First, the economic system is founded on the rational pursuit of efficiency and therefore on the maximisation of the labour power of the worker. This system leaves little room for the personal and familial. Second, Elliot argues that the maximisation of income and status (in other words success in the breadwinning role) is in many circumstances related to the time and energy invested in the work role: in the salaried professions and in senior management success depends on promotion up a career ladder and therefore on high performance standards, the acceptance of ever-increasing responsibilities and long hours of work; in manual occupations earning power may be increased by overtime work, shiftwork and moonlighting. Thus in senior professional positions and in skilled manual work, the working week may exceed the 'standard' 40–hour week. Third, Elliot suggests that the work role, precisely because it is defined as men's primary role, is central to their standing in society and their images of self-worth. It therefore competes with the family role for ego-involvement as well as for time and energy.

Elliot maintains that the male work role always limits men's familial involvement but that the extent to which it does so varies between occupations. Men, Elliot says, are least likely to be highly work-involved in occupations in which work does not have intrinsic satisfactions, brings neither status nor power and provides few opportunities for rewarding relationships. Broadly speaking, manual and white-collar work is of this kind and for the most part research findings of men's participation in family life relate to these occupations. However, in the older professions and senior management, work offers intrinsic satisfactions, prestige and power and generates a professional culture which demands devotion to the task and commitment to the colleague group. In these occupations, work constitutes a 'central life interest' (a term used by Dubin, 1956), and wives' self-sufficiency in managing the household and support for their husbands' single-minded capacity for work are highly valued. Elliot emphasises that the work-orientated traditions of the established professions are incompatible with a family ideology that stresses men's active involvement in family life. Similarly, in a study of male managers and their wives, Pahl and Pahl (1971) find that an ideology of 'closeness' in marriage is not readily realised because of the demands of the husband's job. They suggest that this clash between family ideals and the male work role is an important source of conflict in middle-class life.

(ii)   Women's re-involvement in productive activity outside the home

Throughout the 1950s, 1960s and the first half of the 1970s married women's involvement in paid work (particularly in part-time work) increased markedly. This trend reached its peak in 1977 when just over 50 per cent of married women were 'economically active' (that is in full-time or part-time employment or seeking employment) compared with just under 22 per cent in 1951 (Equal Opportunities Commission, 1982, Table 3.1).

This return to paid work seems to have been facilitated by two (apparently unrelated) events. First, family limitation made motherhood a 'phase of life' rather than a lifetime's activity. Titmuss (1963) shows that in the mid-twentieth century the typical mother experienced two or three pregnancies whereas the typical working-class mother of the 1890s experienced ten. The Victorian mother spent fifteen years of her life in a state of pregnancy and in caring for children during their first year of life. When her youngest child left school she was in her mid-fifties and then, because life expectation was low, had only a few years to live. In contrast the mid-twentieth century mother spent four years of her life in a state of pregnancy and infant care and, despite the extension of the school-leaving age, finished with child-rearing by the age of forty. With lengthening life-expectancy conditions, she then had another thirty-six years to live. Titmuss emphasises that family limitation, together with changes in life expectancy, have freed women from continuous child-rearing and for involvement in other areas of life. The late 1950s and early 1960s did in fact see a moderate boom in births and child-bearing at very young ages, but these trends were short-lived and family-building patterns have increasingly facilitated women's paid employment. The average number of children women have has fallen since the late 1960s (Table 4.1) and the average age of married women at the birth of their first child has risen (Table 4.2). This latter trend may in part indicate a growing tendency to lay career-foundations before 'starting a family' (*Population Trends*, Winter, 1984, p. 6).

The second development which has been commonly identified as affecting women's position in the division of labour is the labour shortage which was created by the expansion of the service sector of the economy and by the growth of the Welfare State in the 1950s and 1960s. Married women (and immigrants) filled this gap. Conversely, the current recession seems to have halted the increase in married women's paid employment. The proportion of married women who were economically active in 1981 (just under 50 per cent) was virtually the same as it had been in 1977 (Equal Opportunities Commission, 1982, Table 3.1).

A further and important element in women's increased participation in paid work is the speed with which they now return to it after child-bearing. Martin and Roberts (1984), in a recent survey of women and employment, show that half of the women who had a first baby between 1975 and 1979 returned to work within four years; the comparable figure for women who had their first birth between 1950 and 1954 was 9.6 years. The survey also shows that the proportion of women ultimately returning to work has in fact

Table 4.1   *Post-Second World War fertility trends, England and Wales*

Year	Total period fertility rate[1]
1964 (post-war maximum)	2.93
1977 (post-war minimum)	1.66
1980 (latest peak)	1.88
1983	1.76

[1]   Average number of children women would have if they experienced current fertility rates throughout their childbearing period.

SOURCE   *Population Trends*, Winter, 1984, p. 6.

Table 4.2   *Mean age of women at birth of first child in marriage, England and Wales, 1973 and 1983*

	1973	1983
Women married to men in professional or managerial occupations	26.3	27.9
Women married to men in semi-skilled or unskilled manual occupations	22.7	23.7

SOURCE   *Population Trends*, Winter, 1984, p. 6.

been high for much of the post-war period: 87 per cent of women whose first birth was in the early 1940s and 90 per cent of women whose first birth was in the late 1950s and early 1960s returned to full-time or part-time paid employment at some stage. Taken together, these figures suggest a new and significant change in the extent to which mothers of young children work outside the home. They also indicate that although few women adopt the typical male pattern of continuous participation in the labour market – only 4 per cent of women with children had been in paid work continuously – an increasing proportion of women's lives is spent in paid employment. As a result dual-worker families (in which husbands work full-time and wives work full-time or part-time) are now common.

Women's earnings contribute in important ways to the family's economic standing. McNay and Pond (1980) cite evidence showing that in the mid-1970s the number of couples having an income of less than 140 per cent of Supplementary Benefit would have trebled were it not for the earnings of the wife. McNay and Pond also say that in the 1970s families increasingly required two wage-earners to achieve the relative living standards that could have been achieved in the 1950s by the efforts of one wage-earner. Taking households as a whole, wives' income constituted 16.1 per cent of family income in 1983 (Family Expenditure Survey, 1983, Table 21).

However, all the evidence suggests that the housewife–mother role continues to be defined as women's primary role and to dominate their lives. Wainwright (1978) says that the wife-mother role, because it is defined as involving direct care for individual human needs, demands women's 'exclusive personal loyalty'. Oakley (1974) points to the heavy demands it makes on women's time and energy. She found, in a study of housework, that the average working week of the wife–mother is 77 hours. Oakley further points out that the wife–mother is never off duty; she remains responsible for children even when they and she are asleep. Finch (1983) has recently pointed out that in addition to domestic work and child-care, a wife's role may include active support for her husband in his work: the MP's wife nurtures his constituency; the clergy-wife is involved in the organisation of Church affairs; the army officer's wife pays welfare visits to the wives of other ranks; the businessman's wife entertains his colleagues and clients; the wife of the self-employed man provides secretarial services and so on. Finally, some writers have emphasised that women's domesticity extends beyond the care of husbands and children to include the expectation that they care for the old, the sick and the disabled (Briggs, 1983; Finch and Groves, 1983).

Two consequences for women's employment seem to flow from their familial commitments. First, it has been shown that the attempt to combine motherhood with paid employment presents women with intense overload dilemmas and conflicts of loyalty and commitment (Rapoport and Rapoport, 1976) and may involve considerable mental and physical stress (Shimmin *et al.*, 1981). Leisure activities and kin and neighbourhood relationships may be crowded out (Rapoport and Rapoport, 1976) and the wife's career goals tend to be subordinated to the needs of her family and to her husband's career (Edgell, 1980; Finch, 1983).

Second, it has been shown that women's familial commitments, in conjunction with the way in which labour is utilised and rewarded in modern Western economies, entail their relegation to a position in the labour market that is low-paid, low in status, without power and related to cultural conceptions of femininity. Three ways in which this happens have been identified:

1. The American sociologist, Caplow (1954) suggests that because women move in and out of the labour force to have children (and he might have added to care for relatives) their working-life is discontinuous and their occupation one in which employment is short-term and 'the gain in skill achieved by continuous experience is slight, in which interchangeability is very high and in which the loss of skill during long periods of inactivity is relatively small' (Caplow, 1954, p. 245). Caplow's statement pinpoints a perception of women's work potential which seems to have been fairly general and which helps explain how, in an economic system founded on the rational pursuit of efficiency and the maximisation of profit, women workers came to be concentrated in semi-skilled and unskilled work and to/have low earning power. In Britain in 1983, women's full-time hourly earnings were just over 74 per cent of men's (Equal Opportunities Commission, 1983, p. 89).

2. Some writers (for example, Barrett, 1980) suggest that women are expected to, and believe that they should, assume only those occupational commitments which are compatible with their family commitments. This means that they tend to seek part-time work and homework, though this work is low-paid, low in status and vulnerable to redundancy. Three-quarters of working women with a child under five work part-time, as against 7 per cent of childless women (Martin and Roberts, 1984). In 1981, 42 per cent of female employees were working part-time compared with only 6 per cent of male employees (*Social Trends*, 1984, p. 63). Relatedly, Coser and Rokoff (1971) say that married women's access to the professions and to other high status occupations is limited because these occupations typically demand a degree of commitment to work that is incompatible with expectations of the wife–mother.

3. Women are concentrated in occupations which involve caring for others or which are socialised forms of domestic labour such as teaching, nursing, social work, office work and catering. In 1983, 60 per cent of all female manual workers were employed in catering, cleaning, hairdressing or other personal services. In non-manual employment, 52 per cent of female workers were

in clerical and related occupations and 27 per cent were in professional and related occupations in education, welfare and health (Equal Opportunities Commission, 1983, p. 79). That is, women seem to have readiest access to occupations that are in some sense an extension of their familial roles. Moreover, women entering 'masculine' occupations tend to be located in 'feminine' areas: women lawyers take up matrimonial work; women doctors take up obstetrics, gynaecology and paediatrics; women police deal with female offenders; women sociologists specialise in the sociology of gender divisions.

In sum, it seems that in re-entering productive labour, women have entered a specifically female labour market, a market that is low-paid, low in status, and in which there is little or no control over the allocation of resources. They have done so not merely because paid work is defined as secondary to their role as wives and mothers, but also because 'success' in the modern occupational world depends on the worker's total commitment to that world. Commitments to one sphere do not mesh easily with commitments to the other.

(iii)   Male/female power and the sexual division of labour

In the 1950s and 1960s beliefs in men's greater participation in family life together with married women's return to paid work led to the assumption that women had achieved equality, or near equality, with men. Paid employment was very generally interpreted as giving women some measure of economic independence and as increasing their options, including the option to leave an unsatisfactory marriage. Some researchers reported joint decision-making within marriage (Gavron, 1966) and the perception by young couples of their marriages as egalitarian (Zweig, 1961; Gavron, 1966). Moreover, women's civil rights were extended in the 1970s and this was again interpreted as reflecting and establishing women's improved social position. Notably, the principle of equal pay for like work was formally established under the Equal Pay Act 1970 (operative from 1975) and sex discrimination in employment and in various other areas of social life was prohibited under the Sex Discrimination Act (1975).

However, the interpretation of post-war developments as establishing gender equality is vigorously countered by the feminist argument that the continued domination of women's lives by their wife–mother roles, together with their overwhelming location in poorly-paid, low-status and part-time employment, place women in a position of subordination to men. Women's position in the labour market, says Wainwright (1978), means that they remain economically dependent on men. This material dependence turns personal relationships between the sexes into relationships of power and subjugation and leaves women without power in the public world. In Wainwright's view, women's achievement of legal and political rights has not been matched by the equalisation of their social conditions and consequently a formal equality coexists with the reality of dependence and subordination.

The husband's dominance within the family and its connection to his role as family breadwinner is demonstrated by Edgell (1980). In a study of middle-class couples, Edgell shows that decisions about house purchase, children's education, holidays and leisure activities are made jointly by husband and wife, that routine housekeeping decisions are made by the wife but that career-related decisions are made by the husband. Edgell argues that these decisions have important consequences for family life. For example, where the couple live, the scheduling of family activities and the amount of family income are determined by the husband's career decisions. Edgell suggests that the husband is given the right to make decisions over a whole range of career-related activities which have important consequences for his wife and family because his occupational role constitutes the economic basis of family life and its demands are regarded as pre-eminent. Consequently, considerable power to order the life of family members accrues to the husband. Edgell emphasises that the husband's power derives not simply from his access to resources which his wife, as homemaker, does not have but from the fact that his occupational role is also the family's principal source of income and status.

That men exercise a considerable control over women's sexuality and reproductive processes is also a prominent theme in certain strands of feminist thought and research. This feminist literature shows that the ever-present threat of rape, assault and sexual harassment limits women's movements, their encounters with other people and their autonomy (see, for example, Brownmiller, 1976; Smart and Smart, 1978). It also suggests that popular beliefs in the urgency of male sexual 'need' are a form of male privilege, emphasises that the sex act itself is defined in male terms and for male pleasure (see, for example, Campbell, 1980) and points out that the management of pregnancy and childbirth is in the hands of a male-dominated profession (see, for example, Oakley, 1981). Furthermore, it is argued that women's freedom to choose whether or not to have a child is limited by the less-than-total satisfactoriness of available methods of contraception, by the fact that abortion is not available on demand, and by the general cultural belief that married motherhood is the 'natural' goal of all 'normal' women (see, for example, Macintyre, 1976).

Women's lack of power in the public world has also been extensively elaborated by feminist writers. They have argued that educational, medical, legal and political, as well as economic institutions are controlled by men and operate in terms of male-defined goals and interests and on the assumption that women's 'proper' place is in the home. Often cited as indicators of women's limited role in the public world are their under-representation in trade union leadership (Table 4.3) even in unions with a predominantly female membership, in the membership of professional institutes (Table 4.4) and on public bodies (Table 4.5). As at October 1984, there were only 25 women MPs in the House of Commons (House of Commons Weekly Information Bulletin, 3 November 1984, p. 23), only one woman on the Opposition Front Bench (House of Commons Weekly Information Bulletin, 3 November 1984) and only one woman (albeit the Prime Minister, Margaret Thatcher) in the Cabinet (House of Commons Weekly Hansard, Issue No 1324, 6–9 November 1984, p. xi). Finally, feminist writers have shown that in one way or another male domination is reflected in and supported by the images of men and women that appear in the media, in literature and art, in children's reading materials, in our myths and folklore, and in the language that we use. Greer (1971) observes that even terms for sexual intercourse in popular use are male-orientated and emphasise male initiative, domination and penetration.

(iv) The effects of recession

The current recession carries a potential for restructuring gender roles through the development of strategies for role-sharing – that is, through the development of strategies whereby women and men share available jobs by working part-time and share domestic labour. There are however few indications that this potential is being

Table 4.3 *Representation of women in trade unions*

Union	Membership % Women	Executive members		Full-time officials		TUC delegates	
		Total	Women[6]	Total	Women[6]	Total	Women[6]
APEX[2]	53.2	15	4 (8)	50	2 (26)	12	5 (6)
ASTMS[2]	22.5	22	2 (5)	97	7 (22)	31	6 (7)
BIFU[5]	49.0	31	3 (15)	54	6 (26)	20	5 (10)
CPSA[1]	72.7	29	12 (21)	37	8 (27)	15	7 (11)
GMBATU[2]	28.8	31	1 (9)	290	16 (84)	86	3 (25)
NALGO[2]	52.0	71	18 (37)	181	16 (94)	72	18 (37)
NUPE[1]	66.7	26	10 (17)	161	10 (107)	31	10 (21)
NUT[3]	72.2	47	6 (34)	27	2 (19)	27	3 (19)
NUTGW[4]	92.7	14	7 (13)	38	3 (35)	12	4 (11)
TGWU[1]	14.7	39	1 (6)	502	10 (74)	83	3 (12)
USDAW[1]	55.6	17	1 (9)	125	8 (69)	36	6 (20)

1 Figures were supplied by the individual trade union and are as at December 1983.
2 Figures were supplied by the individual trade union and are as at September 1983.
3 Membership figures are as at December 1982; TUC delegates are for the 1983 conference; Executive members and full-time officials are as at February 1984.
4 Membership figures are as at December 1983; TUC delegates are for the 1983 conference; Executive members and full-time officials are as at April 1984.
5 Membership figures are for the year ending December 1980. Figures for Executive members and full-time officials were supplied by BIFU. TUC delegate figures are derived from the TUC Annual Report 1981.
6 Figures in brackets show how many women there would be if they were represented according to their share of the membership.

KEY   APEX   Association of Professional and Executive Staff   NUPE   National Union of Public Employees
ASTMS   Association of Technical and Managerial Staff   NUT   National Union of Teachers
BIFU   Banking, Insurance and Finance Union   NUTGW   National Union of Tailors and Garment Workers
CPSA   Civil and Public Services Association   TGWU   Transport and General Workers' Union
GMBATU   General, Municipal, Boilermakers and Allied Trades Union   USDAW   Union of Shop, Distributive and Allied Workers
NALGO   National Association of Local Government Officers

SOURCE   Equal Opportunities Commission, *Eighth Annual Report*, 1983, Table 5.4, adapted.

Table 4.4 *Female membership of selected professional institutes or associations, 1983*

Professional institute	Total no. of members	% Women
Hotel Catering and Institutional Management Association	21 811	47.1
Institute of Personnel Management	25 095	37.2
British Medical Association	65 393	23.4
Institute of Health Service Administrators	2 850	18.9
Institute of Bankers	114 674	14.4
The Law Society (solicitors)[1]	54 697	14.2
The Chartered Insurance Institute	59 408	11.4
Royal Town Planning Institute	8 743	10.5
Association of Certified Accountants	26 052	8.7
The Rating and Valuation Association	4 953	7.1
Institute of Chartered Accountants of England and Wales	76 993	5.6
Institution of Chemical Engineers	15 191	4.2
Institute of Marketing	21 099	3.9
British Institute of Management	73 483	2.4
Royal Institute of Chartered Surveyors	50 337	1.6
Institution of Mechanical Engineers	63 758	0.7
Institute of Building	27 030	0.5
Institution of Production Engineers	15 852	0.5

[1] These figures are as at January 1982.

SOURCE Equal Opportunities Commission, *Eighth Annual Report* (1983), Table 5.3 (adapted), compiled by the EOC from information supplied by individual professional institutes.

Table 4.5 *Appointments to public bodies,*[1] *1983*

Parent department	Male appointments	Female appointments	Women as a % of total
Scottish Office[2]	3095	1319	29.9
Home Office[2]	2499	1023	29.0
Trade and Industry[2]	1057	320	23.2
Health and Social Security	9606	2840	22.8
Environment	6158	966	13.6
Employment	5329	806	13.1
Education and Science	661	85	11.4
Welsh Office	813	94	10.4
Transport	385	34	8.1
Foreign and Commonwealth Office	288	23	7.4
Energy	211	16	7.0
Inland Revenue and HM Customs and Excise	5206	282	5.1
Defence	409	18	4.2
Agriculture, Fisheries and Food	1481	50	3.3
HM Treasury	91	3	3.2
Overall	37 289	7879	17.4

[1] Public bodies refer to organisations for which Ministers have a degree of accountability, such as nationalised industries, public corporations, advisory bodies, tribunals and National Heath Service Authorities.

[2] Sex of some appointees was not known; these were therefore excluded from this analysis.

SOURCE Equal Opportunities Commission, *Eighth Annual Report* (1983), Table 5.2, compiled by the EOC from information supplied by government departments.

realised. In general, responses to the recession reflect, and perpetuate, the sexual division of labour.

First, the evidence suggests that unemployment is widely perceived as problematic for men but not for married women. It is, it seems, interpreted as depriving men of the role that defines their place in the family and in society, but as leaving married women with an alternative approved role, that of full-time housewife and mother. Thus, unemployed married women are unlikely to be labelled scroungers; unemployed men may be. Studies of the consequences of unemployment suggest that deprived of the role that defines their place in family and society men become disorientated and defeated and may be prone to a variety of 'pathologies'. It has been shown that unemployed men are nineteen times more likely than employed men to attempt suicide and six times more likely to be suspected of child abuse (Harris 1984), are particularly likely to get divorced (Table 6.4), and may become impotent or alternatively may attempt to 'prove' their masculinity by sexual aggressiveness (Chappell, 1982).

Second, there are few indications that the recession is leading to greater flexibility in the allocation of domestic labour. Marsden's findings (1982) suggest that men do not generally compensate for the loss of a work role by significantly increasing their participation in domestic labour. Married women, on the other hand, may feel guilty about taking paid employment, believing that in a recession the available jobs are a male prerogative. Nor is there any evidence that role-reversal is taking place. Wives of unemployed men are less likely to be in paid employment than married women in general: only about 10–15 per cent of the wives of long-term unemployed men are in paid employment (Harris, 1984). This may relate to the way in which social security benefits are paid since wives' earnings reduce entitlement to supplementary benefit but may be too low substantially to raise the family's living standards (Martin and Roberts, 1984).

Third, it has been shown that women's employment opportunities in recession are related to their position in the labour market. Walby (1983) notes that married women are particularly vulnerable to redundancy in that they are heavily located in part-time work and, because they move in and out of the labour market, are liable to be dismissed before men on the 'last in, first-out' principle. However, a further critical factor in the relative vulnerability of men and women to recession is the sex-segregation of the labour force. This, as Walby notes, may have varying effects. In the first half of the 1970s, women's concentration in the service sector protected them from the worst effects of the recession since this sector of the economy continued to expand while manufacturing industry contracted. Thus, although women in manufacturing industry were more likely than men to lose their jobs, the continuing expansion of the service sector provided an area of expanding employment opportunities and the proportion of married women in work increased. However, this degree of protection may be under threat for traditional female occupations are now endangered by technological advance (for example, by the automation of clerical work, *New Society*, 15 March, 1984) and by cuts in the social services (Edgell and Duke, 1983). As has already been indicated (p. 87), the upward trend in women's paid employment came to an end in the late 1970s.

Finally, some writers (for example, Edgell and Duke, 1983) suggest that attempts to cut public expenditure – by rationalising or reducing the personal social services, pre-school facilities and other welfare provision – extend women's caring role in the home and may result in their reducing or giving up paid work. Smart (1984) claims that the political strategies of the Right are combining with the recession and a male backlash to create a powerful reaction against married women's participation in productive labour outside the home.

4.2   THEORETICAL PERSPECTIVES

Because it is generally assumed that gender divisions are rooted in the relations of human reproduction (that is, in child-bearing, rearing and socialisation) and because these relations are in general located in the family, theoretical accounts of the bases of change in the sexual division of labour complement or supplement the theoretical accounts of the development of the conjugal family which we examined in the last chapter. Four main positions have been taken: (i) that the sexual division of labour is functional for society as a whole and its members in general; (ii) that it maintains in a variety of ways the capitalist mode of production; (iii) that it serves male interests, and (iv) that it serves both capitalist and male interests. The first position is associated with the functionalist tradition and dominated the 'old' family sociology. The second position is associated with Marxism, the third with radical-feminism and the fourth with a particular Marxist-feminist stance. Arguments advanced from a functionalist stance have been primarily concerned with the sexual division of labour and have not seen women as oppressed. In contrast, arguments advanced from the other perspectives assert women's subordination and tend to see the sexual division of labour as one aspect of that subordination.

This section looks at some of the very diverse arguments which have been advanced from each of these points of view.

Functional for the Family and Society?

Accounts of the sexual division of labour as functional for society are based on the assumption that the identification of the housewife–mother role with women and of breadwinning with men is a practical and efficient way of allocating societal tasks, given differences between men and women in biological reproduction and in physical strength. However, task-differentiation is not necessarily seen as entailing gender inequality; rather the different roles of men and women may be seen as complementary and of equal value in maintaining the society as a functioning whole. Men and women may then be seen as united by the essential homogeneity of their interests and as bound together in marriage by their shared parenthood and shared class position.

Parsons (1949, 1955, 1964) provides a sophisticated exposition of this functionalist argument. Family tasks, Parsons argues, are either 'expressive' (nurturant/emotionally supportive) or 'instrumental' (directed towards material goals) and it is in principle possible for women and men to perform either set of tasks. However, 'the bearing and early nursing of children establish a strong presumptive primacy of the relation of mother to the small child and this in turn establishes a presumption that the man, who is exempted from these biological functions, should specialise in the alternative instrumental direction' (Parsons, 1955, p. 23). This, says Parsons, explains the primacy of the housewife–child-carer role for women. He also argues that the sexual division of labour, however it may have come about in the course of bio-social evolution, contributes to the functioning of contemporary society in specific ways and is consequently reinforced. He identifies three ways in which this happens. First, he suggests that the separation of home and workplace intensifies task specialisation. Second, he argues that women's limited participation in paid employment eliminates tension-producing rivalries between husband and wife for occupational status and success. Third, he claims that the restriction of the number of the family's status-giving occupational roles to one role, that of the husband, makes the family's status in the community relatively definite. In Parsons' view, this makes for certainty in social interaction and therefore for psychological security.

Parsons recognises that there is a contradiction between the emphasis modern Western societies place on freedom and egalitarianism and women's relegation to home-making and child-rearing. The married woman, he says, is 'debarred from testing or demonstrating her fundamental equality with her husband in competitive occupational achievement' (Parsons, 1964, p. 193). However, Parsons seems to believe that the roles of men and women are functionally complementary and have equality of recognition. He believes that individuals are treated as equals within the kinship system, notes that wives take the social status of their husbands and so occupy the same position in the stratification system, and argues that the marriage relationship, resting as it does on affective attachments, places a premium on the equality of the partners as human beings.

Parsons' argument has been widely criticised (Beechey, 1978; Edgell, 1980; Morgan, 1975; Oakley, 1976) on the grounds that (i) it is biologically based; (ii) familial and occupational roles cannot adequately be categorised as expressive or instrumental – an argument that is supported by the observation that familial tasks such as washing, ironing and cleaning are scarcely expressive tasks and occupational roles involve expressive elements such as the containment of interpersonal frictions; (iii) the economic significance of women's domestic labour and wage labour is not recognised; (iv) the way in which mothering limits women's political and economic power and leads to their subordination is not recognised; and (v) the tensions and dilemmas which women experience and which have led to pressures for change are unrecognised and unexplained.

These criticisms are not entirely justified. Parsons does in fact recognise that the identification of women with domesticity clashes with the egalitarian and individualistic values of modern society.

Further, correctly interpreted, Parsons is to be seen as saying, not that gender roles are biologically determined, but that given women's child-bearing and given the way in which modern economies use labour, it is more efficient for the family and society if she performs nurturing and home-based tasks while men perform economic roles. This, says Harris (1983, pp. 60–2), is a plausible argument, does not deserve to be lightly dismissed and is, moreover, not very different from that developed by some Marxist-feminist writers. The real complaint against Parsons is that he appears to suggest that social life cannot be effectively organised in other ways; he accepts, and provides a justification for, the sexual division of labour.

Supportive of Capitalism?

Unlike Parsons, Marxist theorists tend to assert women's subordination to men within the family and in the wider society and this, rather than the sexual division of labour, is their primary concern. However, men as men are seen as benefiting only indirectly from women's subjugation. Marxist theorists tend to locate women's subordination to men in the logic of capitalism, see it as benefiting the capitalist system and argue that socialism would achieve women's liberation from capitalist exploitation and therefore from male domination.

The foundations of this approach to gender were laid by Engels (1884) in his account of the emergence of the monogamous family as a social arrangement for the protection of private property (see pp. 62–3). In Engels' view, early hunting and gathering societies were characterised not only by the communal ownership of property and group marriage but, because paternity was uncertain, by matrilineal descent systems and 'mother-right'. Engels also assumed that there was a sexual division of labour in early human societies: men hunted and were the main food providers, women cared for children and did the 'housework' and each sex owned the tools they used. He then argued that the domestication and breeding of animals created surplus wealth within men's sphere of labour and, as a result, men's position in the group was strengthened. Matrilineal descent was replaced by patrilineal descent, and monogamy evolved as men sought to control the sexuality and fertility of women so as to ensure the legitimacy of heirs to their property. Moreover, household management, which had been a public activity in primitive communal societies, now became a private service, performed by the woman for the man. Women were thus excluded from social production and became mere sexual property and domestic slaves.

Engels believed that 'progressive' tendencies were at work in capitalism: the absence of private property from the proletariat had, he declared, removed the incentive to male domination; further, capitalism's demand for female labour had made economic independence a possibility for proletarian women. Even so, the proletarian wife had to choose between carrying out her familial duties properly and taking part in social production, and the bourgeois wife had to produce legitimate heirs in return for her upkeep, and so differed from the prostitute only in that she did not hire out her body, like the wage worker, on piece work but sold it once and for all into slavery. In Engels' view, full equality between the sexes could and would be achieved only through a socialist revolution. He presumed that with the communal ownership of the means of production, the bourgeois wife would cease to be mere sexual property for the production of heirs; housework and child-care would become the responsibility of the community and women would re-enter social production and thus achieve economic independence. Male domination, which had first appeared as a result of the emergence of private property, would disappear with the disappearance of private property. So too would the indissolubility of marriage, since this too was a product of private property. No motive for marriage would be left but mutual inclination and, not being constrained by economic interests or responsibility for children, sexual relations could be based on equality and 'true' sex-love.

In short, the subjugation of women was for Engels closely linked to the monogamous nuclear family and both were related to the emergence of private property. However, as the discussion in Chapter 3 (pp. 62–3) of his account of the evolution of the nuclear family indicated, the criticisms levelled against this thesis are legion. First, the assumption that matriarchy characterised early human societies has been rejected by modern anthropologists along with the assumption of primitive group marriage. Second, Himmelweit and Mohun (1977) point out that his entire analysis was based on the assumption that a sexual division of labour existed in early human societies and has hardly changed throughout history. This is taken for granted and is not explained. Third, Barrett (1980, pp. 221–2) suggests that his central argument, the need to secure the legitimacy of heirs, does not help us to understand the persistence of male domination within capitalism. (See p. 63 for the further elaboration of this argument). Fourth, Blackburn and Stewart (1977) reverse Engels' argument. Pointing to women's disadvantaged position in the labour force, they say that women's paid employment has not mitigated their inequality, but reflects and reinforces it. Finally, all the evidence suggests that, contrary to Engels' predictions, male domination has not been overthrown in societies which have attempted to establish a socialist order (Morgan, 1975, p. 139; Barrett, 1980).

These criticisms have proved lethal and Engels' specific arguments have been abandoned. However, his general orientation – that is, his perception of women as subjugated and his belief that this is related to the forces and relations of production – has profoundly influenced attempts to develop and expand Marxist theory to take account of the position of women.

A major stream of contemporary Marxist theorising focusses on women's position as housewives and child-rearers and argues that the housewife role is a mechanism through which capitalism secures, at one and the same time, the reproduction of the labour force at the lowest possible cost and a 'reserve army' of cheap and flexible labour. This is seen as bringing about the subordination of women to men by rendering them dependent on the male wage. This argument may be illustrated by looking at two important contributions to the debate: Seccombe (1974) and Beechey (1977).

Seccombe focusses on the importance of domestic labour to capitalism, its assignment to women and the dependence that stems from it. As we have already seen (pp. 63–4), Seccombe believes that the family is essential to capitalist industrial production in that it reproduces labour power, on a daily basis as well as a generational basis, and socialises children into the values and class relations of capitalism. Seccombe further argues that these tasks (domestic labour) fall to women: capitalist industrialisation, he says, was accompanied by a sex-based split in the labour force with industrial labour being assigned to men and domestic labour to women. Women were thus removed from any direct relation with capital. Furthermore, Seccombe points out that a wage is not paid in the domestic unit and the husband's wage, though it is in reality payment for her labour as well as his, presents itself as payment for his labour only. The housewife is therefore divorced not only from the means of production but also from the means of exchange and is dependent upon the private redistribution of the wage between herself and her husband. This, says Seccombe, is the basis of his authority and her dependence.

As critics were quick to point out, Seccombe's focus on the housewife as a domestic labourer neglected women's participation in industrial labour. Analysing this aspect of women's activity in capitalist society, Beechey suggests that the housewife is useful to capital as a source of unskilled, cheap, flexible and relatively docile reserve labour. Her argument hinges on the notion that married women can be paid wages at a level which is beneath the value of labour power and can, moreover, be drawn upon or discarded as changes in the economy require a different distribution of the labour force or a smaller labour force. Capital, Beechey argues, can use married women in this way because part of the costs of producing and reproducing their own labour power is borne within the family and by the husband's wage. Moreover, married women have a world of their own, the family, into which they can disappear when discarded from production. In developing this argument, Beechey explicitly recognises that a family system based on a sexual division of labour pre-dated capitalism but she sees capitalism as using and perpetuating this family system.

The strength of these Marxist arguments lies in the fact that they reveal the economic value of women's domestic labour and their particular significance as a 'reserve army'. Moreover, some writers have pointed to contradictions between the roles of housewife–mother and wage-labourer which constitute pressures for change in the family and in gender roles. Beechey (1977) points out that the difficulty of combining within the woman two vital forms of labour is the source of pressure for the state to play a greater part in the reproduction of labour power (for example, by providing day nurseries) and may lead to the dissolution of the family. Wainwright (1978) suggests that women's movement into the labour market gives them basic rights as wage workers and thus comes into conflict with, and challenges, the assumption that 'natural' family commitments make women a special and subordinate group.

However, arguments which see women's subordination as the by-product of capitalism's need for domestic labour and/or for a reserve army of labour have been vigorously attacked by some feminist writers. Barrett (1980) claims that such arguments are problematic in that women's subordination and dependent position tend to be seen as functional for capital, and reductionist in that gender relations are reduced to an effect of the operation of capital. Barrett supports this contention by pointing to specific difficulties. First, she says that this Marxist argument cannot explain why it is that it is women who are exploited in this way. It does not tell us why married women, rather than men or the aged or some other category of persons, occupy the dependent, subordinate and exploited position of domestic labourer and/or reserve wage labourer. In fact it assumes – may even, as Beechey does, explicitly recognise – the prior existence of the sexual division of labour, but does not explain it. Second, Barrett emphasises that the sexual division of labour and female subordination pre-dated capitalism in present-day capitalist societies and are found in societies which have attempted to establish socialism. Male domination, says Barrett, was not a creation of capitalism and is not specific to capitalist societies, and so cannot be explained without reference to pre-existing gender divisions. Third, Barrett argues that it has not actually been shown that the housewife role is the most beneficial arrangement for capitalism. She points out that though women are unpaid as domestic labourers and poorly paid as wage labourers, the costs of reproducing their labour power are borne within the capitalist economy, partly through the payment of a wage to the husband and partly through various state welfare benefits. In other words, women's labour is paid for by the system as a whole, even though they are not directly paid for it. (See also Barrett's arguments on the doubtful utility of the family to capitalism, pp. 66–7.) Finally, Barrett suggests that the capitalist-imperatives argument slides into portraying women's subordination as the unfolding of an inevitable plan directed by the logic of capital. This, she says, is inadequate because it does not take account of historical conflicts and struggles, the outcome of which was not pre-given in terms of the needs of capital but reflected capitalist interests, the interests of sections of working-class men and the assumption that the relegation of women to child-care and domesticity was natural and desirable.

Underlying Barrett's critique of the capitalist-imperatives argument is the contention that a properly constituted Marxist feminist argument would take account of a pre-existing and enduring ideology of female domesticity and mothering, and seek to show

how it has been incorporated in capitalist relations of production – and become an important element of those relations – during the course of struggles between men and women and between the bourgeoisie and the working class.

In the Interests of Men?

Accounts of the sexual division of labour and of women's subordination as serving the interests of men stem from a radical-feminist approach to gender divisions. Radical-feminist theory maintains that gender structures are specific to the male–female relationship and are always based on male domination. From this viewpoint, men as men are oppressors, the beneficiaries of women's subjugation are men not capital, and all women, irrespective of their social class, share a common oppression around which they may be organised. Men and women are thus seen as constituting sex classes which are independent of economic class. Further, sex class divisions are seen as more important for determining the general character of social life than economic class relations. Society is said to be patriarchal (male-dominated) and patriarchy is said to be universal and transhistorical. Radical-feminist theory tends also to stress the way in which husbands benefit from the daily services of their wives (that is to emphasise the marriage relationship as oppressive) whereas Marxist accounts which see women's oppression as derived from capital's long-term needs for future labour power implicitly or explicitly see the labour of child-care as the more intractable aspect of women's oppression. Finally, from a radical-feminist perspective women's liberation is to be achieved not through the class struggle and a socialist revolution but through women's struggle to overthrow patriarchal structures and establish a new ordering of male–female relationships.

Given this general orientation, radical-feminist theorists face the task of accounting for patriarchy. Attempts to theorise patriarchy have moved in three major directions. Firestone (1970) roots patriarchy in the relations of human reproduction. Millett (1970), on the other hand, sees patriarchy as an ideological and psychological structure, while Delphy (1977) develops an account of patriarchy as a system of material (economic) relations.

Firestone presents a sophisticated feminist version of the view that gender relationships are a function of the different roles of men and women in human reproduction. Her argument has as its starting-point the 'biological reality' that women bear the greater part of the burden of procreation. This fundamental biological inequality, she argues, gives rise to the dependence of women on men for survival and therefore to an unequal power relationship. Out of these differences in material conditions arise the sexual division of labour and a sex class system in which women are dominated by men. Firestone also argues that the power which men have over women promotes ego-gratifications and gives rise to a power psychology (a desire to dominate others) which generates other forms of domination. She claims that the psychosexual configurations of men's domination over women is the source of all domination, including economic class domination.

Thus, to Firestone the economic class system as well as the sex class system arises out of the reproductive roles of men and women. For Firestone the relations of biological reproduction determine historical development: inverting Engels, she declares that 'the ultimate cause and the great moving power of all historic events' is to be sought 'in the dialectic of sex: the division of society into two distinct biological classes for procreative reproduction and the struggles of these classes with one another; in the changes in the modes of marriage, reproduction and child-care created by these struggles' (Firestone, 1970, p. 12).

She does not, however, see the sex class system as a biological inevitability. According to Firestone, the development of human society represents the gradual transcendence of biology by culture and in advanced industrial societies the means of transcending biological differences between men and women are at hand. She points out that the unequal burden of procreation has already been alleviated by birth control and she urges the development of artificial reproduction and of communal child-caring so that women may be completely free of their 'biological burden'. This development, Firestone claims, is necessary for true equality between the sexes and will, by providing the basis for overthrowing the family and the power psychology associated with it, destroy the economic class system as well as the sex class system.

For Millett, as for Firestone, the dominion of the male over the female is the fundamental political division in society. Patriarchy, she says, is more vigorous than class stratification, more uniform and more enduring, and is so deeply entrenched that it runs through all political, social and economic forms. It denies women independent economic status and consequently women, whatever their class by birth or education, have less investment in the class system than the male. Women, she says, transcend the economic class system and constitute an oppressed sex class. However, for Millett, patriarchal rule lies not in biology but in the acceptance of a value system which gives males the right to rule over women. The 'birthright priority' whereby males rule females, says Millett, is the most pervasive ideology of our culture. It is sustained through socialisation in the family and by peers, the school, the media and other learning sources, formal and informal. It is 'interiorised' to become part of the psychological make-up of both sexes. The image of women as we know it, she says, is an image created by men and fashioned to suit their needs. Millett's analysis implies that the liberation of women is to be achieved primarily through a change in human consciousness and the destruction of the ideology of male supremacy and of the institutions (of which the family is the most important) which socialise us into acceptance of male supremacy.

***

Delphy provides a third approach to male–female relationships. She attempts to root patriarchy not in biology, nor yet in ideology, but in the economic relationships which exist between men and women. She argues that the family is a domestic mode of production in which child-rearing takes place, domestic services are provided and some goods produced. It exists alongside, but independently of, the industrial mode of production. The industrial mode of production is the arena of capitalist exploitation, the family that of patriarchal exploitation. Delphy argues that the productive and reproductive activities which take place in the family are controlled by husbands, that women's labour in the family is performed free and that the main beneficiaries of women's labour are husbands. This situation is sustained by marriage, which is for Delphy an arrangement whereby men gain control over women's labour. Moreover, in Delphy's view, women's entry into paid work does not bring women independence, for they continue to provide domestic services free and their wages from paid employment are likely to be controlled by their husbands. Women are thus in a common and oppressed class position, men are their oppressors, and marriage is the main instrument of their oppression. Delphy concludes that women should mobilise autonomously to overthrow this patriarchal system of production and reproduction.

***

In highlighting the pervasiveness throughout history and across cultures of patriarchal power, these radical feminist writers have convincingly shown that gender structures are not simply the by-product of economic relations and the class struggle. They have provided a trenchant critique of traditional Marxist theory. They also provide considerable insight into the way in which male power permeates the social fabric and show that gender relations are central to existing social relations and forms of power. These are their achievements. However, some writers, arguing from a point of view that is sympathetic to Marxism, have criticised radical-feminist theory for (i) failing to take account of the different forms that patriarchy takes in different societies and periods of history; (ii) not providing a systematic account of the relationship between patriarchal forms in contemporary society and the capitalist mode of production; and (iii) obscuring social class differences in women's experience of oppression and in the power which men have to define their world (see especially Barrett, 1980; Beechey, 1979; Middleton, 1974). Some writers have also pointed out that the origins of patriarchy are not satisfactorily explained. Thus Beechey (1979) says that Millett's account of patriarchal ideology does not tell us what it is about the organisation of all human societies that leads to the institution of male domination, while Delphy's account of men's control of women's labour does not explain why women are exploited both within the labour process and within the family. In effect, Beechey is saying that Millett's patriarchal ideology and Delphy's male control of female labour are presented as 'givens' and are not explained. In contrast, Firestone's energetically argued thesis does explain the origins of male power and in doing so confronts head-on the reality of biological differences between the sexes. However, this approach, though endorsed and further elaborated in some strands of feminist thought, is not generally liked because it slides into biologism, makes women's liberation dependent on the uncertain future of technological developments in human reproduction and does not deal adequately with the problem of how women are to gain control of reproductive technology.

The Marriage of Marxism and Feminism

The belief that the strengths of traditional Marxist theory are the weaknesses of radical-feminist theory and that the strengths of radical-feminist theory are the weaknesses of Marxism has led to attempts to unite the two theories. This brand of Marxist-feminism is a diverse enterprise and cannot easily be summarised, but broadly speaking it takes as its starting-point the notion that men and women are located in relations of reproduction which are essentially patriarchal in structure *and* in relations of production. According to Hartmann (1981):

> There is no such thing as 'pure capitalism' nor does 'pure patriarchy' exist, for they must of necessity coexist. What exists is patriarchal capitalism, or patriarchal feudalism, or egalitarian hunting/gathering societies, or matriarchal horticultural societies, or patriarchal horticultural societies and so on (Hartmann, 1981, p. 17).

It seems also that patriarchy is to be seen as ever-present but as taking different forms. The theoretical task then becomes the task of identifying the forms taken by patriarchy in different societies and determining how they are interrelated with, though always distinct from, the social relations of production. This approach implies that women's liberation depends on a twofold struggle to transform both capitalist relations and patriarchal relations.

Writers in this tradition tend to take one of two approaches. They may see gender relations as material relations in which men control women's labour. Or they may see gender relations as ideological or psychological structures, deriving, for example, from the meanings which we give to biological sex differences. In both approaches the development of capitalism is said to influence and be influenced by the structure of gender relationships.

Hartmann (1976 and 1981) provides one of the clearest examples of the first approach in her account of the exclusion of women from rewarding positions in productive labour. Hartmann contends that capitalism created a hierarchically ordered labour structure, but that patriarchy (which is based on men's control over women's labour power) determined which places were occupied by men and which were occupied by women. She then proceeds to argue that in capitalist societies 'a healthy and strong partnership exists between patriarchy and capital'. This, she says, may be explained in terms of the strength of pre-existing patriarchal social forces. She points out that men occupied a privileged and dominant position in the household economy of the pre-industrial period so that when industrial capitalism developed women were already in a weak position. She then argues that men acted to protect their patriarchal privileges. Male workers, says Hartmann, fought for a 'family wage' for a 'male breadwinner', reserved union protection for themselves, and supported legislation to restrict women's employment. Job-segregation by sex and low pay for women's jobs then ensured women's continued economic dependence on men and encouraged the choice of housewifery for a career. However, Hartmann argues, capitalism also benefits from this arrangement in that women's location in the family represents an effective arrangement for the reproduction of the labour force. The terms of the 'bargain' between capitalism and men alter over time but ultimately remain one in which women's work in the family serves capitalism by reproducing a labour force and serves men by providing them with domestic and child-rearing services *and* by giving them privileged access to productive resources. Capitalism and patriarchy thus reinforce each other and the subordination of women in the family is to be seen neither as simply a by-product of capitalism nor as independent of capitalism.

Hartmann breaks new ground in that she gives priority to labour-market processes and locates women's subordination in men's exclusion of women from the workplace and capitalism's manipulation of labour. She thus presents gender divisions, not as inherent in the logic of capitalism, but as the outcome of economic and sex class struggles in which women, because they were in a weak position at the onset of industrialisation, were pawns.

The most notable attempt to treat patriarchy as a universal ideological structure which nevertheless takes different forms in different modes of production is found in the work of Juliet Mitchell. In her first major work (1966), Mitchell locates women in four structures – production, biological reproduction, sexuality and its regulation, and the socialisation of children – and argues that women's oppression must be understood in terms of the restriction of sexuality, reproduction and socialisation to the family and the identification of women with the family. In her later work (1975), Mitchell seeks to identify the origins of the patriarchal order and to account for its persistence. Her starting-point is the conception of the social order as founded on networks of social relationships wider than the nuclear family. She then argues that the incest taboo and exogamy (rules which forbid marriage within one's group) were established at the dawn of civilisation, not as a means of avoiding the biological hazards of incest, but as a mechanism by which families exchanged their members and established wider social networks. The incest taboo and marriage laws, Mitchell argues, were the essential prerequisite for breaking out of the cul-de-sac of the biological family and inaugurating a cultural order. But it was always women who were exchanged and they were exchanged by men. This primary sex division, says Mitchell, was the basis of patriarchy (here defined as 'the law of the father'). Mitchell further argues that the patriarchal law and, with it, ideas of femininity and masculinity were embedded in the unconscious structures of the human mind and are reproduced over the generations in the context of the family. Pressing Freudian theory into service, Mitchell describes how, in each generation, we develop in the context of the family the gender identity appropriate to the patriarchal order and learn to look outside the family and to the opposite sex for mates.

Patriarchy, Mitchell contends, is a universal ideological and psychological structure. However, its form varies. She then argues that in capitalism, social relations are established through the exchange of commodities, not through kinship structures. There is therefore no longer any need for the incest taboo, the exchange of women and the family. The patriarchal law is redundant and would have disappeared but for the invention of a new idea of the family as a basic biological unit and of a new function for it as a unit for reproducing the labour force. Women thus remain defined by kinship relations while men enter class relations.

Mitchell has been criticised for failing to give patriarchy a material base (Hartmann, 1981; McDonough and Harrison, 1978), for making patriarchal ideology autonomous (McDonough and Harrison, 1978), and for ignoring the historical development of patriarchy and the concrete forms which this assumes (Beechey, 1979). She has also been criticised for presenting an incoherent two-spheres theory (McDonough and Harrison, 1978) and for failing to specify just how patriarchy and the relations of production interconnect (Charvet, 1982). Finally, she has been criticised for failing to provide a satisfactory theory of the foundations of patriarchy since she does not tell us why it is that at the dawn of history it was women who were exchanged and men who did the exchanging (Beechey, 1979).

These criticisms of Mitchell's thesis point to the difficulty of forging a union between Marxist and radical-feminist theory. There is a basic tension between radical feminism's insistence on the universality of patriarchy and Marxism's insistence on the historical specificity of social relations. There is also a basic tension between the radical-feminist claim that patriarchy is specific to male–female relationships and the Marxist claim that the economic is always, if only in the last resort, primary. For these reasons the union of Marxism and feminism remains, in Hartmann's phrase (1981), an 'unhappy marriage'.

Finally, there are problems in radical-feminist conceptions of male power and female subordination. Radical-feminist thought, whether it appears in its 'pure' form or as a marriage of Marxism and feminism, seems to equate women's domesticity and men's breadwinning with male domination and the subordination of women. This is problematic because the sexual division of labour and gender inequality are analytically independent concepts (Rossi, 1977; Harris, 1983, p. 227). Moreover, some scholars have argued that men are not unambiguously advantaged and women unambiguously disadvantaged by gender role differentiation. Barrett (1980, pp. 216–17) notes that the male breadwinning role locks men into wage labour, pressurises them into being politically docile in order to safeguard their jobs, deprives them of significant access to their children and defines masculinity in terms that may be oppressive for some men. Conversely, Zaretsky (1982) argues that the nineteenth-century enhancement of the idea of a family wage earned by a male breadwinner was compatible with women's interests since pregnancy and breast-feeding covered most of the married woman's life-span and limited their earning power. Again the location of married women in the home has been seen as a working-class strategy, supported by women as well as men, for controlling the supply of labour and so raising wages (Humphries, 1977). Moreover, Roberts (1984) has recently shown that within the working-class home of the late nineteenth and early twentieth centuries women exercised considerable moral power, controlled the spending of money, made family decisions and limited their husband's leisure. Wives, says Roberts, were seen as managers, husbands as providers and working-class women saw emancipation as moving away from paid work and into full-time housewifery. The working-class women of this period, says Roberts, did not feel exploited and oppressed by their men. Rather, they interpreted the world in terms of class conflict and saw themselves as sharing a common oppression with their men. In Roberts' view, this evidence suggests that a patriarchal model of male domination is not particularly helpful to the analysis of male–female relationships. Again, Stacey and Price (1981) cite evidence for the medieval period and for the sixteenth century which shows that women, although they had little formal standing in the public world, exercised considerable practical authority in the private world through their participation in productive activity. Moreover, Stacey and Price show that some women (the wives of powerful men) used their private power and family connections to influence the decisions men made in the public domain and exercised power over women and men of the labouring classes.

All these arguments suggest that there are dangers in assuming, as some feminist theorising has tended to do, that the mid-twentieth century experience of the sexual division of labour as oppressive can be imposed on the experience of other periods and that women are entirely subordinate and totally oppressed. These arguments also imply the need for a theory which recognises not only reciprocities in the interests of women and men but also women's (sometimes successful) efforts to combat and circumvent male power.

5

The Conjugal Family: Haven or Prison?

As the preceding chapters have indicated, 'traditional' family sociology emphasises the importance of the conjugal family in meeting basic human needs in an urban–industrial society. It stresses the necessity of stable and intimate relationships to child development and celebrates marriage as an affective, psychologically-fulfilling relationship in a rootless and bureaucratised social world. However, as the proceding chapters have also indicated, the family sociology of the 1970s challenges the idea of the conjugal family as 'haven in a heartless world' (a phrase used by Lasch, 1977). This 'new' family sociology presents us with a critical analysis of the conjugal family as oppressive, repressive and confining.

This chapter looks more closely at these opposing evaluations of the conjugal family, at their links with 'everyday' family ideals, and at the implications for change which they contain. Positive evaluations are considered in the first section, negative evaluations in the second section. The concluding section considers the view that the conjugal family is a two-sided institution, both haven and prison.

5.1 A HAVEN?

Images of the conjugal family as a 'haven in a heartless world' appear in their strongest form in functionalist sociology. On the one hand, modern society is characterised as rootless, competitive, impersonal, bureaucratised. On the other hand, the conjugal family is said to be a system of affective relationships which meets basic human needs for love and intimacy. The work of Talcott Parsons (see especially Parsons, 1955) epitomises this viewpoint. As we saw earlier (pp. 35–8 and p. 56), Parsons maintains that relationships within the conjugal family have intensified in response to the disintegration of kin groups. In his view, the erosion of kin bonds has left the individual without structured sources of support outside the conjugal family and consequently husband and wife, parents and children have been 'thrown together'. Marriage has come to be of particular importance as a source of companionship and psychological support and parenthood has been enhanced. Parsons also maintains that the conjugal family provides two conditions necessary to the successful socialisation of children: (i) a small primary group in which children may invest all their emotional concerns, and (ii) models of the adult male and female roles.

Goode (1963) adds a further dimension to the argument. He suggests that the conjugal family by its emphasis on emotionality counterbalances the frustrations of a psychologically burdensome occupational world: it counterbalances the competitiveness and insecurity that result from the struggle for success in middle-class work and the tedium that results from the repetitiveness and monotonous nature of working-class jobs. Similarly, Litwak (1965) says that familial intimacy complements the work of bureaucratic institutions in that the latter are based on an impersonal and utilitarian rationality and so cannot meet the individual's need for affective, intimate relationships. The conjugal family, these analyses suggest, is essential to individual happiness and social order in a bureaucratically organised society.

Writing from a phenomenological perspective – that is from a perspective which emphasises the social construction of reality – Berger and Kellner (1964) present us with a view of the conjugal family which is very similar to that of functionalist theorists. Every society, say Berger and Kellner, has specific ways of defining and perceiving reality, particular sets of shared meanings through which its members interpret and order their experiences. This socially constructed world is supplied to us through socialisation and so exists for the individual as a ready-made world that simply is there to be lived in. However, it is in constant need of validation (precisely because of an ever-present glimmer of suspicion as to its social manufacture and relativity). Berger and Kellner go on to argue that 'the world' is confirmed and validated through intensive interaction with 'significant' others. They further argue that in modern Western societies marriage occupies a privileged place as 'a social arrangement that creates for the individual the sort of order in which he [sic] can experience his life as making sense'. The public world, they say, is alien, incomprehensible, anonymous, and in the private sphere groups other than the conjugal family have been destroyed by social and geographical mobility. Consequently, stable, all-embracing and significant relationships can only be found in the conjugal family. Moreover, say Berger and Kellner, contemporary societal ideologies provide us with an image of marriage as the appropriate setting for self-discovery and self-realisation. Within the context of this image of marriage, newly married couples centre all significant conversation upon their relationship with each other, talk through and match their images of themselves, their experiences and their interpretations of their worlds, and so gradually arrive at a shared and stable definition of reality. With the advent of children, the marital conversation becomes a 'family symposium' and the couple's social world gains in density, plausibility and durability. Ambivalences are converted into certainties, and images of self and others are stabilised.

Berger and Kellner write of the conjugal family as facilitating the construction of stable images of the world and of our place in it. Functionalist sociologists write of emotional supportiveness. However, their message is the same: Berger and Kellner, like functionalist theorists, suggest that the conjugal family meets basic human needs and stands in sharp opposition to the cold impersonality and merciless competitiveness of a rootless and bureaucratised public world. This argument is frequently supported by citing evidence of the greater 'stability' of married persons as against unmarried persons (as measured by such indications as their lower suicide rates). Moreover, the family-is-a-haven thesis is complemented by the psychological thesis that stable intimate relationships are necessary to 'healthy' personality development in children (see Section 2.2). In a recent defence of the family, Berger and Berger (1983) combine their phenomenological perspective with this psychological theory and with evidence of high personnel turnover in professionally-managed child-care facilities to maintain that in modern societies the conjugal family is the arrangement that best provides a basis for the stable, predictable, intimate relationships necessary to the development of the child's sense of self.

Stresses and strains do not go unrecognised in these accounts of the importance of the family to personal well-being. Parsons notes that the adult feminine role is rooted in the family and that this denies women equality with men in access to occupational status.

This, he says, is incompatible with the democratic values of Western society. Goode notes that married women are without the support of kinswomen in their child-rearing role and that this may be stressful. Berger and Kellner argue that the very fact that the conjugal family is a small, isolated sub-world makes the task of constructing stable images of the social world particularly difficult. They say that because marriage involves only two people it must make up in intensity for the numerical poverty of the arrangement and is therefore potentially unstable. All these observations imply that the conjugal family makes heavy demands of its members. Costs and potential dangers are thus recognised. Nevertheless, these writers see the conjugal family as the best solution to the problems that confront the individual in a bureaucratised and rootless industrial society and emphasise its overall beneficence.

In the 1950s and early 1960s, these functionalist and psychological theories fell on fertile ground. They were in harmony with everyday ideas about the family. Moreover, they seemed to provide a scientific basis for maintaining the nuclear family as the fundamental unit of society. They therefore appealed to an age in which science was taking on the role that religion had once played in moulding everyday thought (North, 1972; Smart, 1984). These theories influenced social policy (Wilson, 1977), were given practical application by social workers, health visitors and other 'experts' in child-rearing and personal relations (Berger and Berger, 1983; Donzelot, 1980; North, 1972) and were popularised by women's magazines and by other self-appointed mentors of the public. Traditional family ideals were thus refurbished in the light of social science thought, given renewed legitimation and sustained.

However, the positive view of the family which these schools of thought promulgated is now hotly contested. Some writers have questioned the uniqueness of the conjugal family as a psychological support system. Morgan (1981) argues that alternative sources of support are available in some social situations. He points to the 'traditional working-class extended family' as an example and reminds us that in such families the wife's chief confidante and supporter was her mother, not her husband. Again, studies of occupational cultures suggest that some occupations, particularly at the middle-class level, provide a firmly structured career, intrinsic work satisfaction and expressive colleague relationships. In such circumstances, meaningful and absorbing relationships may be found in work, and family life may have limited salience (Elliot, 1982).

More importantly, it is passionately argued that the overall emphasis on the conjugal family as beneficent obscures the contradictions and tensions that in reality permeate family life. 'Dysfunctions', says Morgan (1975, Chap. 3), are recognised in the functionalist tradition, but often seem to be regarded as residual, pathological or unusual phenomena, which may or may not be present, which may be resolved through remedial action and which are not therefore to be incorporated into the ideal typical model of the conjugal family. Morgan argues that the functionalist tradition thus directs attention away from a critical analysis of the family as a social institution. It prevents us from considering whether the family may not simply have problems but may itself be a problem and whether radical change may be desirable. Morgan further argues that the incorporation of accounts of dysfunctions into the family-is-a-haven thesis only leads to a further problem: the need for criteria by which we may evaluate dysfunctions against eufunctions. To this may be added the need to discover who determines which groups shall bear the costs and which groups shall reap the benefits.

These questions bring us to the problem of power. It has been widely argued that the family-is-a-haven thesis treats the wider society as an integrated whole and the family itself as a unified entity and thereby ignores the reality of power. At the heart of this criticism are two notions: (i) that there are disparities in the life situation and interests of families in different class positions and in the power they have to realise their interests, and (ii) that husband and wife, parents and children are in different situations, have different interests and differential power. Critics therefore argue that we must ask: 'For whom is a given family system functional'? They further argue that when we seek to answer this question we will find that it serves the interests of those who have power but oppresses and represses those who do not.

5.2 A PRISON?

Those who view the conjugal family as oppressive, repressive and confining present us not so much with a critique of the functionalist approach as with divergent theories and alternative evaluations. Three major positions have been taken: (i) that the conjugal family helps to preserve the oppressive capitalist system; (ii) that the conjugal family oppresses and represses individuality, and (iii) that the conjugal family oppresses women. From each of these positions radical change in, even the abolition of, the conjungal family is to be struggled for.

An Instrument of Capitalist Oppression?

In Marxist theories the construction of the conjugal family as a psychological-support system is presented as an effect of capitalism. This may be viewed negatively or positively. For some writers (for example, Hunt and Hunt, 1974), the elevation of immediate personal experience within the conjugal family maintains capitalist society by making love the panacea for all ills. For other writers, the conjugal family is created within the context of capitalism but is for its members. Thus Dorothy Smith (1975) argues that the working-class family provides its members with a private space in which they are free from capitalist surveillance. Corrigan and Leonard (1978) say that the family, though utilised by capitalism, at times defends its members against exploitation and may be the context for affection, co-operation and altruism, values which stand in direct ideological opposition to the dominant values of the capitalist system.

Zaretsky (1976) provides one of the most fully elaborated and sophisticated versions of this construction-within-capitalism argument. Zaretsky maintains that when the family was a unit of production, as in the medieval period and in the early stages of capitalist development, family members understood their domestic life and personal relations to be rooted in mutual labour. He also notes that Puritanism 'meshed' with early capitalist endeavour to celebrate labour as 'a calling' and the family as part of the God-given order of productive and spiritual activity. Puritanism, says Zaretsky, represented an expansion of self-consciousness and a specific perception of the family as an arena of a shared labour and common love. Zaretsky then goes on to argue that capitalist industrialisation created a separate world of the personal. The immediate effect of industrialisation, he says, was the creation of a wage labour force and the removal of work from the centre of family life. Work thus becomes the means whereby family life was maintained rather than the family's central task. Further, as capitalism advanced, productive property came to be monopolised by a small, centralised ruling class, social authority shifted from the property-owning family to remote centres of power and the labour process was increasingly rationalised. Consequently, individual identity could not be realised either through work or through the ownership of property and individuals felt isolated, ranged against a society they could not affect. Zaretsky (1976, p. 57) writes:

> On one side appeared 'society' – the capitalist economy, the state, the fixed social core that has no space in it for the individual; on the other, the personal identity, no longer defined by its place in the social division of labour. On one side the objective social world appeared, perceived at first as 'machinery' or 'industry', then throughout the nineteenth century as 'society' and into the twentieth as 'big business', 'city hall', and then as 'technology' or 'life', as the domination of the proletariat by the capitalist class became more difficult to perceive.

Zaretsky goes on to argue that the modern world of subjectivity – of emotionality, individuality and personal relationships – was created in opposition to this harsh world. A new form of the family developed – one that understood itself to be separate from production and that placed a primary emphasis on the personal relations of its members. The family, says Zaretsky, came to be seen, first by the bourgeoisie and later by the proletariat, as a protected enclave within industrial society, as standing in opposition to the terrible anonymous world of commerce and industry. Within it personal life developed. Filial relationships were intensified and women came to be seen as maintaining the human values crushed by modern life. The split in society between personal feelings and economic production was thus integrated with the sexual division of labour; men were identified with the struggle for existence, women with emotional life within the family.

Zaretsky seeks to establish that our very notion of 'the personal' and its location in the conjugal family is a social construction and argues that this is an effect of capitalism. He emphasises the consequences for women – their separation from production and location in a limbo of private space and time. He notes also that the pressure of being the only refuge in a brutal world may bring the family 'inner torment'. Nevertheless, Zaretsky asserts the value of the family in establishing a real sphere of personal freedom. In his view, the root cause of our problems lies in capitalism, not in the family. From this standpoint, salvation is to be achieved through the destruction of capitalism.

Zaretsky's argument, like other Marxist accounts of the construction of the family as a psychologically-supportive system, presents us with a critique of capitalism and recognises family dilemmas. Nevertheless, this Marxist version of the family-is-a-haven thesis has a certain similarity with functionalist arguments. It presumes that the family has been successfully established as a haven in a heartless world. We are thus again left with an image of the conjugal family as a unified entity and of family members as bound together by their mutually supportive endeavours. This Marxist formulation is therefore subject to the criticism that, like functionalist theory, it mistakenly assumes that family life can be insulated from the tensions and contradictions that permeate the public world. It is also subject to the criticism that it obscures the inequalities which exist within the family. Relatedly, it is criticised by some feminist writers (see, for example, Barrett, 1980; Hartmann, 1981) for not attributing to the family a specifically patriarchal content.

Oppressive of Individuality?

A major challenge to the conjugal family-is-a-haven thesis comes from those who see it as repressing and destroying individuality. The radical psychoanalytic theorist, R. D. Laing, is a leading exponent of this argument (see especially, Laing, 1971; Laing and Esterson, 1970; Laing, Phillipson and Lee, 1966). Laing focusses particularly on the parent–child relationship and the power that parents have to impose their interpretations of the world on the child. For Laing parental love is two-edged. It is warm and protective, but it is also suffocating and ultimately destructive.

Laing (whose views of the family were based on his analysis of the family lives of schizophrenics) is not, as functionalists and Marxists are, concerned with the relationship between the family and other social institutions. Rather, he provides us with an account of the 'psycho-social interior' of the family (Morgan, 1975, p. 131). He conceives of the family as a complex set of dyadic (two-person) relationships, each of which is played out in terms of a triadic (three-person) relationship. That is, Laing sees the family as a set of dyadic relationships, as between husband and wife, each parent and each child and each child and each of the other children, each of which takes place in the context of relationships with each of the other members of the family. Alliances are formed and re-formed and family members play each other off against the others to achieve their own (often warped) ends. Opportunities for confusion, misunderstanding, deception, manipulation and attempted manipulation are manifold.

Laing goes on to argue that the individual's identity is shaped and structured within the context of the dyadic and triadic relationships of the family. According to Laing, each family member synthesises and internalises the family's interaction patterns as he/she perceives them. Through this process of reciprocal internalisation, family members become a part of each other and of the family as a whole. They thus bear the 'stigmata' of their family drama and find their individuality absorbed by their family. Moreover, the family drama goes on over the generations; parents bring the dramas of their own families of origin to their family of procreation, project them on to their children – as, for example, when they liken children to grandparents – and thus perpetuate them. Family members, Laing seems to be saying, live through each other and true privacy and autonomy are not experienced in the family.

Laing also suggests that images of the world, including images of the family itself, are moulded within the family. It seems to be his view that parents define the family and the world for the child and, in particular, delineate boundaries between family and non-family and therefore between 'us' and 'them'. The perception of the world in terms of our family and others parallels and, Laing seems to suggest, gives rise to other binary distinctions – between good and bad, male and female, white and black, gentile and Jew. In this way the family constructs for us a world of differences rather than similarities, antagonism rather than brotherhood. Moreover, the world may be defined as alien, dangerous, hostile, persecutory while the family (which defined the outside world as hostile in the first place) is defined as the only refuge from this world. Its suffocating grip is thus tightened.

Laing, like Parsons, is saying that the family plays an important part in forming personality and in shaping the individual's interpretation of his or her world. Parallels may also be drawn between

Laing's emphasis on ways in which images of the family and of the social world are produced and reproduced in interaction within the family and Berger and Kellner's (1964) emphasis on the construction and negotiation of reality. However, Laing's emphasis on the family as a set of dyadic and triadic relationships is radically different from the functionalist model of the family as a monolithic and homogeneous entity. Further, Laing sees the family's influence as baneful whereas the functionalist tradition sees it as generally beneficent. Where Parsons highlights the needs of the social system, Laing emphasises the importance of individual autonomy, freedom and self-awareness, and from this point of view sees the close bonds of family life as suffocating. For Laing, the family restricts individuality and smothers self-awareness while expectations of reciprocal concern accumulate constant and unremitting obligations.

Laing has emerged as 'symbolic leader' of a school of thought which focusses on the destructive and violent in family life. Echoes of his images of the family reverberate throughout the ideology of anti-family movements. Yet Laing himself gives little indication as to the way in which we may escape the dilemmas he describes (Morgan, 1975, p. 130). He offers no assurance that alternative ways of ordering sexual and intimate relationships and parenting could lead to a more satisfactory state of affairs, for there is a profoundly pessimistic world view in his work. This goes unnoticed by those who find in it a rationale for the family's abolition.

Laing's thesis is important as a counterbalance to glib accounts of the eufunctionality of the conjugal family. However, it has not withstood sociological criticism. In a valuable critique, Morgan (1975, Chap. 4) raises three pertinent sets of issues.

First, at one level Laing seems to be saying that family bonds are supportive as well as suffocating and this paradox lies at the heart of family living. However, he addresses himself almost entirely to its suffocating elements. This preoccupation with the 'dark side' of family living may be unbalanced. Morgan observes that our images of the social world include notions of similarities as well as differences, of a shared humanity as well as basic oppositions and these notions of a shared humanity are frequently expressed in familial terms such as 'the brotherhood of man'. If, Morgan not unreasonably asks, interpretations of the social world based on us–them dichotomies can readily be attributed to primary experiences within the family, cannot interpretations of the social world based on a shared humanity also be attributed to the family?

Second, Laing focusses on the parent–child relationship as the key relationship in socialisation, and, therefore, as critical in shaping children's personalities and structuring their interpretations of the social world. Morgan suggests that this view of the parent–child relationship implies that socialisation flows from parent to child. However, Morgan argues, children are not passive recipients of parental definitions. They quickly learn means of resistance and redefinition, and exploit differences between parents. Further, Laing obscures the role of siblings, playmates, teachers, welfare workers and the media as socialising agents and thus attributes to parents an all-determining power which they may not in fact have. Furthermore, Laing's account of the power that parents have to interpret the world for the child tells us little about the images of the world that are presented to the child. In Morgan's view it is not sufficient to say that the family, by establishing boundaries between us and them, leads us to see the world in terms of binary structures – good and bad, white and black, and so on – for the culture defines which categories are socially relevant, and in any case the social world is too complex and diverse to be encompassed within simple binary divisions.

Third, Laing, says Morgan, does not locate the family in a social context. In one sense his family exists in a social vacuum. In another sense it is universalised. We thus find that he fails to consider the way in which child-rearing practices are defined in the culture, the links between the family and other social institutions, or the options available to family members. He fails also to take account of class and other variations in family structure and values. In effect he fails to ask whether or how the family dramas he describes are shaped by the social structure in which they are embedded.

Some writers have attempted to locate the Laingian madhouse in the contemporary isolation and privatisation of the conjugal family. Thus Leach (1967) claims that in the modern isolated conjugal family there is an intensification of emotional relationships between husband and wife, parents and children and, in their isolation, family members expect and demand too much of each other. The result is stress and conflict within the family, but also suspicion and fear of the outside world. The conjugal family with its narrow privacy and tawdry secrets is, says Leach, the source of all our discontents. Similarly, Harris (1977) suggests that where work is alienating and community ties attenuated, family members focus all their interests and energies on the family and live through each other. The resulting concentration of creative and emotional energies within the family becomes oppressive, repressive and claustrophobic. These arguments strike at the very core of the conjugal-family-is-a-haven thesis. They suggest that where public life is rootless, individualistic and bureaucratised and the family isolated and privatised, family relationships become claustrophobic and overcharged and so cannot in fact serve as a supportive counterbalance to the psychic strains of the public world.

Lasch (1977) advances a different argument. He argues that accounts of the isolated but oppressive conjugal family perpetuate a fundamental mistake of Parsonian theorising: the assumption that family life is insulated from the wider society. In Lasch's view, the family is not in itself destructive. However, the modern family has been invaded and distorted by the destructive forces of capitalism. Modern family relations, Lasch seems to be saying, reflect the menace and the self-interested individualism of the market place.

An Agency for the Oppression of Women?

The belief that women are oppressed and repressed by and through 'the family' is most forcibly and extensively articulated by feminist writers. Like Laing, feminist critics of the family say that behind an ideology of love and nurture lie conflict and oppression. They also remind us that the family is not a monolithic and unified entity but a set of power relationships. However, where Laing focusses on the repression of individuality in general and of children in particular, feminist writers identify women as the main victims of the family's power to oppress. Barrett and McIntosh (1982, pp. 56–9) say that men may experience the family as a mental prison but can steer clear of the house if they want to, and children may be abused physically and psychologically within the family but have another life in the school and peer group into which they can escape. However, women, for whom motherhood and home-making are expected to be fulfilling and rewarding, are more fully imprisoned. They are trapped by the apparent inevitability with which they are destined to be wives and mothers and by the all-absorbing nature of the housewife–mother role.

Though feminist critiques of the family vary in their emphases and orientations, three aspects of the present-day family are commonly identified as oppressive for women: (i) its regulation of women's labour through the housewife role, (ii) the control it gives men over women's sexuality and fertility, and (iii) its structuring of gender identities.

The identification of women with the housewife role and the control which this gives men over women's labour and material circumstances is a central theme in feminist discussions of the family. Feminist writers (see pp. 89–93) have shown that the priority which it is assumed the housewife role should have over all other roles for women limits their participation in paid work outside the home and so cuts them off from opportunities for self-realisation and self-fulfilment, makes them economically dependent on men and denies them a say in the allocation of public resources. Men thus have privileged access to, and control over, the public world and therefore control over women.

Some writers have also pointed to the alienating nature of women's work in the home. Oakley (1974) characterises housework as monotonous, fragmented, repetitive, relentless and lonely. She notes that housework, because it is unpaid, is regarded as non-work and has low social status. In Oakley's view, housewives experience greater alienation from their work than the most alienated of industrial workers. Barrett and McIntosh also say that the housewife role is solitary, continuing and unrelieved. They say that the housewife's daily regime in 'the prison' of the home entails:

> long hours of working banged up in a solitary cell while the guards attend to other more important business. It is the mundane stuff of cartoons: it is 5.45 p.m. in a block of council flats. In each of fifty boxes a women is frying the children's fish fingers, bathing the baby, putting its dirty nappies into the washing machine and peeling the potatoes for the husband's tea. All the same, but all in isolation (Barrett and McIntosh, 1982, p. 58).

The second way in which the family is seen as oppressing women is through the power which it gives men over their sexuality and fertility. Feminist writers emphasise that historically marriage has been constructed as the site of sex and sex conflated with reproduction, so that reproductive sex has become the model of normal heterosexuality and male penetration the organising principle of sexual pleasure. Consequently, says Campbell (1983), women's sexuality is conventionally confined to heterosexual marriage, haunted by the ever-present risk of pregnancy and motherhood, and bound up with their plight as economic dependants. Feminist writers have also highlighted the way in which marriage has historically co-existed with ideals of female, but not male, chastity and fidelity, and with a failure to define rape by a husband as a criminal offence. According to these arguments, marriage is an institution through which women are denied the right to control sexual access to their own bodies and to control their own fertility. In addition, feminist writers have drawn attention to the power which men have over women through the use of physical force, and have identified the family as a major site of male physical abuse of women. In an analysis of official statistics on offences involving violence in two Scottish cities, Dobash and Dobash (1980) found that wife-assault represented 26 per cent of all serious assaults and 76 per cent of all family violence. They show that wife-battering is not a rare phenomenon, the action of disturbed or drunken men, but is widespread and has cultural support. They say that wife-beating is seen by many men as the natural extension of a husband's authority. They also point out that beliefs in the family's right to privacy and independence mean that the police are reluctant to intervene, that penalties for wife-battering are relatively light and that women are cut off from public protection. Thus, Dobash and Dobash confront us with the irony that the family, where nurture and affection are supposed to be located, is also the place where violence against women is most tolerated.

The third way in which the family is said to imprison women is through the promulgation of ideals of femininity and masculinity which locate women in the private world of the family and men in the public world. This argument is elaborated in various ways. Leonard (1980) claims that marriage is in reality a labour relationship in which a woman pledges her labour for life to her husband, provides him with sexual services and bears his children in return for upkeep and protection. According to Leonard, notions of romantic love mask this reality and lure women unawares into marriage. Oakley (1976, Chaps. 7 and 8) identifies beliefs in the 'naturalness' of the sexual division of labour and in the importance of the mother–child relationship as central elements in the ideology of the conjugal family. In Oakley's view, these beliefs secure women's psychological identification with the domestic world while the belief that the family is particularly important as a system of affective relationships tightens the noose by privatising the home and romanticising marriage. Mead (1954) sees theories of maternal deprivation as 'a new and subtle form of anti-feminism in which men – under the guise of exalting the importance of maternity – are tying women more tightly to their children'. Similarly, Mitchell (1966) maintains that motherhood, when used as a mystique, 'becomes an instrument of oppression'; it denies women lives, needs, activities and relationships that are apart from, or may conflict with, mothering. In short, these writers see the ideology of the family as containing within it and sustaining ideas of romantic love, female nurturing and male breadwinning which imprison women and men in particular gender identities.

Barrett (1980, pp. 204–8) emphasises that gender identities are constructed and reproduced within an ideology of the family *and* through socialisation in actual families. She points out that socialising agents other than the family – peers, the school, the law, the state, the media – are engaged in constructing and reproducing gender identities. Barrett further points out that within families definitions of appropriate gender behaviour rely strongly on general social definitions; thus particular families seek to achieve the characteristics attributed to 'the family' by representations of it, for example, in the media and, conversely, the efforts of 'liberated' parents to raise their children in non-conforming ways may be defeated by the strength and pervasiveness of the ideology of the family. 'Families' says Barrett 'are enmeshed in and responsive to the ideology of "the family" ', which is produced in the society as a whole. At the same time the ideology of the family is, in Barrett's view, 'most pervasively and intensively articulated in the processes of gender socialisation that take place in families themselves'. She emphasises that parents encourage little girls to be helpful, dependent and caring and little boys to be active, independent and protective. She notes also that the intense emotional and psychological forces deployed in family life pressurise children into appropriate gender identities. Ideas of domesticity and maternity for women and of breadwinning and responsibility for men, says Barrett, are articulated very strongly within families. It is not surprising, she concludes, that feminists have defined the family as a positive agent of gender socialisation and, therefore, of women's oppression.

For many feminists, change in familial arrangements is essential to the liberation of women. They therefore seek to overturn particular aspects of the family which they consider to be problematic or to confront the system as a whole. Reformist proposals aim at achieving greater equality between men and women by modifying family structures. Such proposals tend to centre on the incorporation of men into domestic labour, on the one hand, and the greater and more equal participation of women in employment outside the home, on the other hand. They include the expansion of day-care facilities for children so as to remove some of the burden of child-care from the family. Radical proposals advocate that marriage be superseded by a range of options – free-love unions, group marriage, homosexual relationships, celibacy – and that the family as a child-care unit be replaced by communal child-rearing and/or professional parenthood.

However, the feminist critique of the family has itself been criticised, by feminist as well as by non-feminist writers. Four interrelated issues have been raised.

First, feminism has been charged with portraying the family as wholly oppressive. Feminism, says Nava (1983), has taken over the image of the monolithic family found in functionalist theorising, but has inverted it. Instead of being wholly good, the family is now wholly bad. The widespread appeal which motherhood and family life has for many women is thus either ignored or treated as some form of false consciousness. Relatedly, Thorne (1982) says that feminist accounts of women's subordination often slide into portraying women not only as subordinates but also as helpless and passive victims of patriarchal forms. They thus fail fully to recognise the complex dialectic of men's control and women's (sometimes success-ful) efforts to combat and circumvent it. Nineteenth-century struggles for the vote, for temperance and moral reform and for increased welfare for mothers and children, as well as the contemporary women's movement, demonstrate women's power to resist and to effect some change in family structures.

Second, there is an important ambiguity in the feminist critique of the family. On the one hand, feminism has emphasised cultural variability in family patterns (see Chapter 2) and denied the modern Western family privileged status as 'the family'. On the other hand, accounts of women's oppression often slide into writing of the family as though it were everywhere the same and thus seem to deny the complexity and diversity of family life which feminism has itself emphasised.

Third, some writers have doubted that there is a necessary connection between the family, the sexual division of labour and patriarchal power. As we saw in Chapter 4 (pp. 113–14), some writers have suggested that women have sometimes exercised some measure of power within and through the family. Conversely, the persistence of a conventional division of labour in communes organised on a non-familial basis (see Section 7.4) and in unmarried cohabitation (see Section 7.2) suggests that the abolition of the family may not of itself accomplish a restructuring of gender relations.

Finally, insistence on the family as the major site of women's oppression runs the risk of divorcing the family from wider political and economic structures. Yet the consequences of women's mothering for their standing in society is clearly related not only to the way in which the family is organised but also to the way in which productive activity is organised. In contemporary capitalism, the organisation and ideology of the workplace is based on the maximisation of labour power and does not admit to full membership those who have important commitments to other spheres (see pp. 85–91). It is reasonable to suppose that it is this circumstance, as much as the ideology and structure of the conjugal family, which leads to women's oppression. This supposition is supported by evidence of women's greater standing in the public world in societies in which work is not organised on the principle of maximising labour power (see, for example, Steady, 1981). This interaction between work and family is obscured in accounts of the family as the root of women's oppression.

5.3   A HAVEN AND A PRISON?

The preceding sections have shown that the conjugal family is viewed by some writers as a refuge from the psychic strains of the public world, by other writers as imprisoning and oppressive. We have also shown that each of these positions contains analytical weaknesses. The conjugal-family-is-a-haven thesis has been challenged on the grounds that it obscures the diverse ways in which family life may be experienced, mistakenly assumes that family life can be insulated from the tensions and pressures which permeate the wider society, ignores the fact that some people have the power to order family life in terms of their own interests but others do not, and pays insufficient attention to the 'dark side' of family life. It cannot therefore account for the intensity of the 1970s reaction against the conjugal family as imprisoning and oppressive. On the other hand, accounts of the conjugal family as oppressive have been challenged because they also fail to recognise the diverse ways in which life within the conjugal family may be experienced, fail to trace the interconnections between the oppressive family and wider society and, in emphasising the 'dark side' of family living, fail to take account of its widespread appeal. The family's critics do not, Hirst (1981) suggests, take account of the fact that the family is the product of voluntary association. It is structured by laws, social policies, dominant ideologies, but it is also formed by the acts of choice of two individuals in marrying and having children.

These arguments imply the need for a theory which recognises the family as having negative and positive aspects and which takes account of the rejection of the family as well as of its wider appeal. We are pointed in this direction by Fletcher's (1973) old and spirited defence of the modern conjugal family. Fletcher claims that the modern family provides in an admirable way for the careful upbringing of children and the emotional and sexual needs of the married pair. However, he also recognises that the conception of marriage as a relationship of personal affinity entails a continuous process of matching expectations and life-styles and therefore continuous effort in working out a successful relationship. It can be 'most rewarding and enriching if it is successful' but, precisely because so much is expected of it, 'the most miserable and intolerable of human experiences if it is a failure' (Fletcher, 1973, p. 140). Fletcher also points out that the family, as the locus of affective relationships, is the locus of destructive as well as of positive emotions. He writes:

> The family is that group within which the most fundamental appreciation of human qualities and values takes place – 'for better for worse': the qualities of truth and honesty, of falsehood and deceit; of kindliness and sympathy, of indifference and cruelty; of co-operation and forbearance, of egotism and antagonism; of tolerance, justice and impartiality; of bias, dogmatism and obstinacy; of generous concern for the freedom and fulfilment of others, of the mean desire to dominate – whether in overt bullying or in psychologically more subtle ways (Fletcher, 1973, p. 42).

Images of the conjugal family as both haven and prison lead to ambivalence and neutrality and are not well developed in the literature. Yet attention to the nurturant and supportive as well as the oppressive sides of families is not just an ambivalence. It is, in part, a recognition of the fact that family life may be experienced in different ways by different people and, in part, a recognition of the tragic paradox that security in personal relationships implies commitment and loss of freedom. It recognises that not only love and altruism but the whole range of human feelings find expression in family life.

6

Remodelling the Conjugal Family

Pressures for change in the way in which sexual and parental relationships are ordered have had as an important outcome the legitimation of marital breakup. Over the past thirty years most Western societies have introduced relatively liberal laws allowing the termination of marriage by divorce. Moreover, the number of marriages ending in divorce has shown varying, but in general marked, increases. As a result, lifelong marriage has effectively been replaced by serial monogamy and one-parent families and remarriage families have become part of the family scene.

These developments are the concern of this chapter. The institutionalisation of divorce is examined in Section 6.1, the one-parent family in Section 6.2 and the remarriage family in Section 6.3. Opposing views of the significance of these changes for 'the family' are briefly considered in the final section.

6.1 THE INSTITUTIONALISATION OF DIVORCE

The Christian ideal of marriage as a holy bond which could not be broken while the partners were alive was established in most parts of Western Europe by medieval times (Chester, 1977a). This did not mean that marriages were not sometimes broken by separation or desertion. Nevertheless, from medieval times onwards, lifelong marriage was the basic principle of family organisation; separation and desertion left the marital bond unsevered in law and the persons involved without the option of remarriage. It is only in modern times that the termination of marriage by divorce, and serial monogamy, have come to be permitted. The process of legitimation has varied between societies. In some societies divorce is still not available and even where it is available it may not be fully approved. It is not yet sanctioned by the Roman Catholic Church, for example.

To understand why and how marriage has come to be seen as a voluntarily terminable contract we must look at the introduction and liberalisation of divorce law, the resort to divorce and the reasons for marital breakdown.

The Introduction and Liberalisation of Divorce Law

The establishment in the Western world of laws for the ending of marriage by divorce is usually explained in terms of changing religious and familial ideologies (see, for example, Goode, 1966). Thus, the decline of religious belief is commonly seen as leading to the erosion of beliefs in the divinely-ordained nature of marriage, and as a critical factor in the development of conceptions of marriage as a personal contract serving individual needs and dissoluble at the wishes of the partners. In addition, or alternatively, the ideology of the conjugal family is said to entail the legitimation of divorce: it is argued that a family ideology which emphasises individual rights and achievement of personal happiness through sexual and emotional fulfilment presumes that marriages which do not provide these satisfactions are without a *raison d'être* and should be dissolved.

The foregoing arguments emphasise the effect of ideas, beliefs and values on social practices. Arguments which relate the institutionalisation of divorce to changes in the economic basis of society have also been advanced. Thus it has been asserted that lifelong marriage is irrelevant to the capitalist mode of production but was necessary to feudal-type societies since divorce would have undermined security of land tenure, created problems over inheritance and disrupted household production (see, for example, Sachs and Wilson, 1978). However, attempts to relate the development of divorce law to the logic of capitalism are problematic. Harrison and Mort (1980) point out that they gloss over: (i) the fact that pressure for divorce did not build up until after the Second World War, and (ii) the powerful influence which the Church and religious ideas exercised over the regulation of marriage and its dissolution in the feudal and early capitalist periods. In addition, Marxism cannot readily explain why societies in which Roman Catholicism is dominant have been relatively slow to establish divorce procedures and Catholic peoples within Protestant countries relatively slow to use them. Moreover, theories which emphasise the utility of the family to capitalism, as Marxism has tended to do, cannot readily explain how so fundamental a change in the family system has taken place within the capitalist system. Feminist theories which stress the family's utility to patriarchy and the continuing dominance of patriarchal forces run into the same kind of difficulty. The institutionalisation of divorce has, in fact, received scant theoretical attention within these schools of thought and its significance tends to be underplayed (see Section 6.4).

In England divorce law has passed through three major phases. In the first, marriage was regulated by the Church and divorce was not allowed. In the second, the regulation of marriage passed to the civil authorities but continued to be governed by religious and collectivistic ideals and divorce was allowed on very limited terms. In the third, secular and individualistic ideals became dominant and divorce law was liberalised.

The exclusive jurisdiction of the Church over marriage was established in England by the twelfth century. Under this jurisdiction, marriages could be declared invalid and set aside under a decree of nullity. This was available where rules against marrying near relatives had been broken. Further, spouses could separate but not remarry under what was, more or less, the equivalent of modern judicial separation, a decree of divorce *a mensa et thoro*. However, until the passing of the Matrimonial Causes Act in 1857, valid marriages could be dissolved only by a Private Act of Parliament. The use of private parliamentary acts to dissolve a marriage was a device developed towards the end of the seventeenth century for overriding the spiritual authority of the Church by invoking that of Parliament. It was expensive, slow and cumbersome and available only to the wealthy and influential. Between 1715 and 1852 only 244 marriages were dissolved in this way (Report of the Royal Commission on Marriage and Divorce, Cmd. 9678, 1956).

The Matrimonial Causes Act 1857 significantly changed this situation in that it transferred jurisdiction over marriage to the civil courts and allowed judicial divorce. However, it did not go very far towards making marriage a voluntarily terminable contract. For one thing, divorce remained expensive and so remained an aristocratic and upper-middle-class privilege (Harrison and Mort, 1980). More importantly, the 1857 Act retained the notion that church and/or state have an interest in the continuation of marriage which takes priority over the wishes of the parties involved. Furthermore, it based divorce on the doctrine of the 'matrimonial offence'. This doctrine defined certain acts, adultery in the case of wives and adultery aggravated by some other offence such as cruelty, desertion, bigamy or incest in the case of husbands, as incompatible with the undertakings entered into at marriage and as absolving the innocent partner from his or her marital obligations. Divorce was thus defined as arising out of the contravention of basic moral principles. The 1857 legislation, say Harrison and Mort (1980), was structured by religious ideals (even though the jurisdiction of the Church had been replaced by that of the state) and contained no trace of the individualistic, privatised, person-focussed ideals which were to lead to pressures for divorce by consent in the 1960s.

The gender inequality inherent in the 1857 Act was removed in 1923 and wives, like husbands, were allowed to sue for divorce on the basis of adultery alone. In 1937 matrimonial offences were extended to include wilful desertion for three years or more, cruelty and incurable insanity after five years confinement. Legal aid for divorce became available in 1950 (under the Legal Aid and Advice Act, 1949). Nevertheless, the basic principles of the 1857 Act, the doctrine of the matrimonial offence and the idea that marriage was not a voluntarily terminable contract, remained unchanged.

However, a divorce law which sought to maintain the overall stability of marriage by making access to divorce difficult was out of step with the increasingly individualistic, person-focussed and privatised ideals of the mid-twentieth century. Three factors are commonly cited as eventually effecting change. First, in the absence of 'easy' divorce, many couples simply separated and formed new and illicit unions while others colluded in the fabrication of a matrimonial offence. This disjunction between the principles embodied in divorce law and social practice seems to have constituted a considerable pressure for change. Second, some writers maintain that with women's increased participation in paid labour and with the establishment of a welfare state, the overall stability of marriage began to seem less necessary to the economic security of women and children. Third, the argument that easy access to divorce would be detrimental to children was now countered by the argument that an uncongenial divorce law damaged children by imprisoning them in a home torn apart by marital conflict.

Confronted by these very considerable pressures for change, the Established Church suddenly withdrew its opposition to reform, and in 1969 the Divorce Reform Act (operative from 1971) made the irretrievable breakdown of marriage the sole basis for divorce in England and Wales. Seven years later (in 1976) its provisions were extended to Scotland under the Divorce (Scotland) Act. Five criteria were established as evidence of marital breakdown: (i) the respondent's adultery and the petitioner finds it intolerable to live with the respondent; (ii) unreasonable behaviour; (iii) desertion for at least two years; (iv) separation for two years where both partners consent; or (v) separation for five years where one partner is opposed to the divorce. This reform did not entirely banish connotations of fault from divorce since some of the criteria for establishing marital breakdown (adultery, unreasonable behaviour and desertion) were modified versions of the old matrimonial offences. However, the 1969 Act is generally viewed as transforming the divorce scene. It has been seen as putting an end to the public blaming of one of the partners as guilty of a moral offence, as providing for the reality if not the letter of divorce by consent (McGregor, 1972) and as formally redefining marriage as a secular and terminable arrangement between a man and a woman (Sachs and Wilson, 1978, p. 143).

The Incidence of Divorce

The post-war period has seen not only the liberalisation of divorce law but also marked increases in the proportion of marriages ending in divorce. In England and Wales (see Table 6.1), the divorce rate (that is the number of persons divorcing in a given year per 1000 married persons) was always below 1 per 1000 married persons during the first four decades of the century. It stood at 12.2 per 1000 persons in 1983 – an all-time high. According to some estimates, *if the trends of the 1970s persist*, one in three marriages will end in divorce (Haskey, 1982a) and one in five children will experience their parents' divorce before reaching their sixteenth birthday (Haskey, 1982b). Wives more often than husbands petition for divorce. In 1983 about seven out of ten divorce decrees were granted to wives, with the husband's unreasonable behaviour being the 'fact' most often cited as evidence of marital breakdown (Table 6.2).

The trends in divorce found in England and Wales are also found in other Western societies, though the timing and rate of increase vary from country to country. The divorce rate in England and Wales is below the level found in the USA where it is estimated that if recent trends continue the proportion of marriages ending in

Table 6.1   *The increase in divorce in England and Wales, 1911–83*

Year	Divorce rate[1]
1911	0.09
1921	0.47
1931	0.44
1937	0.52
1947[2]	5.60
1951	2.60
1961	2.10
1969[3]	4.10
1970[3]	4.70
1971	6.00
1978[4]	11.60
1979	11.20
1980	12.00
1981	11.90
1982	12.00
1983	12.20

[1]   Number of persons divorcing per 1000 married persons.
[2]   Represents the peak of an upsurge in divorcing – the result, it is usually said, of disturbed war-time conditions. During the 1950s the divorce rate declined from this 1947 peak but remained higher than in the pre-war period.
[3]   Divorce rose sharply throughout the 1960s, that is, before the 'liberal' 1969 legislation. These figures show the rate of divorce in the two years before the 1969 Divorce Reform Act became operative.
[4]   The divorce rate continued rising sharply until 1978 and since then has shown small annual fluctuations.
SOURCE   Office of Population Censuses and Surveys.

divorce could be close to 40 per cent (Levitan and Belous, 1981, p. 29). Increasing divorce is also a widespread phenomenon in Europe but levels there seem to be generally lower than the levels found in England and Wales (Figure 6.1). The rate in Scotland, though it rose considerably after the Divorce (Scotland) Act 1976, is still relatively low: it stood at 3.2 in 1976 and 4.6 in 1982 (*Annual Abstract of Statistics*, 1984, Table 2.14).

Some commentators have interpreted the increase in divorce as indicating the particular susceptibility of present-day marriage to breakdown, but others have argued that it indicates, not that

Table 6.2 *Grounds on which divorce was granted, England and Wales, 1983*

	Total	Party to whom granted		
		Husband	Wife	Both
Dissolutions:[1] all grounds	146 645	41 221	104 860	564[2]
Adultery		18 151	25 571	
Unreasonable behaviour		5 243	48 849	
Desertion		678	1 803	
Any two or all three of adultery, behaviour and desertion		91	348	
Separation (2 years) with consent		12 219	22 850	
Separation (5 years)		4 820	5 384	
Others		19	55	

[1] Excludes annulments, and petitions filed prior to 1, January 1971.
[2] Not distributed.
SOURCE OPCS Monitor FM2 84/1, Table 9, adapted.

marriages are more likely than in the past to be unsatisfactory, but that unsatisfactory marriages are less likely to be endured, more likely to be ended. These competing interpretations cannot readily be tested since we can identify and count divorce and legal separation only. Other forms of marital breakdown – 'failed' but intact marriages, informal separation and desertion – cannot easily be identified and counted. We therefore have no way of measuring the total amount of marital breakdown (seen as including 'failed' but intact marriages, formal and informal separations and desertion as well as divorce) or how it has changed over time.

However, some indication of how the ratio of divorce to other forms of marital breakdown has changed may be derived from Chester's analyses of divorce numbers and rates, applications to magistrates for maintenance orders and social security returns (Chester, 1971, 1972a, 1977a). Chester maintains that if the increase in divorce represented only a shift from covert to manifest instability (that is, from unrecorded to recorded breakups), then – given the magnitude of divorce in the 1970s – the level of informal separations in, say, 1960 would have been very much greater than the level of

Rate per 1000 existing marriages

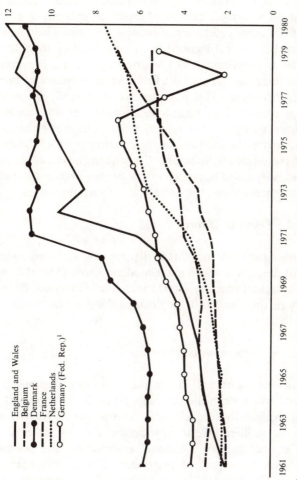

England and Wales
Belgium
Denmark
France
Netherlands
Germany (Fed. Rep.)[1]

[1] 1977 and subsequent years are not comparable with earlier years. The First Law Reforming Marriage and Family Legislation came into force on 1 July 1977.

SOURCE: Demographic Statistics, 1980 (SOEC)

FIGURE 6.1   Divorce rates: international comparisons

divorce, but none of the evidence suggests that this was so. Further, using as evidence social security applications by unsupported wives, Chester suggests that the level of informal separations has also increased (though the 'redistribution hypothesis' would lead us to expect a decrease). The adequacy of the indices which Chester uses is unproven. Nevertheless, his analyses suggest that the increase in divorce cannot be explained in terms of a shift to divorce from other categories of marital breakup. There would seem to have been a real increase in marital breakup though the extent of this is exaggerated by the divorce statistics. It remains possible that there has been a shift from the maintenance of failed marriages to divorcing. This hypothesis cannot really be tested. Because expectations of marriage have changed over time, ideas of what constitutes a successful or a failed marriage have also changed. By the same token, the kind of marriage that now ends in divorce may once have seemed satisfactory. Consequently, we can neither define and identify failed but intact marriages nor make meaningful historical statements about the prevalence of such marriages.

Explaining the Resort to Divorce

Explanations of the modern resort to divorce have variously sought to identify (i) the factors which make modern marriage breakdown-prone; (ii) the factors which facilitate the ending of an unsatisfactory marriage by divorce, and (iii) the distinguishing characteristics of those who divorce.

(i)   Sources of strain in modern marriages

The accounts we examined in Chapter 5 of the tensions and contradictions which permeate the conjugal family system point to the kind of explanations which have been advanced for marital breakdown in modern Western societies. For example, it is commonly argued that the emotional gratification and personal fulfilment which we expect of marriage are not easily realised. According to Fletcher (1973), mutuality of consideration and freedom for personal development within marriage require continuous individual effort in working out a satisfactory relationship. We have, in Fletcher's view, come into an age of more complex expectations but of more explicit discontents, made marriage potentially more rewarding but also potentially more unstable. Moreover, specific sources of stress which may make it difficult, if not impossible, to find the expected satisfactions have been identified. Some writers, as we saw in the preceding chapter, have argued that the isolation of the nuclear family from wider kin, together with the fragility of neighbourhood networks, have deprived marital partners of sources of support, companionship and tension-release outside marriage, imprisoned them within a self-contained little den and placed a heavy burden on them to be all things to each other. Marriage is thus seen as overloaded and charged with a heavy potential for stress and conflict. Other writers point to the contemporary reinterpretation of women's roles as leading to stress and conflict. Hart (1976) suggests that there are ambivalences and difficulties in combining the role of wife and mother with that of paid employee and in working out a marital relationship which does not, as hitherto, merge the wife's aspirations with those of the husband but treats husband and wife as independent and equal persons. Again, it has been argued that because conventional gender structures define women as almost totally responsible for, and men as marginal to, the family's expressive tasks, women go largely unnurtured and unsupported in marriage and so are unlikely to find the satisfactions they had been led to expect (Feldberg and Kohen, 1976). Moreover, it is likely that the feminist view of marriage as inherently oppressive for women has lessened women's commitment to their marriages. Finally, there is the argument advanced by Goode (1966) that failure to realise personal fulfilment goals is now seen as a sufficient reason for abandoning the marriage. Priority, says Goode, is given to the achievement of personal satisfactions and we ask whether the disruption of marriage suits our needs, not whether it is 'moral'.

All these arguments seem to suggest that a tendency to marriage breakdown is inherent in the elevation of the conjugal family to a position of supreme importance as a system of affective relationships.

(ii) The opportunity structures of divorce

It is often argued that whether or not unsatisfactory marriages end in divorce or continue to function as unsatisfactory marriages is related to the opportunity structures of divorce – that is, to the ease with which the marital partners may extricate themselves from their marriage and the alternatives available to them for restructuring their lives. Thus changes in the opportunity structures of divorce have been seen by some writers as contributing to upward trends in divorce. Hart (1976) identifies four factors as facilitating the modern resort to divorce. First, she reiterates the often-made argument that the liberalisation of divorce law has made it easier to end a stressful marriage. Second, she argues that legal aid has reduced the cost of divorce to the poor and widened its availability. Third, she suggests that the growth of state welfare has facilitated the establishment of one-parent families. Fourth, Hart argues that the lessening rigidity of the sexual division of labour (described in Section 4.1) has not only increased the autonomy of women and men and their ability to dispense with marriage but has also increased social interaction between the sexes and widened their access to potential new partners. Hart suggests also that at an individual level the decision to divorce may be influenced by the availability of alternative accommodation, access to other sources of economic support or domestic labour and, importantly, the potential availability of a new partner.

These 'opportunity' arguments have gained wide currency, but are at best only partially validated by research findings. Clearly the ability to divorce depends on the state of the law regarding divorce. However, as we noted earlier, Chester has shown that the upward trend in divorce cannot be attributed in its entirety to the increased availability of divorce. Chester (1972b) has also declared that hypotheses which account for increasing divorce in terms of the facilitating agency of legal aid fail to fit the facts of petitioning and ascribe too much significance to a somewhat limited welfare scheme. Again, data from the United States suggest that there is little or no relationship between the availability of welfare benefits and increases in divorce (Thornes and Collard, 1979, p. 3). Some commentators have also argued that the liberalisation of divorce does not simply provide a *solution* to marital breakdown but is itself a *cause* of marital breakdown. This argument maintains that 'easy' divorce leads to marital instability because it makes marriage a terminable contract in which minor disputes can readily develop into disruptive conflicts and which is vulnerable to the predatory activities of the interloper. This is an unfashionable argument for it is effectively an argument against liberal divorce. Moreover, it is not easily testable. What is true, however, is that the liberalisation of divorce law embodies new norms of marriage behaviour: it represents acceptance of marital *breakup* as a solution to marital *breakdown*.

(iii) Divorce-prone categories

Research in the USA and in Britain has consistently shown that divorce is not evenly distributed across the population but is related to (i) religious commitment, (ii) social class, and (iii) the demographic characteristics of the marriage.

Religious commitment seems to be associated with relatively low levels of divorce (Thornes and Collard, 1979, pp. 52–8). In addition, American data suggest that the divorce rate of Roman Catholics is lower than that of other religious groups (Levitan and Belous, 1981, p. 32). The mechanisms whereby religiosity protects the couple against divorce are unclear. Thornes and Collard (1979, pp. 58–9) say that it could be that the marriages of 'religious couples' are as unhappy as the marriages of other couples but that religious commitment represents a barrier to divorce; alternatively, their marriages could be happier because of the security, support and direction they find in religion.

Social class differences in divorce have been amply documented. American census data (report Thornes and Collard, 1979) have consistently shown an inverse relationship between social class and divorce – that is, the lower the social class of the husband (as measured by such indicators as occupational status, income level or educational attainment), the higher the rate of separation and divorce. In Britain, class differentials are more complex. Gibson's (1974) analysis of data for 1961 suggests that divorce peaks in those classes which are at the bottom of their own broad occupation groups, that is, in Social Class III Non-Manual, the group at the bottom of the non-manual classes and in Social Class V, the group at the bottom of the manual working classes (Table 6.3). A more recent study (Haskey, 1984) shows a similar though less marked peaking in Social Class III Non-Manual and a marked peaking in Social Class V, and is perhaps better interpreted as showing that Social Class I is relatively divorce-free and Social Class V divorce-prone, with the intervening groups having moderately high rates (Table 6.4). The armed forces and the unemployed, whom Haskey treats as distinct categories, are also shown to be divorce-prone. The divorce-proneness of couples at the bottom of the class structure

Table 6.3   *Social class variations in divorce, England and Wales, 1961*

Social class of husband	Divorces per 10 000 married women under 55 yrs.
I	22
II	25
III non-manual	43
III manual	29
IV	25
V	51
All	30

SOURCE Gibson (1974) 'The association between divorce and social class in England and Wales', *British Journal of Sociology*, 25, p. 83.

Table 6.4   *Social class variations in divorce in England and Wales, 1979*

Social class of husband		Divorces per 1000 husbands aged 16–59
I	Professional occupations	7
II	Intermediate occupations	12
IIIN	Skilled occupations – non-manual	16
IIIM	Skilled occupations – manual	14
IV	Partly skilled occupations	15
V	Unskilled occupations	30
	Armed forces	47
	Unemployed	34
All husbands[2]		15

[1] Based on a representative national sample of 2164 divorces in 1979.
[2] Based on all divorces in England and Wales in 1979.

SOURCE Haskey (1984) 'Social class and socio-economic differentials in divorce in England and Wales', *Population Studies*, 38, p. 429.

has been explained in terms of the acute material disadvantage which such couples typically experience and the stress this produces (see, for example, Thornes and Collard, 1979, pp. 37–47). Alternatively, their proneness to divorce has been attributed to their more limited economic investment in marriage. Goode (1966) suggests that upper-class husbands are constrained from divorcing by their long-term investments in mortgages, insurance policies and the like, and upper-class wives by their access to a life-style based on their husbands' income. Lower-strata husbands on the other hand are relatively free of long-term economic investments and lower-strata wives may not be substantially less well-off divorced than married. Goode's argument suggests that the economic 'costs' of divorce are greater in the upper strata than in the lower strata and represent a barrier to divorce even where marriages are unsatisfactory. However, neither the material-stress argument, nor the economic-costs-of-divorce argument seems to explain the particular susceptibility of Social Class III Non-Manual workers to divorce; just why this group is divorce-prone is unclear.

Finally, the demographic features of a marriage appear to be associated with its stability/instability. It has been consistently shown that marriages in which (i) one or both of the partners were in their teens at marriage, (ii) the bride was pregnant, (iii) the parents of one or both of the partners had divorced, (iv) the bride was of higher socio-economic status than the groom, and (v) one or both of the partners had been previously married, are likely to founder. Spouses who marry in their teens are almost twice as likely to divorce as those who marry for the first time between the ages of 20 and 24 (Haskey, 1983). A high proportion of teenage marriages are marriages in which the groom is in an unskilled or semi-skilled occupation and the bride is in manual work (Ineichen, 1977). Moreover, many teenage marriages are precipitated by pregnancy (Figure 6.2). It has been shown that marriages which combine these features are often attended by stress-generating conditions such as a short courtship period, parental opposition, inadequate housing and low and uncertain incomes, and are singularly unstable (Ineichen, 1977; Thornes and Collard, 1979). (Remarried divorce will be discussed in Section 6.3.)

The Divorce Experience

A growing body of 'divorce research' has shown that the divorce experience reaches beyond the lives of the marital partners to encompass their children and to some extent their kin and social networks. It involves five major ruptures. First, divorce represents the severance of what, within the context of contemporary family

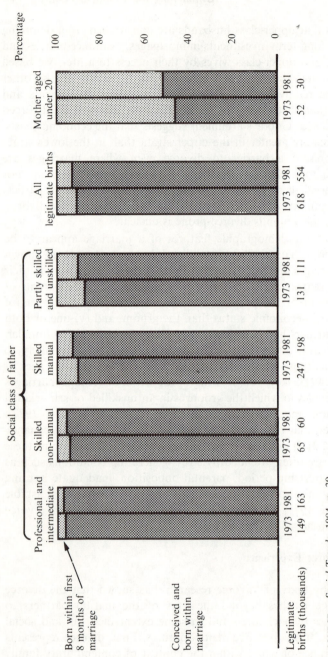

SOURCE: *Social Trends*, 1984, p. 39.

FIGURE 6.2 *Legitimate live births: by conception inside or outside marriage, social class of father and age of mother, 1973 and 1981, England and Wales*

ideologies, was expected to be a close, intimate, affective relationship. Second, divorce ruptures parental relationships, with one partner (usually the husband) effectively losing his (or less often her) parental role, while the other gains custody of the children but loses the support of a spouse in parenting (see also Section 6.2). Third, divorce ruptures the social networks of the partners (Hart, 1976). Joint friends may solve the dilemma of 'siding' with one partner by abandoning the couple altogether, while friendships which emanated from the husband's workplace may be lost to the wife, neighbourhood and other friendships cultivated by the wife may be lost to the husband, and both partners may lose their in-law kin relationships (see also Section 6.2). Fourth, resources which had once sustained one household must now be redistributed between two households; consequently, both partners and their children are deprived of material resources which had been theirs during the marriage (see also Section 6.2). Fifth, on divorce the status of 'married person' is superseded by that of 'divorced person' so that the individual's social identity is ruptured. The former status, Hart (1976) emphasises, is firmly structured and socially honoured, the latter is weakly structured and stigmatised.

The literature suggests that few couples negotiate these divorce ruptures without discomfort to one or both of the partners and/or to their children.

The nature of the divorce experience for children is poignantly depicted in a recent study by two American psychoanalysts, Wallerstein and Kelly (1980). This study observed the children of sixty Californian divorcing couples for a five-year period following their parents' separation. It suggests that marital breakup brings unpredictability, unreliability and insecurity into the child's world. Bewilderment, anxiety, anger, grief, shame, but above all a yearning for, and/or a sense of rejection by, the departing parent (the father in nearly all of these cases) are common responses. Further, Wallerstein and Kelly maintain that a major hazard of the divorce experience for children is the parents' diminished capacity to parent throughout the marital breakup period. The effects of this, they assert, may be consolidated to create long-term maladjustments. Wallerstein and Kelly say that the central factor in the child's response to divorce is the parents' own adjustment to it. They find that children experience most psychic pain where they are dragged into their parents' conflicts, where divorce brings their parents little relief, and/or where the departing parent maintains irregular or little contact with them. Finally, and somewhat surprisingly, Wallerstein and Kelly report that many marriages which had been unhappy for the parents had been reasonably comfortable for the children; many of the children would have preferred to 'hobble along' in the marriage. Five years after the breakup, over half the children in their study did not regard the divorced family as an improvement on the pre-divorce situation.

The traumatic nature of the divorce experience for husbands and wives is vividly portrayed in a number of American and British studies (see especially Ambrose *et al.*, 1983; Hart, 1976; Wallerstein and Kelly, 1980). These studies show that divorce may bring release from a relationship in which one or both of the partners had been demeaned, neglected and/or betrayed, but it may also bring a range of destructive emotions – anger, resentment, guilt, despair and disillusionment, a sense of rejection or loss, feelings of failure and intense isolation. Marital breakup has been linked with physical and mental ill-health and some studies have suggested that the separated and divorced are at particular risk of suicide, accidents and admission to psychiatric hospitals (see Ambrose *et al.*, 1983, for a review of some of the findings). Further, it has been shown that the trauma of marital breakdown and divorce can be long-lasting. Wallerstein and Kelly report that, while it is not unusual for one of the partners to relegate the divorce to the past, it is unusual for both of them to do so. Usually the divorce remains a live issue for one partner.

There are also indications that men more often than women experience divorce as a lasting trauma. Wallerstein and Kelly (1980, p. 193) say that five years after separation one-third of the men but only one-fifth of the women in their study were 'troubled and unhappy'. A Scottish study shows that divorced men are twice as likely as divorced women to be referred for psychiatric treatment (Robertson, 1974). In a recent British study, half of the men compared with just over one in four of the women 'would have preferred to have stayed married'. What is more, one in three of the men who had remarried and one in five remarried women wished they had remained married to their first partners (report of a study in Bristol, *Sunday Times*, 28 October 1984).

In sum, there is now substantial evidence that divorce is not only traumatic for some women and for a substantial proportion of men and children but also does not necessarily resolve the tensions and conflicts that had been associated with the marriage. However, these findings must be interpreted with caution. It is, in the first place, possible that mental health problems preceded, and even led to, marital breakdown. Second, the divorce experience is mediated by the alternatives available to the partners. For one or other or even both the partners, divorce may be a stepping-stone to a new (but not necessarily happier) relationship through remarriage (see Section 6.3) or cohabitation (see Section 7.2). A few may find in same-sex pairings (Section 7.3) or group living (Section 7.4) a preferred alternative to marriage. For others divorce may mean single-parenting (Section 6.2). For yet others divorce may mean a life of isolation and loneliness. The eventual outcome of the divorce experience for the persona of the people involved is clearly different in each of these cases. Finally, it is possible that the severity of the divorce trauma is a function of all the expectations that 'go with' the traditional ideal of a lifelong loving marriage and with the privileged status of the monogamous nuclear family. As divorce becomes more common, as alternatives to the monogamous nuclear family gain legitimacy, and as women establish themselves as independent persons, the ideal of the loving couple may lose its hold. In this event, divorce may become a less significant and less traumatic experience. However, the evidence does not point in this direction: despite nearly twenty years of relatively high divorce in Britain (and longer in the USA) there is no evidence that suggests that couples divorce with ease.

6.2 ONE-PARENT FAMILIES

Marital breakup has, as one of its by-products, the creation of one-parent families. In Britain six out of every ten couples who divorced in 1981 had children under 16 (*Social Trends*, 1984, p. 37) and most of these children were projected, for a while at least, into one-parent (usually lone-mother) family situations.

One-parent families may be created by the death of one of the parents or by unmarried parenthood as well as by divorce, and are not new. In the pre-industrial and early industrial periods, widowed one-parent families were a relatively common phenomenon. Laslett (1977) estimates that in sixteenth-century and seventeenth-century

England about 20 per cent of dependent young persons lost a parent (or parents) by death. However, in Britain as in many other Western societies, the latter part of the nineteenth century and the early twentieth century saw substantial declines in mortality at young ages and, consequently, in widowed one-parent families. The General Household Survey (a continuous government survey based on a national sample of private households) suggests that throughout the 1970s families headed by a widowed mother did not exceed 2 per cent of all families (Table 6.5).

Unmarried procreation, the third cause of solo parenthood, is found in all periods of history and in all places, but its prevalence and the circumstances in which it occurs vary. In Britain, unmarried parenthood has shown a marked upward trend since the late 1970s. The processes which have led to this result are complex. The total number of conceptions outside marriage rose from 208 000 in 1971 to 245 000 in 1981 (Figure 6.3). This reflected an increase of about a quarter in the number of unmarried women of child-bearing age in the population and not an increased tendency for women who were not married to conceive (*Social Trends*, 1984, p. 41). At the same time, the outcomes of extra-marital conceptions changed in contradictory ways. Between 1971 and 1981 the proportion terminated by abortion rose sharply, while the proportion ending in a legitimate birth declined and the proportion ending in illegitimate births increased only marginally (Figure 6.3). Further, an increasing proportion of illegitimate births – 58 per cent in 1981 compared with 45 per cent in 1971 in England and Wales (OPCS Series FMI, No. 8, Birth Statistics, 1984) – were registered by both parents and this is usually taken to mean that an increasing proportion of illegitimate births occur within the context of a cohabiting relationship; where this happens the child is in an unmarried two-parent family situation. On the other hand, the proportion of illegitimate births ending in adoption has declined dramatically: between 1971 and 1979 the number of non-parental adoptions of illegitimate children fell from 11 000 to 4000 and has since remained fairly constant (*Social Trends*, 1984, p. 41). The net outcome of the interaction of these contradictory trends was a doubling between 1971–3 and 1981–3 of families headed by never-married mothers as a proportion of all families (Table 6.5). At the latter date (1981–3) 2.5 per cent of all families were headed by lone never-married mothers.

Table 6.5 *Families with dependent children[1] by type and, for lone mothers, by marital status: Great Britain 1971–83*

Family type	1971–3	1973–5	1975–7	1977–9	1979–81	1981–3
			Percentages			
Married couple	91.8	90.7	89.8	88.9	88.1	87.0
Lone mother	7.1	8.0	8.8	9.7	10.4	11.6
Single	1.2	1.3	1.5	1.7	2.2	2.5
Widowed	1.8	1.9	2.0	1.9	1.7	1.7
Divorced	1.9	2.5	3.2	3.8	4.1	4.9
Separated	2.1	2.2	2.1	2.3	2.5	2.4
Lone father	1.2	1.3	1.3	1.3	1.5	1.4
All lone parents	8.2	9.3	10.2	11.1	11.9	13.0
Base = 100 per cent	14 105	13 655	13 972	13 178	12 984	11 540

[1] Children aged under 16 or aged 16–18 and in full-time education.
SOURCE GHS Monitor 84/1, 1984, Table 5.

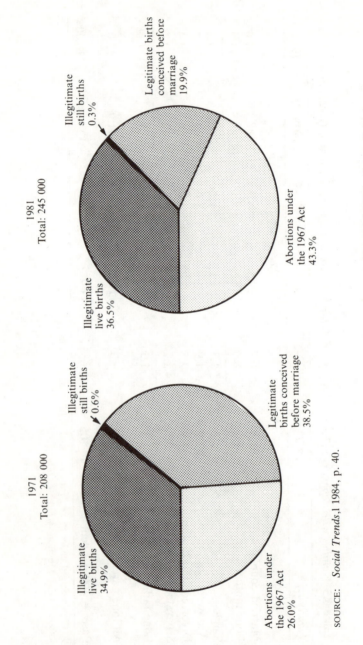

1981
Total: 245 000

Illegitimate
still births
0.3%

Legitimate births
conceived before
marriage
19.9%

Abortions under
the 1967 Act
43.3%

Illegitimate
live births
36.5%

1971
Total: 208 000

Illegitimate
still births
0.6%

Legitimate births conceived
before marriage
38.5%

Abortions under
the 1967 Act
26.0%

Illegitimate
live births
34.9%

SOURCE: *Social Trends,*1 1984, p. 40.

FIGURE 6.3 *Extra-marital conceptions: by outcome, 1971 and 1981, Great Britain*

However, divorce is the major factor in the increase in the numbers and proportions of lone mothers which Britain has experienced in recent years. In 1981–3 nearly 5 per cent of all families in the GHS samples for those years were headed by a divorced mother, compared with just under 2 per cent in 1971–3 (Table 6.5). Overall, the proportion of lone-mother families increased from just over 7 per cent (approximately one in fourteen families) in 1971–3 to just under 12 per cent (or approximately one in eight families) in 1981–3. The proportion headed by a lone father remained fairly constant and accounted for 1.4 per cent of all families in 1981–3.

Different sectors of the population have a differential propensity to produce one-parent families. Evidence from the National Child Development Study (Ferri, 1976, p. 41) found that at age 11 the proportion of children not living with both parents was lowest in Social Class I and II (one child in 18) and highest by far in Social Class V (one child in every seven). This reflects social class differences in divorce. There is also evidence of ethnic differences in lone parenting. Data for 1974 show that at that date 13 per cent of West Indian families and only 1 per cent of Asian families were headed by a lone parent compared with 9 per cent of all families (Royal Commission on the Distribution of Income and Wealth, Report No. 6, Cmnd. 7175, 1978, p. 125).

An increase in the proportion of one-parent families is also found in many other West European countries (Cockburn and Heclo, 1974) and in the USA, though the timing, rate of increase, total levels and ratio of divorced to widowed and unmarried lone parenthood vary from country to country. In the USA, with its somewhat higher divorce rates, the proportion of lone parent families is greater than in Britain. Whereas in Britain in 1981 6 per cent of children under 16 were living in one-parent households (1981 Census data), in the USA in the late 1970s 19 per cent of children under 18 were living in one-parent households. In the USA, as in Britain, the heads of most one-parent households are female. In the late 1970s nine out of every ten American children who were living in a lone-parent household were in lone-mother households; roughly two-thirds of the children in lone-mother households were in this situation because their parents had divorced or separated, 15 per cent because their mother had never married and 10 per cent because their father had died (data cited by Levitan and Belous, 1981, pp. 62–9).

Structural Characteristics

The one-parent family is defined in the Finer Report (the Report of the Committee on One-Parent Families, Cmnd. 5629, 1974) as a 'father or mother living without a spouse (or not cohabiting) with his or her never-married dependent child or children aged either below 16 or 16–19 and undergoing full-time education'. This definition focusses on child-dependence and the presence in the household of only one parent.

However, this focus on the absence from the child-rearing household of one of the parents obscures other important structural features of 'the one-parent family'. In the first place the one-parent tag obscures the role the 'absent' parent may continue to play in child-rearing (in economic provision, for example) and the psychological identification of child with absent parent. Second, it presents the one-parent family as a static phenomenon. However, with the exception of the never-married-never-cohabiting mother and child, one-parent families move into their one-parent status from a two-parent family situation, and many will be reconstituted as a two-parent family through the remarriage, often within a relatively short period of time, of the parent (see Section 6.3). Third, the focus on the parental dimension obscures the fact that the parent lacks a cohabiting sexual partner and companion. It also obscures the weakening of links to the absent parent's kin. Fourth, the one-parent tag seems to assume the homogeneity of divorced, separated, never-married and widowed families. Yet social research suggests that the different circumstances of their formation are associated with differences in their economic circumstances (see pp. 160–4) and official statistics reveal differences in their demographic features. For example, never-married mothers tend to be younger than other lone mothers, more often live with their parents and more often have only one child (GHS, 1982). Further, the significance of the one-parent family for the family system as a whole and for its members depends on the circumstances of its formation. Widowhood, though it creates a one-parent family when it occurs at an early rather than a late age, is an integral part of the life cycle of the monogamous nuclear family and does not represent a breach of traditional family ideals. Divorce, on the other hand, takes place in the context of a redefinition of marriage as a terminable relationship. Lone unmarried parenthood may be the unintended result of a more or less casual sexual relationship, or the result of planned procreation by formerly cohabiting partners, or the planned result of a desire for unpartnered parenthood; each of these circumstances is linked to the rejection or unavailability of other possible courses of action – marriage to the father of the child, abortion or adoption. Thus, in some circumstances, unmarried parenting represents the rejection of the father of the child as a married partner but not of marriage *per se*, and, in other circumstances, the principled rejection of marriage.

This chapter is about the changes in family structure associated with the institutionalisation of divorce, and so our primary concern is with separated and divorced one-parent families. However, never-married one-parent families (which could be regarded as coming within the remit of Chapter 7) and widowed one-parent families will also be dealt with as their separate treatment is impracticable (they are often 'lumped' together in research) and cumbersome. It must, however, be borne in mind that the degree to which members of separated, divorced, unmarried and widowed one-parent families adhere to, and are perceived as adhering to, the orthodox two-parent family ideal varies considerably.

We look at one-parent families in terms of (i) child-care; (ii) breadwinning; (iii) the experience of being without a spouse, and (iv) the implications for kin relationships.

(i)   Child-care

The general conclusion to be drawn from accounts of one-parent families is that child-care arrangements are structured in important ways by conventional gender assumptions.

In the first place, the conventional identification of child-rearing with femininity ensures that child-care and custody falls to the mother in the majority of divorces. Lowe (1982) maintains that, although statute law now defines mothers and fathers as having equal parental rights, the 'best interests' of the child are the primary consideration in determining child custody and the idea that young children, are, all things being equal, 'better off with their mother' is firmly entrenched in custody proceedings. Eekelaar and Clive (1977) found that just over three-quarters of custody orders are made in favour of the mother and less than one-tenth in favour of the father (with custody going to a third party, to both parents jointly or with no order being made in the remaining cases). Moreover, it seems that when marriages break down parents make arrangements between themselves which are in line with conventional assumptions about women's mothering so that the courts are in most instances simply confirming the status quo. Richards (1982) claims that fathers may be deterred from seeking custody by the belief that the 'odds' are stacked against them and may be so advised by their solicitors; Lowe (1982) suggests that welfare reports are more often asked for and the status quo more often set aside when the father is claiming custody; and Parker (1983) maintains that in disputed cases men are assumed to be unskilled in parenting and must prove otherwise, whereas the mother's 'fitness' for parenting is assumed and it is her 'unsuitability' that must be demonstrated. Feminist accounts of biasses in family law (see, for example, Smart, 1984) have emphasised that certain categories of mothers, notably in the past mothers 'guilty' of adultery and in the present mothers judged to be 'unstable' or known to be lesbian, are unlikely to be granted child custody. However, in general the belief that 'the mother not as a matter of law but in the ordinary course of nature is the right person to have charge of young children' (Sir John Pennycuick in a leading judgement, cited by Poulter, 1982) prevails.

'Mother care' is also deeply entrenched in unmarried parenthood. Accounts of the legal position of cohabiting parents have highlighted the fact that unmarried fathers have virtually no legal parental rights, not even within a stable cohabiting relationship (see Section 7.2). However, they may apply for child custody under the Guardianship of Minors Act, 1971, and may achieve parental rights in this way. Parker (1983) suggests that they are then in the same *de facto*, though not the same *de jure*, position as married fathers: the interests of the child will be regarded as paramount and as best served by 'mother care' so that the unmarried father must establish the unsuitability of the mother as a parent. However, unmarried fathers have rarely figured in reported custody cases (Parker, 1983). They are also absent from studies of solo parenting.

The second way in which the sexual division of labour structures child-care arrangements in one-parent families is in its impact on the child-care responsibilities of the present parent. Community norms define full-time child-care as appropriate for lone mothers but not for lone fathers and lone fathers are significantly more likely to be in full-time employment than are lone mothers (see pp. 160–

164). There are also indications that lone fathers, more often than lone mothers, are assisted in child-care by a relative or by a housekeeper (Ferri, 1976).

Finally, conventional gender assumptions mean that the absence of one parent is very generally perceived as creating a not-easily-filled emotional and psychological vacuum. George and Wilding (1972) and Hipgrave (1982) report that fathers are anxious about handling children's emotional difficulties (which, in the two-parent family, is generally viewed as the mother's province), while Marsden (1973) found that lone mothers experience difficulty in trying to be a source of both authority (generally seen as the father's province) and affection. American and British studies describe lone fathers as confronting social reservations about their suitability as rearers of daughters (Hipgrave, 1982; Orthner *et al.*, 1976), boys in lone-mother families as having greater adjustment problems than girls (Wallerstein and Kelly, 1980; Hetherington, Cox and Cox, 1979) and lone fathers and mothers as striving to counteract the dangers they believe to be inherent in opposite-sex lone parenthood. Whether this gender vacuum would be experienced if gender roles were less sharply differentiated is a question that is raised but not answered by these findings.

The gender vacuum of lone parenthood is a function not only of the absence from the household of one parent but also of the very limited contact that children have with the absent parent. The disappearance of the unmarried father from child-care is a long-established theme of folklore and of the social work literature. The divorced non-custodial parent may also disappear from the child-rearing scene. British (Ambrose *et al.*, 1983; Eekelaar and Clive, 1977; George and Wilding, 1972; Marsden, 1973) as well as American (Wallerstein and Kelly, 1980) research has shown that contact between non-custodial parents (mothers as well as fathers) and their children diminishes in frequency and regularity over time, may be particularly weakened by the remarriage of either the non-custodial or custodial parent, and is maintained into the child's adulthood only in a minority of cases. Some of the custodial parents in these studies see contact with the absent parent as presenting the child with conflicts of affection and/or as inhibiting the burial of an unhappy marriage, and therefore discourage it; conversely continued friendliness between the parents seems to foster the absent parent–child bond. It may also be the case that the weakness of the bond between absent parent and child is related to gender norms. Greenberg (1979), finding that twice as many custodial mothers as fathers have support from their ex-spouses, suggests that the absentee-parent role is much more sex-role incongruent for women than for men; in her view, absentee mothers avoid their children because of their inability to deal with such a marginal status. Conversely, the limited involvement of the absent father in the life of his children has been seen as a symptom of men's more general lack of involvement in child-rearing. Moreover, some writers (notably, in Britain, Richards, 1982, and, in the USA, Wallerstein and Kelly, 1980) maintain that the restricted nature of access rights (which typically concern the rights of fathers) reflects the traditions of a society that has customarily relegated to secondary importance the father's role in child-care. These writers advocate the greater use of joint custody orders as a way of reaffirming and reinforcing the absent parent–child bond. Joint custody and split custody orders are now in favour in some American states.

(ii)   Breadwinning

Analyses of the economic conditions of solo parenthood suggest that in economic provision, as in child-care, conventional assumptions about the sexual division of labour structure the life of one-parent families in important ways.

Social definitions of men-as-breadwinners are, it seems, extended to lone fatherhood. George and Wilding's survey (1972) of community attitudes shows that child-care responsibilities are not perceived as overriding a man's obligation to be self-supporting. 78 per cent of their respondents felt that lone fathers with children under school age should go out to work. In contrast, 86 per cent of their respondents felt that lone mothers with children under school age ought to stay at home. Moreover, most lone-fathers are in employment. Data from the 1981 census show that in that year 71 per cent of lone fathers were in full-time work, 2 per cent in part-time work and 19 per cent unemployed and seeking work; only 8 per cent were economically inactive (OPCS, 1984). However, income may be less than in the two-parent family even where the father remains in full-time work. George and Wilding (1972) find that for 44 per cent of their lone-father families income was less than before the family broke up but only half of these fathers had given up work. They point out that in the lone-father family, income is not supplemented by a wife's earnings and that child-care reduces overtime and weekend working.

Men's breadwinning responsibilities have also been elaborated so as to cover their widows and orphaned children, their illegitimate children, their separated or divorced wives, and their legitimate children of former marriages. The needs of widows may be anticipated by life insurance policies and occupational pension schemes. Unmarried mothers may, on obtaining an affiliation order, claim support for their children from their former partner and the amount awarded may include an element for their own support while they are caring for children of the union (Eekelaar, 1984, p. 139). Divorce law has from its inception defined a husband's support obligations as continuing after divorce and under the 1973 Matrimonial Causes Act earlier and somewhat tentative measures were substantially improved. This Act established the principle that on divorce the assets and income of husband and wife were to be pooled and redistributed so that each of the partners may, insofar as is 'practicable and having regard to their conduct, just', continue to maintain the living standards they had enjoyed during marriage. Though wives could be required to support their former husbands if their resources were the greater, their lower earning capacity almost always meant that support obligations were placed on the husband.

However, most men have not the means to support themselves and their families in separate households and in practice lone mothers receive very little support from their former partners. Official statistics suggest that private maintenance is the main source of income for only just over 6 per cent of all lone mothers (see Table 6.6). Furthermore, the principle of lifelong support obligations between spouses – which in the late 1970s was increasingly attacked by feminist writers as incompatible with the ideal of independence for women, by former husbands as ignoring their partners' transgressions, and by second wives as absorbing their husbands' resources – has now been abandoned. The Matrimonial and Family Proceedings Act of 1984 retains the principle of parental (for all practical purposes paternal) support for children and gives overriding priority to their needs, but bases maintenance for a former spouse on the principle that each of the partners should achieve self-sufficiency as soon as possible. The Act also reasserts the notion that 'conduct' should be taken into account where 'it would be inequitable to disregard it'. In effect the principle of lifelong support between spouses has been jettisoned but formal parental responsibility for children has been enhanced. This is the logical outcome of the conception of marriage as a terminable contract. However, it does not deal with the root problem of the divorced-mother and her family, a man's inability (or unwillingness) to support two households. Further, it ignores the fact that the earning capacity of most divorced women would have been severely impaired by their marital and child-rearing commitments.

In attempting to combine paid employment with child-care, lone mothers confront all the problems encountered by working mothers in general (see Section 4.1) but may also face particular difficulties because of their sole responsibility for child-care. In the GHS sample for 1980–2 about 48 per cent of lone mothers, compared with 51 per cent of married mothers, with dependent children, were in paid employment but lone mothers were more likely to be in full-time employment: 22 per cent of lone mothers, compared with 15 per cent of married mothers were in full-time employment (GHS 1982). Some (limited) evidence suggests that lone-mothers are over-concentrated in typically low-paid women's jobs and have lower earnings than women in general (Popay *et al.*, 1983, p. 50–1).

The failure of a support system based on the extension of men's breadwinning responsibilities, together with women's weak employment opportunities, mean that lone-mothers are heavily dependent on state benefits (Table 6.6). However, social security policies are informed by the ideal of the self-sufficient male-breadwinning nuclear family and have been modified only marginally to take account of the growth of lone-mother families. Popay *et al.*, (1983, pp. 51–3) say that with the exception of widows, for whom a specific state benefit – the Widow's Pension – has been provided, one-parent families are dependent on the *ad hoc* adaptation of measures which were designed for other purposes and which may not be appropriate to their needs. Among these adaptations are an addition to the child benefit for the first child (now known as one-parent benefit) and relatively favourable treatment under the Family Income Supplement and Supplementary Benefit schemes.

None of these means of support – state benefits, paid employment and private maintenance – nor any combination of them provides lone-mother families with an income which is at all comparable

Table 6.6 *One- and two-parent families by main source of income: Great Britain, 1979*

	State benefits	Earnings	Maintenance	Other items	Total number of families with head under pension age
One-parent families headed by a woman	360 000	330 000	(50 000)	(10 000)	740 000
One-parent families headed by a man	(30 000)	70 000	—	—	100 000
Two-parent families	270 000	5 960 000	—	(30 000)	6 260 000

NOTES
1 These broad estimates are based on a Department of Health and Social Security analysis of income and other information recorded by respondents to the 1979 Family Expenditure Survey. They are subject to statistical error; those in brackets are subject to very considerable proportionate error.
2 The estimates relate to the population living in private households in Great Britain. Families and other people living in institutions are not included in the family expenditure survey.
3 The figures are based on the normal employment of the head of the family. For example, where the head of the family has been off work because of sickness or unemployment for less than three months at the time of the survey, he or she is classified according to the income received when working.
4 Figures relate to families where the head was under pension age.

SOURCE House of Commons, Written Answers, *Hansard*, 24 June 1982, cols 175 and 176.

with that of the average two-parent family. The National Council For One-Parent Families have used data from the Family Expenditure Survey (an annual Government Survey of the income and expenditure of a national sample of private households) to show that in 1983 in the UK the average total weekly income of all one-parent families was less than half (42 per cent) that of two-parent-two-child families (National Council For One-Parent Families Information Sheet No. 24). These data do not distinguish between lone-father and lone-mother households, but it can be assumed that they are a fair indication of the relative position of lone-mother households since they constituted 90 per cent of the sample. It can also be assumed that lone-father households are far less 'disadvantaged' than lone-mother households since, as we have seen, most lone-fathers do not have care of very young children, are in full-time employment and have earnings as their main source of income (see Table 6.6) while lone mothers tend to have very young children in their care, are in a weak position in the labour market, receive little support from their former partners and for the most part rely on limited state benefits. They are amongst the poorest in our society.

The plight of the lone mother in Britain is replicated in the USA. In some states 'alimony' has been superseded by the concept of 'community property' but in all states child-support after divorce is a legal obligation. However, a review of the data by Levitan and Belous (1981, pp. 72–5 and pp 111–16) suggests that two out of three divorced, separated and never-married mothers do not receive child-support payments from the father and, when they do, the amount they receive is inadequate. Child-support payments represent less than 20 per cent of the total income of half of all women getting them. Levitan and Belous claim that the father's ability to pay, as measured by his earnings before divorce or separation, is a key factor determining both the chances that payment will be made and the size of the payments. They emphasise that lone–mother families depend on welfare benefits to a greater extent than do two-parent families. Poverty, say Levitan and Belous, haunts one out of every nineteen two-parent families, one out of every nine lone-father families and one out of every three female-headed families.

(iii)   The absence of a spouse

In the one-parent family not only are the children without one parent but the parent is without a spouse. Greenberg, in her American study (1979) of middle-class lone fathers and mothers, finds that this 'spouseless' state is regarded by many of the men and women in the study as bringing beneficial autonomy, freedom and opportunity for self-development. In general, however, research findings emphasise the lacunae created by spouselessness within the context of present-day gender divisions and social conventions.

First, lone parents are without a partner in the child-care and household management task. One aspect of this is that they are without the customary provider of certain kinds of domestic services: men are without their 'domestic labourer', women are without their 'handyman'. There are some indications that lack of the respective skills may have its problems. Hipgrave (1982), for example, suggests that some lone fathers experience difficulty in managing the household budget. However, this gap is little discussed in the literature and we are left with the general impression that the requisite skills are either developed without undue difficulty or delegated. On the other hand, some of the literature has emphasised that lone parents are without support in, and relief from, the insistent demands of child-care, and confront responsibility-overload and task-overload dilemmas (see, for example, Chester 1977b and Cherlin 1981).

Second, the lone parent is without an established and socially legitimated sexual partner. Research findings suggest that they are also without the sexual freedom of the single person. Greenberg (1979) shows that the presence of children limits the lone parent's relationships with the opposite sex. Chester (1977b) notes that cultural stereotypes foster beliefs that the divorced or separated mother is both sexually needy and sexually predatory and consequently lone mothers experience offensive sexual overtures from men and wariness from women. Divorced men, it would seem from George and Wilding's findings (1972, p. 130), are also suspected of uncertain standards of sexual morality. Moreover, in Britain cohabitation makes widows ineligible for the Widow's Pension, and Supplementary Benefit dependent on the aggregate earnings of the couple; as a result lone parents are subject to sexual surveillance by public officials.

Third, lone parents are without the companionship of an age-peer in the home and without a social partner in a society in which the unaccompanied person is not easily included in mixed gatherings and may not easily participate in public social ventures. British and American research suggests that often the agreeable freedom and independence of solo parenthood is counteracted by a sense of loss of emotional intimacy. Lone mothers may find alternative sources of support and intimacy within same-sex friendship networks but lone fathers seem to be cut off from the interests and activities they once shared with male friendship groups by child-care responsibilities and are treated with suspicion if they attempt to establish informal non-sexual relationships with women (Hipgrave, 1982). The American study cited earlier (Greenberg, 1979) suggests that this difference in the availability of same-sex peer groups means that the lack of a spouse is more often translated into loneliness and personal discomfort for men than for women. In this study, 50 per cent of the lone fathers but only one lone mother targeted loneliness as a problem. However, lone mothers have another kind of problem. Chester (1977b) maintains that because women in general have less power and standing in society than men, the lack of a spouse means that the lone mother family is at a relative disadvantage in its dealings with the outside world.

Finally, most researchers emphasise the aloneness (as distinct from loneliness) of the solo parent and their ambiguous status as a not-married-not-unmarried person. To be formerly married, says Chester (1977b), is not at all the same thing as to be unmarried. Lone parents thus confront the world on their own but not as single persons. Their social situation, say George and Wilding (1972), is full of ambiguities which place them outside the normal stream of family life.

(iv)   Kin relationships

Accounts of relationships between the one-parent family and other kin suggest that the loss of a parent weakens ties to that parent's kin so that, for example, a grandparent–grandchild bond may be loosened (George and Wilding, 1972; Hart, 1976; Marsden, 1973). George and Wilding find that separated and divorced lone-fathers are less likely than widowed lone-fathers to be assisted by their spouses' kin. The reason, says George and Wilding (1972, p. 146) is obvious: 'The breakup of a marriage through divorce or separation not only divides the married partners, it also divides each of them from the other's relatives'.

However, links between lone parents and their own kin may be activated. All the studies referred to in the preceding paragraph show that the lone parent's natal kin are important sources of support and may even provide partial substitutes for the absent parent.

Tensions and Contradictions

There is, in nearly all accounts of one-parent families, an overriding emphasis on the difficulties and problems its members experience. As is evident from the preceding discussion, solo parents are commonly depicted as isolated and lonely, as experiencing task and responsibility overload, as finding it difficult to rear their children without the support of a person of the opposite gender and as occupying an uncertain and marginal status as not-married-not-unmarried persons. Children are also depicted as faring badly: a considerable body of research purports to show that children growing up in one-parent families have a lower level of educational attainment than children growing up in two-parent families, and are more likely to be emotionally disturbed, delinquent and confused in their sex-role identification (see Richards and Dyson, 1982, for a recent review of the literature). The material deprivations of one-parent families have also been highlighted, particularly in more recent accounts. Further, it has been shown that the one-parent family not infrequently breaks up. For example, data from the National Child Development Study show that of the children in two-parent families only 2 per cent had, at age 11, been in care, compared with 4 per cent of the children in widowed-mother families, 12 per cent of the children in lone-father families, 12 per cent of the children in divorced and separated-mother families and 24 per cent of the children in never-married-mother families (Ferri, 1976).

This last set of findings suggests a hierarchy of disadvantage within lone-mother families. Ferri (1976) points out that children in never-married-mother families are at greatest risk of coming into care since they may have been in a lone-mother situation since birth and therefore are 'at risk' for a relatively long period. In contrast, children in widowed-mother families typically come into the one-parent situation at a relatively late age and so are 'at risk' for a relatively short period. Further, widowed families, supported as they are by state and privately provided pensions, seem to be relatively well placed economically, whereas never-married-mother families are relatively badly placed (Chester, 1977b). Furthermore, it has been found that on a number of criteria of child-development, children in widowed families perform better than do children in other categories of one-parent families (see Popay *et al.*, 1983, and Richards and Dyson, 1982, for reviews of some of the data).

Older accounts of one-parent families attributed their vulnerability to the absence of a parent *per se*. Such accounts maintain that emotional and psychological vacuums are created by the absence of the mother as a model of the feminine role and primary source of affection and care, and by the absence of the father as a model of the masculine role and the primary source of authority and discipline. This mode of explanation is based on the functionalist presumption, which the theories of Talcott Parsons epitomise, that the attribution of instrumental tasks to men and of nurturant tasks to women is eufunctional for the individual, the family and society (see pp. 99–100). From this point of view, both parents are essential to child-development and the absence of one parent is inherently and inevitably problematic. Factors such as the age and gender of the child, the circumstances leading to the absence of the parent and the family's socio-economic status may be seen as moderating or exacerbating the difficulties experienced, but always the absence of the parent is implicitly and explicitly treated as problematic. One consequence of this theoretical orientation is that one-parent families are depicted as 'deviant', 'broken', 'disorganised', 'abnormal' and the like (Chester, 1977b).

However, more recent accounts challenge this view and relate the vulnerability of the one-parent family not to the absence of a parent *per se* but to society's failure to endorse any family form other than the nuclear family. Some writers have pointed to the state's failure to provide the kind of income-support and/or child-care facilities which could alleviate the financial problems and task-overloads which confront solo parents. Women's disadvantaged position in the labour market has also been pinpointed as making it difficult for the lone-mother family to achieve economic self-sufficiency and material viability. This line of analysis emphasises material disadvantages as the critical factor in the malfunctioning of one-parent families. It is supported by evidence from some studies which suggest that the poor performance of children in one-parent families is largely, though not entirely, associated with material deprivation (see, for example, Ferri, 1976). Other writers have placed greater emphasis on the marginal, ambiguous and/or 'deviant' s one-parent families. For example, Chester (1977b) maintai stigmatisation adds to their difficulties in that it creates problems of reputation, self-validation and the negotiation of a legitimate identity.

However, not all the evidence is negative. Many one-parent families function well. Moreover, though it has been consistently found that children growing up in one-parent families have more developmental problems than children in the unbroken nuclear family, the differences are small and do not necessarily persist into adulthood. Finally, problems of reputation may be receding. There are some indications of a growing, if still ambivalent, acceptance of divorce (Popay *et al.*, 1983, p. 22–3). Lone parents are themselves beginning to counter negative images of one-parent families by depicting solo parenthood as liberating men and women from conventional sex-role scripting and from the dependences of marriage and thus providing scope for personal development (see, for example, Itzin, 1980).

6.3 REMARRIAGE FAMILIES

A significant number of divorced persons remarry, often within a short period of their divorce. In the USA five out of every six men and three out of every four women who divorce remarry and about half of all remarriages take place within three years of divorce (Cherlin, 1981, p. 29). In Britain remarriage after divorce is also common. Leete and Anthony (1979) in a study of divorce and remarriage records found that just over half the persons in a sample of 1000 couples who divorced in 1973 remarried within four-and-a-half years of their divorce. In 268 cases, both partners had remarried, in 212 the wife only had remarried and in 287 the husband only had remarried; in 233 cases neither partner had remarried. In another study, Leete (1979) estimates that if divorce and remarriage rates remain at current levels, 20 per cent of those born around 1950 will have entered a second marriage by age 50. We also find that the number of remarriages – that is, marriages in which one or both partners had been previously married – has increased considerably as a proportion of all marriages: in 1983 36 per cent of all marriages in England and Wales were remarriages compared with 18 per cent in 1970, the year before the Divorce Reform Act took effect (*Population Trends*, Winter, 1984 p. 4). This increase in the number and proportion of remarriages is a reflection of the increase in the number of divorced people in the population and not of an increased tendency for divorced people to remarry. In fact rates of remarriage of divorced persons (that is, of persons remarrying per 1000 of the divorced population in any given year) have been falling since 1972 (Haskey, 1982a). There has also been an increase in the proportion of births occurring within remarriage units. In England and Wales in 1983 over 7 per cent of legitimate births were births to women in a second or subsequent marriage (*Population Trends*, Winter 1984, p. 7) compared with 3 per cent in 1971 (*Social Trends*, 1984, p. 38).

Remarriage is not a new phenomenon. Where mortality at young ages is high and social norms permit it, remarriage following widowhood may be relatively common. Laslett (1971, p. 103) reckons that in seventeenth-century England 'something like one-quarter of all marriages were remarriages'. A study of colonial America (Demos, 1970, cited by Cherlin, 1981, p. 29) shows that in the Plymouth Colony one-third of all men and one-quarter of all women who lived 'full' life-times remarried after the death of a spouse. However, with the decline in youthful mortality, remarriage following widowhood became less common. It is remarriage after divorce that is characteristic of our times. Moreover, remarriage following divorce is in one respect significantly different from remarriage following death: in the remarriage of the widowed there is not, as in the remarriage of the divorced, an absent spouse – parent hovering in the wings.

Structural Characteristics

Remarriage units in which neither partner has children from a previous marriage differ from conventional nuclear families only in that they are not based on lifelong monogamy. However, most divorced couples have dependent children (see p. 151); so remarriage will often involve children and will give rise to a unit which differs from the conventional nuclear family in two important ways. First, it creates and adds step-relationships to the kinship universe. Second, remarriage creates links between households through the relationships which children maintain with the non-custodial parent.

The potential range and complexity of these relationships will vary considerably depending on whether or not one or both of the partners have children from a previous marriage, whether their former spouses have remarried and whether there are children of the various remarriages.

This section focusses on the remarriage of a divorced custodial parent. Such a remarriage reconstitutes a one-parent family as a family with two parents in the household, one the natural parent, the other a step-parent (usually the father). GHS data suggest that in Britain in 1982 some 5 per cent of children were living in a mother-and-stepfather unit (GHS, 1982). In the USA, of children in two-parent families, one child in eight is living with a step-parent (Cherlin, 1981, p. 30).

(i)   Step-relationships

Most accounts of step-relationships emphasise the way in which they differ from relationships within the monogamous nuclear family.

First, Cherlin (1978) points out that step-relationships are additions to, not substitutes for, biological kin relationships. For example, the child in a reconstituted family has a stepfather as well as a natural father and is perceived as having obligations to both. Grandparental and other kin relationships multiply in a similar way.

Second, most writers emphasise that step-relationships do not exist from birth and so have not the pre-established, taken-for-granted character of monogamous family relationships. Walker and Messinger (1979) suggest that this means that remarriage family roles differ from monogamous family roles in the degree to which they are ascribed or achieved. They say that in the step-parental relationship, loyalty and affection are earned and bonds are forged through effort and on the basis of performance: the relationship lies at the achievement end of the achievement–ascription continuum. In the monogamous family the pre-established character of the parental link places it at the ascriptive end of the achievement–ascription continuum: affection and loyalty tend to be ascribed on the basis of the relationship and with little reference to performance.

Two studies – Wallerstein and Kelly's (1980) American study of how children and parents cope with divorce and Burgoyne and Clark's British study (1982) of reconstituted families – point to the

.chieved nature of step-parenthood. Wallerstein and Kelly find that children's approval or disapproval of the step-parent emerges cautiously. They also find that relationships are more easily forged where children are very young and where the step-parent is of the same sex as the stepchild. Burgoyne and Clark find that parenthood, which in first marriages is generally perceived as spontaneous and instinctive, in remarriage families is self-conscious and reflective. The step-parent relationship is, they say, tremulously negotiated within the context of the belief that 'blood is thicker than water' and the step-parent not 'a real parent'. Moreover, Burgoyne and Clark find that, because divorce and remarriage are generally perceived as unsettling for children, remarriage parents are conscious of managing a series of difficult transitions in their children's lives and invest considerable energy in arriving at a shared understanding of the step-parent's role during courtship and in the early stages of remarried family life.

Third, remarriage family relationships have been seen as characterised by uncertainty as to appropriate codes of conduct. This uncertainty, says Cherlin (1978) is apparent in the absence of an adequate terminology for step-kin, in the limited relevance of legal regulations to remarriage families, in the absence of a clear 'incest' taboo and in uncertainty as to the rights and responsibilities of the step-parent. The extent of a step-parent's authority over children seems to be a particularly problematic issue in the negotia- tion of a shared reality within the remarriage family (Burgoyne and Clark, 1982; Cherlin, 1978).

(ii) Familial links between households

In the remarriage family, parental bonds are in principle shared with the former spouse. This means, say Walker and Messinger (1979), that the remarriage family lacks the boundary-maintaining conditions available to the monogamous family. It lacks the common residence of natural parents and children and the common household locus of parental authority and economic subsistence; in addition, filial loyalties and affections are divided between two parental households. The research findings of Wallerstein and Kelly (1980) and Burgoyne and Clark (1982) lend empirical support to Walker and Messinger's emphasis on the permeability of family boundaries. Wallerstein and Kelly find that a child's identification with his/her 'natural' father is not diminished by remarriage. Burgoyne and Clark show that for the remarried parent the sense of being an entirely self-sufficient unit is modified by the need to consult with the ex-spouse about visits, holidays, maintenance and so on.

However, interaction between the child and his/her absent parent is, typically, formally planned and intermittent and, as we have seen (p. 159), is likely to diminish on remarriage. Burgoyne and Clark (1982) suggest that this is in part because many remarriage families make particular efforts to contain family life within the household so as to be an 'ordinary family'. They find that even the symbolic presence of the non-custodial parent – as in the giving of birthday presents – is seen as an intrusion, as inhibiting the creation of a 'real' family and as undermining the step-parent's attempt to be a 'real' parent to the stepchildren. Child-support payments by the non-custodial parent may therefore be a sensitive issue. Despite the fact that these payments are a vital component of the family budget in low-income households, the stepfather, say Burgoyne and Clark, may be prepared to accept their cessation if this means that contact between his stepchildren and their biological father is lessened. The stepfather is then able to see himself as the principal source of support of the family he has acquired and the feeling of being like an 'ordinary family' is more easily achieved.

The Vulnerability of Remarriage Families

Functionalist writers have conventionally viewed remarriage as an expression of faith in the conjugal family system. They see people as ascribing the failure of their first marriage to a mistaken choice of partner and as remarrying so as to find with another partner the intimacy, support and personal fulfilment which eluded them in their first marriage but which they nonetheless believe marriage provides. More recently, remarriage has been viewed not so much as an expression of faith in the conjugal family system but more as a means of escaping the dilemmas of the divorced status. Solo parents, says Chester (1977b p. 159), are pressured into remarriage 'as the only normatively-sanctioned and institutionally-provided avenue of relief for their manifold (and at least partially socially-induced) problems'. On this view, the greater unpleasantness of available alternatives is a critical factor in the 'popularity' of remarriage. Whatever the merits of these rival views of the 'popularity' of remarriage, the Burgoyne-and-Clark and Wallerstein-and-Kelly studies suggest that those who remarry are strongly committed to conventional family life.

However, the studies we have been reviewing suggest that the ambiguities of step-relationships present remarriage families with some very specific difficulties. Step-relationships, as we have seen, are commonly depicted as ill-defined, as not having the pre-established, taken-for-granted quality of biological relationships and as faced with the necessity of recognising the parental rights of the non-custodial parent and the grandparental rights of the absent-parent's parent(s). Some studies have suggested that the changing familial arrangements and the constant negotiation of new identities which family members experience as they move through first marriage, divorce and solo parenthood to remarriage may be stressful. Moreover, accounts of remarriage families contain repeated references to the pervasiveness of images of the 'wicked' and uncaring step-parent in our culture, to children's definition of the step-parent as not a 'real' parent and to the limited rights and obligations which step-parents have in law. The general conclusion to be drawn from all this is that remarriage is not accorded full legitimacy. This was neatly and publicly illustrated by the placement of Princess Diana's divorced and remarried parents at the Royal Wedding: her 'real' parents were paired together in the place reserved for the bride's family, while their new spouses were placed in the general congregation.

The precarious unity of the remarriage family is manifest in its proneness to breakdown. Demographic data for Britain (Haskey, 1983) show that the marriage of a divorced woman is twice as likely to end in divorce as that of a woman who marries for the first time at the same age. The marriage of a divorced man is 1.5 times as likely to end in divorce as the marriage of a bachelor of the same age. Data for the USA indicate that more than three out of seven second marriages are likely to end in divorce compared with one out of three first marriages (Levitan and Belous, 1981, p. 34).

Remarriage families would also seem to present children with adjustment problems. Some studies have shown little difference between the intellectual, emotional and social development of children living in monogamous nuclear family units as compared with those living in remarriage units, but when differences are found it is the children in remarriage units who are faring badly. (See

Richards and Dyson, 1982, for a review of some British findings and Cherlin, 1981, for a review of American findings.)

6.4 HOW MUCH CHANGE?

Two main and opposing views of the significance of the institutionalisation of divorce for marriage and the family have been advanced. One view maintains that marriage has neither been weakened nor greatly changed. High marriage and remarriage rates, says Fletcher (1973), are evidence of the continued popularity of marriage and its essential durability as a social institution. Fletcher writes from an implicitly functionalist viewpoint. He believes marriage and the family to be beneficent and is concerned to show that increasing divorce means only that unsuccessful marriages are being replaced by successful marriages, not that marriage as an institution is endangered. Smart (1984) also sees the institutionalisation of divorce as doing little to undermine marriage, but she views it as retaining what is an oppressive institution. Writing from a feminist viewpoint, she maintains that women and men are not free to choose to remarry, as Fletcher assumes, but are pushed into remarriage by material and ideological pressures. In Smart's view, the liberalisation of divorce law enables us to change sexual partners legitimately and eases the transition between marriages, but does not liberate us from marriage and its obligations. Moreover, divorce, says Smart, has legitimated an increased surveillance over families, particularly where there are children, through the power which the courts have to enforce maintenance obligations and regulate the custody of children. Easier divorce, Smart claims, offers only a spurious sense of permissiveness and liberalisation; it is in reality a continuation of modes of regulation over sexual and reproductive relationships through the agency of marriage.

The second view of the institutionalisation of divorce points to wide-ranging changes. It has been argued that the liberalisation of divorce law has given the married couple the power to decide whether or when their marriage has ended (Mount, 1982, pp. 212–18), has transformed marriage from a divinely-ordained and indissoluble contract to a secular and terminable arrangement between a man and woman (Sachs and Wilson, 1978, p. 143), made married persons potentially available to others as marital partners

(McCall, 1966) and allowed for the regular establishment of one-parent families and serial monogamy. It could also be argued that considerable variation in family patterns has followed from the acceptance of divorce in that marriage may now be lifelong or of short duration, the family unit may contain one parent or two, the rights and responsibilities of biological parents may be extended (as in the case of the custodial parent) or truncated (as in the case of the non-custodial parent) and non-biological step-relationships have been introduced into the family system.

7

The Search for Alternatives to the Family

In some Western societies the belief that 'the family' is oppressive has led to vigorous advocacy of 'alternative life-styles'.

This issue brings us back to the problem of defining 'the family', for if, as we found in Chapter 1 is generally argued, variations in arrangements we think of as 'families' make it difficult to delimit 'the family', then it is difficult to say what constitutes an 'alternative to the family'. For example, is a communal endeavour in which several nuclear families share accommodation and pool resources to be seen as an 'alternative to the family' or as a group of families? Moreover, the definitional problem does not end when we draw a boundary round 'the family', for there is the further problem of drawing boundaries round the 'family alternatives'. For example, is an arrangement in which unrelated young adults share accommodation and pool some resources an alternative to the family? Or merely a non-familial household? Is it to be differentiated from communal endeavours? In other words, how is 'the commune' to be defined? These definitional problems have been lengthily discussed in the sociological literature but have not been resolved.

However, advocates of alternative life-styles, like most conventional people, appear to identify 'the family' with a nuclear family unit based on legal marriage and biological parenting. They then identify as 'alternatives' sexual and parental relationships which break with legal marriage and/or biological parenting. Further, advocates of alternative life-styles appear to be thinking of a specific nuclear family form, namely a unit which is independent of kin and privatised (that is, the conjugal family). The search for a non-privatised arrangement may therefore be part of the alternative life-style endeavour. In addition, the nuclear family may be identified with the sexual division of labour and gender inequality, and some alternative life-style endeavours involve attempts to restructure sexual and parental relationships in ways that will restructure the sexual division of labour and bring women equality with men.

This chapter examines alternative life-style trends in Britain but some reference is also made to trends in the USA. The development of alternative life-style ideology and practice is examined in Section 7.1. We then look at unmarried heterosexual cohabitation (Section 7.2), same-sex pairings (Section 7.3) and group living (Section 7.4). These arrangements have been selected for study because they represent different kinds of breaks with marriage and the family. The chapter concludes with a brief evaluation of the impact of the alternative life-style endeavour on conventional ways of ordering sexual and parental relationships in Britain.

7.1   THE DEVELOPMENT OF ALTERNATIVE LIFE-STYLE IDEOLOGIES

Alternative life-style ventures have diverse impetuses and objectives, and comprise diverse groups of people: exponents of self-actualisation, propounders of sexual freedom and gay liberation, sections of socialism and, importantly, sections of feminism. The alternatives proposed include heterosexual living-together arrangements (cohabitation), same-sex pairings, single parenting, group-living and professional child-rearing. None of these arrangements is in fact new in Western societies. The 'free-love' union was a favourite remedy with some groups in the nineteenth century. Group marriage has its nineteenth-century counterpart in the Oneida community and elsewhere. Unmarried procreation and homosexuality have long and varied histories. However, the vigour with which legitimacy is now sought for alternative life-styles, the openness with which they may be practised even in the middle classes, and the sexual freedom which they give women as well as men are new.

Paradoxically, alternative life-style ventures are rooted in ideas and beliefs which, in important respects, are continuous with conjugal family ideals. As we have seen, the conjugal family was sustained by beliefs in individual freedom and in the importance of warm, intimate relationships to personal fulfilment. These ideals are also emphasised in alternative life-style thought but, whereas the conjugal family used to be celebrated as bringing freedom from wide-ranging kin obligations, it is now seen as limiting freedom, impeding self-realisation and confining intimacy by obliging us to contain our sexuality within heterosexual and monogamous marriage and our parenting within the nuclear family. 'Liberationists' therefore seek to extend individual freedom to include the right to choose between a range of sexual and parental relationships. This leads to the celebration of non-binding commitments – of warm but diffuse, easy-going, undemanding and always changeable relationships. It leads also to an emphasis on the mutual negotiation of commitments and the rejection of societally-defined rights and obligations. Furthermore, alternative life-style ideologies embody a shift away from the emphasis on the needs of the child, which had dominated traditional views of the family, to an emphasis on the sexual and emotional needs of adults. Children figure only minimally in alternative life-style literature.

Some writers have sought to explain the emergence of alternative life-styles in terms of the unfolding of these individualistic, person-focussed ideals. For example, Berger and Berger (1983, Chaps 4 and 5 *passim*) say that the ideas and ideals which underpinned the conjugal family have been transmuted over time and are eroding it. Berger and Berger insist on the causal importance of ideation (that is of ideas, values and beliefs) and assert that the individualistic values of the conjugal family contained within it the seeds of its own destruction.

Social science thought has also been seen as playing a part in the development of alternative life-style ideologies. Some writers (for example, Abrams and McCulloch, 1976; Lasch, 1977; Segal, 1983) have noted that Marxist and/or Laingian images of the family as oppressive reappear in a diffuse but consistent way in the rhetoric of alternative life-style movements. Further, sociological accounts of social variability in family patterns and of the role of dominant interests in shaping them have undermined everyday beliefs in biological normality and in moral absolutes, and are persistently used to legitimate alternative life-style practice.

The isolation of the nuclear family and/or the continued identification of women with the housewife–mother role are generally regarded as having provided the structural context for the development of alternative life-style ideals and practice. As we saw in Chapter 5, it is now widely believed that the isolation of the nuclear family has led to a claustrophobic intensification of emotional relationships between husband and wife and parents and children. Further, it is clear that the freedom from continuous child-bearing which birth control technology has given women has made their continued identification with the housewife–mother role seem anomalous. We thus find that pressures for change are frequently explained in terms of the tensions and discontents which these structural conditions generate.

Finally, the implementation of alternative life-style ideals has, *prima facie*, been facilitated by a number of changes in the social environment. Women's increasing economic independence and the expansion of the welfare state mean that support for women and children is available outside the family. Advances in contraceptive technology have facilitated sexual freedom. More fundamentally, the decline in mortality at young ages has made population control rather than population replacement a societal goal. This means that procreation need no longer be a universal obligation. There is therefore greater scope for the celebration of non-reproductive sex. At the same time the expansion of higher education means heightened exposure to radical world views. Further, social and geographical mobility, though not as great as is sometimes imagined, have freed many young people from encapsulation within the conventional value system of parents and neighbourhood groups. The spokespersons for the new morality have come from this section of the population – that is, the young, educated, mobile middle class – and media attention has amplified their influence.

It must not, however, be thought that pressures for change are universal and relentless in the Western world. Roman Catholic countries seem generally to adhere to conventional family ideologies. By contrast, unmarried procreation and cohabitation are well established in Protestant Sweden and Denmark. In Britain and the USA alternative life-style ideologies and practices have established themselves in some social groups but the conjugal family remains a privileged institution and in both societies strong pro-family movements have appeared. The concluding section of this chapter will explore the impact of alternative life-style trends on 'the family' and the growth of pro-family movements. In the meantime, we examine some specific alternative life-styles.

7.2   COHABITATION

Cohabitation (defined in official statistics in Britain as a relationship in which a man and woman live together without formally marrying)

Kinsey Reports on sexual behaviour in men, 1948, and in women, 1953) of the mix of homosexual and heterosexual experiences in the lives of many people is now being used to argue that homosexuality is a diffuse experience which anyone can have. From this point of view, heterosexuality is a 'social obligation' rather than a 'natural tendency', and the 'abnormality' of homosexuality is a social construction rather than a pathological condition. Plummer (1981) suggests that the stigmatisation of homosexuality is related to the threat it poses to our everyday images of the 'natural world'. He points out that homosexuality implies that 'love' and sexuality need not be channelled to the opposite sex, that gender is ambiguous and that life can be led without children and in contexts other than the family. Plummer claims that the stigmatisation of homosexuality is the reverse side of the organisation of societies around the family. Further, some sections of feminism depict lesbianism as the ultimate symbol of sisterhood and 'compulsory heterosexuality' as a means by which men establish rights of access to, and control over, women's sexuality. The lesbian existence, says Rich (1980), is 'an electric and empowering charge between women' – 'a source of energy, a potential springhead of female power, violently curtailed and wasted under the institution of heterosexuality'.

With this reconstruction of heterosexuality as a social institution rather than an innate tendency, and of homosexuality as a life-style that can be chosen and celebrated rather than a condition into which pathologically-disordered women and men stumble, same-sex pairings have become more visible. It is also possible that they have become more common, but we have no way of knowing this.

Structural Characteristics

Homosexual relationships may have very different meanings for women and men. The lesbian experience, says Rich (1980), must be set in the context of women's lack of economic and cultural privilege relative to men and of qualitative differences in female and male relationships. The lesbian experience, Rich maintains, is 'a profoundly female experience, with particular oppressions, meanings and potentialities' (Rich 1980, p. 650). In her view, it is more than a sexual preference; it is a form of marriage resistance, a direct or indirect attack on male rights of access to women, and part of women's age-old struggle against male tyranny.

Rich very clearly shows that the lesbian experience cannot be equated with male homosexuality. Nevertheless, lesbian and male homosexual relationships are alike in that they are same-sex relationships. For both sexes, homosexuality may be part of a life pattern and may be associated with the development of a homosexual identity. Both sexes may also have homosexual encounters in young adulthood or in circumstances (for example when encapsulated within same-sex institutions such as boarding schools or prisons) which are of marginal importance in their lives and are not associated with the development of a homosexual identity. In both sexes, relationships run the gamut from one-night-stands to committed relationships of long duration.

In our analysis, we focus on homosexuality as a life pattern and look at relationships in terms of commitment period and exclusiveness, couple interaction, parenthood and the management of a stigmatised identity. American as well as (still very limited) British research findings are reviewed.

(i)   Durability and exclusiveness

The gay culture seems to be marked by contradictory pressures to relationship-permanence and impermanence. Plummer (1978) notes that the pervasiveness of the couple relationship in the wider society, together with the dominance of the belief that it is natural and rewarding to live one's life with a partner, act as a pressure towards couplehood. Moreover, demands for homosexual marriage with legal contracts and religious ceremonies suggest a desire for permanence and for the equivalent of heterosexual marriage. However, gay thought may also condemn the adoption by gay people of the norms of heterosexual marriage. In this strand of thought, the linking of 'love' with sex is questioned, and the value of a life-style based on diversity and short-term relationships is emphasised.

In practice, the length of male homosexual relationships is variable. However, the dominant pattern appears to be one of brief encounters and/or short relationships. Plummer claims that many gay men (40–60 per cent of most samples) form couple relationships of over a year's duration, but few do so for more than ten years and silver anniversaries are rare. Exclusiveness would also appear to be exceptional. In Plummer's study of nine London couples who had been together for three years or more, only two professed fidelity. The others experienced extra-couple relationships ranging from the casual and impersonal to long-term emotional commitments.

In the lesbian world, older or more conventional women seem to conform to beliefs about female sexuality and seek stable relationships as against casual sex (Tanner, 1978). However, younger 'feminist lesbians' may judge monogamous relationships to be 'incorrect' because they duplicate the nuclear family (Hall, 1978) and in some counter-culture lesbian communities multiple pairing is encouraged (Barnhart, 1975). Evidence from various American studies (reviewed by Peplau and Amaro, 1982) suggests that in general lesbian relationships are somewhat longer than male relationships and are more often based on emotional intimacy. Among older women relationships of twenty years or more are not uncommon. Among younger women relationships are typically of two to three years duration and are based on expectations of sexual exclusiveness and emotional intimacy. However, brief encounters, casual or recreational sex and non-exclusive relationships are also common; in two studies, twenty-five or more partners were reported by 15 per cent of the respondents.

(ii) Couple interaction

Homosexual couples, like heterosexual couples, show a considerable diversity of relationship styles. We look at Plummer's (1978) classification of male relationships and at Tanner's (1978) classification of female relationships.

Plummer identifies three types of couple relationships: the homosexual marriage, the boyfriend relationship and the homosexual partnership. The homosexual marriage mirrors conventional heterosexual marriage. Rituals that simulate marriage rituals – the engagement party, the wedding ceremony and honeymoon – may be performed and the relationship itself may be modelled on the traditional heterosexual marriage, with one partner as chief breadwinner and playing the active role in sex while the other is generally subordinate and plays a passive role in sex. The breadwinning partner is usually of higher occupational status than the other. The boyfriend relationship is a relationship in which the couple do not live together. This pattern may be adopted so that each partner maintains autonomy and/or so that the relationship may remain hidden from family and friends. In the homosexual partnership, the partners seek to establish a life-style that is specific to their needs and interests. They therefore reject as a model the heterosexual marriage and traditional gender divisions, and sexual behaviour may not be restricted to stereotyped notions of a male/female partner. They may do everything jointly, including the household chores, and may share their income.

Tanner's small American study of twelve lesbian couples, aged 20–35, is one of the very few studies to report in any depth on the way in which lesbian couples arrange their lives. Tanner finds that economic independence was, in general, maintained. Rent and household bills were shared, but furniture was individually bought and owned and bank accounts individually maintained. Eight of the twelve couples had joint hobbies, all entertained together at home and six of the couples went on holidays together. However, they did not attend office functions together and did not in general present themselves to the 'straight' world as a couple. All the relationships, says Tanner, had a strong emotional basis. However, six of the couples had had to deal with extra-couple affairs. As in heterosexual relationships, there was jealousy, insecurity, anxiety in relation to other current or past relationships, quarrels over money and time spent alone, disappointed expectations and even violence.

Finally, Tanner categorises lesbian relationships as traditional-complementary, flexible-nurturing-caretaking and negotiated-egalitarian. The traditional-complementary relationship seems to be similar to the homosexual marriage which Plummer describes for male couples. It is, says Tanner, based on a conventional sex-based division of labour, with one partner performing a provider role and the other a wife role. The flexible-nurturing-caretaking relationship, says Tanner, may also be characterised by economic dependence in that one of the partners may be younger and may earn less than the other, but there is no stereotyped division of labour and greater reciprocity than in the traditional-complementary relationship. There may sometimes be emotional dependence and couples tend to relate on an adult–child basis. Tanner says that most of the couples in her study fell into this category; she suggests that this type of relationship may feed into idiosyncratic emotional and economic needs in a mutually reinforcing way. In the third type of relationship – the negotiated-egalitarian – couples are of equal economic status and relate on a basis of equality, independence and self-actualisation. Tanner suggests that few negotiated-egalitarian relationships long survive the mutual drive to autonomy.

(iii) Parenthood

A homosexual couple cannot, *as a couple*, achieve biological parenthood and like any unmarried couple cannot adopt. Previously married homosexuals may be parents but, although mothers in general tend to be awarded child-custody in preference to fathers, custody is problematic for lesbian mothers and, in the case of homosexual fathers, the prejudice against fathers is reinforced. This prejudice against homosexual parenthood has been justified in terms of presumed risks to the child of aberrant psychosexual development and of stigmatisation and/or rejection by peers.

Even so, divorced lesbian mothers may gain custody of their children where their lesbianism is not known and/or custody not contested. Lesbian women may also achieve parenthood through an unmarried heterosexual relationship, or through artificial insemination, or in rare circumstances through single – person adoption. Some indication of the relative prevalence of each of these pathways to parenthood comes from a study by Golombok *et al.* (1983). These researchers found that in their sample of twenty-seven lesbian mothers, twenty-one had been previously married, four had become pregnant in an unmarried heterosexual relationship, one had adopted a child, and one had adopted one child and conceived a second by artificial insemination.

Studies of lesbian motherhood have shown that co-residing lovers share in housekeeping and child-care responsibilities and are regarded as an aunt, big sister or adult friend by the children (see, for example, Golombok *et al.*, 1983; Kirkpatrick *et al.*, 1981; Lewin and Lyons, 1982). However, lesbian mothers and their lovers do not appear to treat parenthood as a joint enterprise. Lewin and Lyons (1982) provide evidence of conflict between mothers and their lovers over child-rearing, of the partner's jealousy of the mother's children and reluctance to share in parental responsibilities, and of mothers' reluctance to give their partners full co-parental status.

No study finds any evidence that lesbian mothers either direct their children's orientation into lesbianism or encourage behaviour 'inappropriate' to their sex. Moreover, there are indications that children of lesbian mothers have more contact with their fathers than do children of heterosexual lone mothers (Golombok *et al.*, 1983). Furthermore, studies which have compared the psychosocial development of children reared in lesbian-mother households with that of children reared in heterosexual lone-mother households have consistently found no differences between the gender identification and sex-role behaviour of these two groups of children (see, for example, Golombok *et al.*, 1983; Hotvedt and Mandel, 1982; Kirkpatrick *et al.*, 1981). However, this evidence is of limited value. Few of the children studied were post-pubertal. Many would not therefore have had any sophisticated awareness of their mother's sexual orientations. Moreover, it could be argued that to compare the children of lesbian mothers with the children of heterosexual lone-mothers is to compare them with a group which also lacks a male figure in the household and in which children have been shown to be disadvantaged. Finally, in the studies under review, lesbian parenthood generally followed marriage and children's earliest years had been spent in heterosexual households, so their results may not hold for situations in which lesbian motherhood follows a non-cohabiting heterosexual relationship or artificial insemination.

(iv) The management of stigma

To be known as a homosexual, says Plummer (1975, p. 175), may mean shame and ostracism, or it may simply mean that one becomes 'an interesting curiosity of permissiveness', but the costs are always high and, even where not positively ostracised or discriminated against, the homosexual couple relationship is neither recognised nor validated. In a later work, Plummer says of the homosexual couple relationship:

> The law does not protect it, nor does the church give it its blessing 'till death do us part'. Family, community and society, if not outrightly hostile, refuse to recognise the couple as a unit . . . the tax man grants no relief; hospitals do not recognise partners as 'next-of-kin' in emergencies; observers look mockingly or violently upon homosexuals kissing each other goodbye; hotel-keepers refuse to give a double bed to two men; heterosexual colleagues and friends ignore the existence of a partner in a way that would be offensive to heterosexual couples (Plummer, 1978, pp. 187–8).

The management of a stigmatised identity is thus central to the homosexual relationship. The literature suggests that this may be accomplished in two ways. First, homosexuals may wrap their sexuality and their relationship in the 'protective cloak' of secrecy. Ponse (1978), in an American study of lesbianism, suggests that they may accomplish this by 'passing', that is by presenting themselves as 'being just like everyone else', by avoidance of 'straight' people as friends, by the separation of gay and 'straight' friendships and by counterfeit secrecy through collusion between the couple and their audience so that, though the relationship is known about, it is not admitted. Second, homosexuals may generate, and live out their life within, their own community of homosexual bars, organisations and friendship networks and their own culture. Ponse (1978) suggests that the homosexual community provides support, friendship, opportunities for sharing common problems and a positive homosexual identity, and thus neutralises the stigmatising labels of the heterosexual world.

Sources of Tension

The data we have been reviewing suggest that same-sex pairings, though they range from one-night stands to committed relationships of long duration, are typically short-term and often not exclusive. Moreover, homosexual couples are typically defined as independent persons by straight friends and kin who either may not know of the relationship or may tacitly ignore it. Typically they will be childless, though children from an earlier heterosexual relationship may sometimes be present in lesbian households and parenthood may sometimes be achieved through artificial insemination.

Such a life-style was conventionally defined in traditional family ideologies as the outcome not only of a pathological sexual orientation but also of a pathological inability to sustain long-term relationships. However, some homosexuals, like some heterosexuals, are seeking to establish the idea that a relationship pattern, based on diversity, change and non-exclusiveness is a stimulating, liberating and viable alternative to long-term, exclusive relationship patterns. Same-sex pairings may also be celebrated, particularly by feminist lesbians, as bringing freedom from the dilemmas and tensions which beset relationships between the sexes.

However, as in heterosexual cohabitation, a life-style based on diversity and change does not preclude conflict and tension over extra-couple relationships and pain in the ending of a relationship. This difficulty is cross-cut by the opposite problem of asserting couplehood in a society in which the homosexual couple relationship is not supported, even where it is not positively ostracised. Writing of male relationships, Plummer (1978) points to three circumstances which militate against couplehood. First, access to gay groups is neither instant nor easy. Moreover, the gay world is small and its inhabitants have little in common. Consequently, says Plummer, homosexuals find it difficult to meet partners of like interests and for the most part interact on the basis of their shared homosexuality. Second, many gays operate on the assumption that a relationship embarked upon with a stranger will quickly result in sex and an anonymous departure and thus avoid the involvement which might lead to disclosure. Third, the fact that the homosexual relationship receives neither recognition nor validation from the heterosexual world means that gay relationships are without the social supports which would bind them together. Homosexual partners, whether they seek permanence or non-permanence in their relationships, have to manage a discreditable identity as persons who are homosexual, unmarried and childless.

7.4   GROUP LIVING

Experiments in group living are based on an ideological commitment to the creation of a system of intimate but open, non-exclusive relationships. They take various forms ranging from co-residential arrangements such as the commune to 'open' marriage arrangements.

Group residential arrangements have a long but sporadic history. In the past most such arrangements revolved round particular religious or political ideals. The present spate of communal ventures dates from the late 1960s. Their primary intention may not be the restructuring of family relations; they may have as their core projects mystical or religious exploration, economic co-operation, or the rational reorganisation of housing. They are also organised in varying ways. Given this diversity, co-residential ventures are not easily defined and delimited, as the extensive discussion of what constitutes a commune shows (see, for example, Abrams and

McCulloch, 1976); but, whatever their primary aim and however they are organised, group residential ventures expand the range of intimate relationships beyond the narrow confines of the conjugal family.

'Open' marriage legitimates and brings into the open 'that constant shadow of the bourgeois marriage', the affair (McCulloch, 1982). The affair, says McCulloch (1982), is one means of resolving the conflict between the conception of marriage as a relatively permanent relationship for child-rearing and the conception of marriage as a relationship for personal satisfaction, but a clandestine affair is damaging because it involves deception. However, in the open marriage, as described and advocated by O'Neill and O'Neill (1973), extra-marital sexual activities become an openly admitted part of the everyday life of the married couple. In their view, the open marriage, by freely acknowledging the affair to be a natural concomitant of marriage, opens up opportunities for personal development.

'Swinging' (regularised spouse-swapping) is a version of the open marriage. In swinging arrangements the marital partners may share a wide variety of other sets of partners or swapping may take place only between couples who have been long-standing friends. Swinging establishes a single standard of sexual behaviour for men and women. Husbands, however, are its usual instigators (Henshel, 1973).

McCulloch (1982) suggests that open marriage arrangements are essentially private and supplementary to conventional marriage. They are not readily visible and have been little researched. By contrast, group-residential arrangements are readily visible and have been much researched. They may therefore be studied in more detail.

Structural Characteristics

Lee (1979) distinguishes between two types of experimental co-residential groups, the collective household and the communal household. In the collective household the nuclear family remains as the basic unit but each family shares resources, facilities and activities with other families. The collective household is segmental in structure and negotiation with the group is formal, tends towards the contractual and is on a family basis. In the communal household the individual is the basic unit and the sharing is between individuals not between families. The quest for self-realisation is more strenuous than in collective households and negotiation with the group is informal and on an individual basis. These distinctions appear clear-cut but are not always easily applied since many co-residential groups appear to be engaged in a continuous process of exploring the range of arrangements which lie between the two modes. Nevertheless, the distinction may usefully be used as a means of identifying the range of relationships found in group residential ventures.

In this discussion, we look at the way in which the couple relationship, parenting and economic provision are handled.

(i)   The diffusion of the couple relationship

Abrams and McCulloch's (1976) description of the large religious community at Findhorn (north-east Scotland) suggests that where the nuclear family is retained as the basic unit of the co-residential endeavour the conjugal bond may be cherished. In such ventures friendship is communal but intimacy is private. In communal households, by contrast, emotional investment is in the group as a whole. Abrams and McCulloch say that in these ventures there is a tendency to deny the idea of sexual love as a unique form of love, to insist that love is love and that its forms are interchangeable. This means that pair-bonding tends to have a lesser salience, to be less clearly defined and less stable than in collective households. In some ventures, such as the Selene Community described by Rigby (1974), group marriage (that is, a commitment to sexual relationships throughout the group) may be adopted as the logical conclusion of the principles and ideologies of communal living. However, the practitioners of group marriage are few and, by all accounts, unsuccessful. The pair-bond, the evidence suggests, is usual in communal as well as collective households (McCulloch, 1982).

Nevertheless, couple relationships are opened up to others. In all co-residential endeavours, economic support and child-care are, in varying degrees, group-based not couple-based (see below). Moreover, intimacy and caring are diffused. This is neatly demon-strated in an American study by Kanter *et al.* (1975). This study shows that needs which cannot be met within the couple relationship may be met by others in the group and conflicts are mediated by the group. At the same time couples have less privacy; Kanter *et al.* show that they do not have the control over their living space and over each other that the couple in the nuclear family or cohabiting household have. Further, definitions of the self change; partners define themselves as members of the group rather than as one half of a couple. Kanter *et al.* say that this changes the way couples relate to each other; they feel freer to act without their partner and to develop relationships not shared by the partner.

(ii) Parenting

In communal households children are in principle defined as children of the commune. In collective households children are children of a particular nuclear family. However, in both settings the relationships of parents and children – like the relationships of couples – are opened up.

For children, group living brings a wide range of relationships with other adults and children. They have, say Abrams and McCulloch (1976), a variety of role models and freedom from the hazards of emotional dependence on, and absorption by, parents. However, Abrams and McCulloch maintain that children are also at risk of haphazard attention to their emotional needs and Kanter *et al.* (1975) say that they are subject to a great number of rule-makers and rule-enforcers and at risk of an over-abundance of rules as well as of inconsistency in rule-definition.

For parents, group living means on the one hand loss of control over their children's experiences, environment and relationships and, on the other hand, freedom from the all-encompassing responsibilities of child-care. Group living also presents opportunities for the reworking of gender relationships because, as Abrams and McCulloch (1976) point out, the home in the communal endeavour is the primary scene of action for both men and women and the ideology of the openness of relationships implies the rejection of conventional gender divisions. However, the evidence seems to suggest that changes in women's position are limited (see, for example, Kanter and Halter, 1976, and Eiduson and Alexander, 1978 – both American studies – as well as Abrams and McCulloch). Abrams and McCulloch say that men make only symbolic concessions to participation in domestic tasks and, although the burden of mothering is alleviated through co-operative action between women, the mother–child link is hardly touched.

(iii) Economic provision

The ideology of group living emphasises economic interdependence and equality. However, the degree of interdependence varies and inequalities are sometimes marked. McCulloch (1982) states that in collective households every family risks some capital in buying-in but, beyond this, property and income are not generally shared. Members of the group participate in the labour force in the conventional way. Inequalities of income are accepted as necessary and are seen as mitigated by the collective form of domestic existence and the economies of scale which this achieves. In communal households, economic interdependence, McCulloch says, is greater. Resources and income may be pooled, economic activities communally organised and expenses shared. Some ventures seek to achieve economic self-sufficiency, for example, through farming or craftwork. Yet, despite the ideology of mutuality and equality, there is a tendency for those with more money invested to enjoy more privileges and for inequalities to emerge.

Sources of Tension

Communal endeavours are not in general long-lived and their membership turnover is high. Rigby (1974) estimates the average life of a commune to be five years. Abrams and McCulloch's (1976) study lasted five years, but only about six of the sixty-seven groups of which they had knowledge lasted through that period and one of these has since disappeared (McCulloch, 1982). At the same time group-living endeavours have, during the latter part of the 1970s, become more modest and less revolutionary in their aims. Collective households rather than communal households may be the more commonly adopted form of group living in the 1980s and their survival may be less chancy than that of communal households has generally been.

In the end the communal experiment, say Abrams and McCulloch (1976), is undermined by the individualism that leads to its establishment in the first place. Their analysis points to four ways in which this happens.

First, the rejection of structural arrangements means that communal households are inherently precarious since problems can only be resolved through constant negotiation and renegotiation.

The larger the group, the less feasible this becomes and the greater the risk of disintegration.

Second, there is tension between the goal of freedom and self-realisation for adults on the one hand and the needs of children for stable attachments on the other hand. Abrams and McCulloch say that in practice a 'balance is struck' between the respective freedoms of the child and the adult in which the parent, especially the male parent, 'spreads the load' of responsibility somewhat while the life of the child is 'haphazard at best and manifestly insecure at worst' (Abrams and McCulloch, 1976, p. 148). The parent is favoured in the balance that is struck since 'the self-determination of the parent is after all the main reason for the existence of the commune and since adults are, as in ordinary families, rather more powerful than children'.

Third, the effort to achieve 'love' faces a twofold problem. On the one hand, interpersonal friction may be exacerbated by an ethos of individual self-realisation and the absence of rules and structures. On the other hand, romantic love relationships are formed and broken, and the problem of sustaining 'love' once romantic love has been withdrawn is both common and profound. Abrams and McCulloch say that the communal ethos creates a world in which one experiences but cannot express the resentment, guilt and jealousy of tangled and broken love relationships. Dilemmas are sometimes resolved on the basis of strenuous 'relationship work' by all concerned, but as often as not both broken love relationships and more general personality clashes result in departures from the group or in the splitting of the group.

Finally, Abrams and McCulloch see the commune as a 'fantasy solution' to the problem of the conjugal family. It is, they say, a fantasy solution because members can decamp at will and because potentially dependent members – such as lone mothers, the aged or 'problem' people – tend to be excluded. Children must leave if their parents leave, despite the notion that children belong to the group. Abrams and McCulloch seem to be saying that communes refuse to face problems that the conjugal family cannot escape.

Paradoxically, of the communal endeavours described by Abrams and McCulloch the one that seems to come closest to the creation of a successful alternative to the family is Findhorn. Findhorn is a religious community and ideals of collective responsibility rather than individual self-realisation are its basis. Its aim is not the dismantling of the conventional structure of family relationships but the construction of a community of families. Abrams and McCulloch describe Findhorn as a community in which marital and parental bonds are cherished, in fact given moral force, and are experienced as achievements not as constraints. The size of Findhorn supports the ideological transformation. The socialisation of children is successfully dispersed because a wide range of adults is constantly there. Domestic tasks are performed by women, but on a communal basis, and are both separated from familial relationships and transformed by the idea that perfection in all tasks is a vital expression of the individual's oneness with the commune.

7.5 FAMILY ALTERNATIVES: A SUCCESS STORY?

The right to choose between a range of sexual and parental relationships now seems to be fairly well established. As we have seen, unmarried cohabitation and parenthood are more common; same-sex pairings are more visible; there is experimentation in group living. In this context, nuclear-family-living has become one of a number of available options. Moreover, the increasing rate of pre-marital cohabitation suggests that marriage is fast becoming the public affirmation of a previous private sexual union rather than the pre-condition of sexual union.

These trends point to a major transformation in conventional ways of ordering sexual and parental relationships. However, there are limits to the 'success' of the alternative life-style endeavour. Most men and women marry and have children within marriage, though they marry at a later date, have fewer children and divorce more frequently than was customary a decade ago. In Great Britain in 1981, less than 6 per cent of women and just over 10 per cent of men in the age group 35–44 had never been married (*Social Trends*, 1984, Table 1.6). In England and Wales in 1983, 84 per cent of children were borne within wedlock (OPCS Monitor FMI 84/4). Further, recent surveys have shown that most people marry in the hope or expectation of a faithful and lifelong union (Guy, 1983), and most women continue to see marriage and motherhood as the primary focus of their lives (Martin and Roberts, 1984). Further-more, the alternative life-style movement now confronts vigorous counter-movements in favour of the family. All these data suggest that large sections of the population remain attached to the conjugal family in practice and as an ideal. Moreover, alternative life-style practice has not, as we have seen, proved to be free of tensions, dilemmas and conflicts. In addition, there are indications that alternative life-style rhetoric is losing some of its vigour.

In order to understand these developments, we look at accounts and explanations of the 'failure' of the alternative life-style endeavour and at 1980s pro-family movements.

The Failure of the Alternative Life-style Endeavour

Accounts of the tensions, contradictions and ultimate failure of alternative life-style ventures fall into two broad categories: (i) accounts which attribute their failure to external patriarchal and/or capitalist forces and (ii) accounts which suggest that they are inherently flawed. Arguments which fall into the first category imply that alternative life-style ventures would succeed in a more 'favourable' social world whereas arguments in the second category imply that they will fail whatever the social context because they are incompatible with fundamental and ubiquitous individual needs and social realities.

The external-pressures argument suggests that, without change in the economic, political and ideological structures of the wider society, experimentation in alternative life-styles is limited and that the difficulties which beset the conjugal family are reproduced in alternative life-style practice. Thus some feminist writers have argued that alternative life-style ventures have not brought about any significant change in women's economic and political position because they leave untouched the male-defined structures of the public world. It has also been argued that in a patriarchal world sexual freedom extends 'macho' male patterns of diversity and casualness as the norm for both sexes (Rossi, 1977), makes women's enjoyment of sex another thing men can demand of women (Barrett and McIntosh, 1982) and creates for men a 'new reservoir of available females' (Firestone, 1970). For some socialists, including feminist socialists, the failure of alternative life-style ventures is to be attributed to the exploitative structures of a capitalist society. Writing from a left-wing position, Lasch (1977) claims that market relations have invaded and distorted all forms of personal life. In his view, the non-binding commitment is indistinguishable from any other relationship founded on self-interest and the manipulation of the emotions of others. On another level, some writers maintain that alternative life-styles remain marginal because patriarchy and/ or capitalism privilege the family and seek to reproduce it. The family, it is argued, is sustained by the media's portrayal of an idealised family life (Barrett and McIntosh, 1982), by family laws and welfare policies which assume nuclear family responsibility for children (Smart, 1984; Wilson, 1977) and by the family itself through its socialising power (Barrett, 1980). Other relationships are made to seem pale and unsatisfactory, say Barrett and McIntosh (1982), because the family is so massively privileged.

The internal-flaw argument points to tensions and contradictions within the alternative life-style project. From this general stance, two particular arguments are commonly advanced. The first points to the uncertainty, insecurity and rupturing of relationships which stem from the freedom which the non-binding commitment brings us to change our partners – and gives to others to take our partners from us. This freedom clashes, it is argued, with the basic human need for stability and security. The second argument is framed within the context of sociological understandings of the construction of social rules, and points to tension between the goal of individual freedom and social realities. The goal of individual freedom, it is here argued, brings not freedom but a new set of constraints and a new set of rules of which 'liberationists' are themselves the key definers. Thus life-style politics may claim to be *the* way everyone should adopt and, in some circles, lifelong monogamy is derided as politically backward, the desire for a conventional family life-style has become a shameful secret and chastity outside marriage has become impracticable. The 'liberation' goal, however, fails to recognise that social rules are constantly being constructed and reconstructed through complex patterns of interaction between diverse groups. Plummer (1981) writes:

'radical' and 'liberating' social movements are never just that; they will always bring their own forms of control. 'Total' freedom and 'total' liberation can only exist in the revolutionary's mind; they are sociological nonsense (Plummer, 1981, p. 56).

Berger and Berger (1983, p. 6) point to a particular but critically important aspect of this: the unfreedom of children. They point out that, whatever consenting adults may decide to do in their private life-styles, there are always their non-consenting children who did not decide to arrive in a particular social locale and who experience their parents' life-style as their destiny.

The Pro-Family Movement

The counter-movement in favour of the family is a complex phenomenon containing diverse and mutually antagonistic elements. In its vanguard are the more conservative sections of the population for whom the 'new morality' was always an affront to ordinary decencies and established verities. The moral vanguard has links with the political Right which is vigorously reasserting the idea of the family as a unit of care. For this section of pro-family thought the establishment of the family as a unit of care and the relocation of women in the home as carers represent a solution not only to male unemployment but also to the 'problem' of rising state expenditure on welfare provision for the aged and the incapacitated (Smart, 1984, Chap. 6). The moral vanguard is joined also by male groups – such as Families Need Fathers (FNF) and the Campaign for Justice on Divorce (CJD) – which seek to redress what they perceive as biasses in favour of women in child-custody and maintenance provisions on divorce and the marginalisation of fathers in families (Smart, 1984, Chap 6). Opposed to all these elements is the pro-family lobby of the political Left. Pro-family sentiment within feminism represents a fifth element in the 'family camp'.

The pro-family sentiment of the 1980s contains many traditional-ist and functionalist arguments. First, it reasserts the child's need for stability and loving care, and suggests that the biological bond between parents and their own children provides a surer foundation for stable adult–child relationships than do other types of arrangements. Rossi (1977) and Berger and Berger (1983) provide examples of present-day re-statements of the needs-of-the-child argument. Second, images of the family as a buffer between the individual and uncontrollable public institutions are reappearing. Mount (1982) and Friedan (1982) have recently defended the family in these terms, the first from a position on the political Right, the second from a position within feminism.

However, the pro-family thought of the 1980s contains new elements and is not identical with traditional views. Though the moral vanguard has spawned crusades against abortion, homosexuality and the portrayal of sex in the media, conservative thought is in general more tolerant of pluralism in sexual behaviour and more sensitive to the 'family problems' – such as rape and sexual violence, child abuse and woman-battering – which radical thought has exposed. It seems less concerned than in the past with maintaining the family as an arrangement for controlling sexuality, and more concerned with establishing the family as a unit of care. It may continue to assert the existence of essential differences between men and women but appears, as in Mount's vigorous defence of the family (1982), to recognise women's equality as persons with men. Socialist and feminist pro-family thinking differs, broadly speaking, from the conservative tradition in that it maintains a vigorous critique of the wider society and of social inequality in all its forms; it implies that 'the mistake' of the conservative/functionalist tradition lies not in its support for the family but in its acceptance of the wider economic and political system (see, for example, Lasch, 1977, on Parsonian sociology). For the socialist and feminist family lobby, the family is to be celebrated, not as a place of retreat from the heartlessness of the public world, but as a challenge to that world. Thus, within the American Left, pro-family thought endorses the family as the site of altruistic values and progressive relationships, sees it as offering the hope of a better life and argues for its incorporation into the socialist reconstruction of society (Barrett and McIntosh, 1982). Within feminism, some strands of thought cherish the nurturant values of motherhood as the opposite of patriarchal values and urge that these values be brought into the public world and used to transform that world (Thorne, 1982).

8

Epilogue

This text has examined two sets of issues: (i) debates about the relationship between urban-industrialisation and change in the family, and (ii) the emergence in the post-Second World War period of Marxist and feminist critiques of the conjugal family as oppressive and of pressures for the legitimation of alternatives to it. The data and arguments we have considered suggest that there have been marked changes in certain aspects of family life and fundamental continuities in others.

As we have seen, many mid-twentieth-century accounts of the family asserted the ubiquity and effectiveness of the nuclear family in providing for basic and universal human needs – for security in sexual relationships and for the rearing and socialisation of children. However, these early accounts also asserted change in the family. They associated industrialisation with major changes in the relationship between the nuclear family and other social institutions and in relationships within the nuclear family. They depicted, on the one hand, the disintegration of large-scale, multi-functional kin groups and the erosion of patriarchal authority and, on the other hand, the emergence of a relatively autonomous nuclear family which had as its core projects, not as hitherto productive activities and the transmission of property, but child-rearing and the stabilisation of personality. The 'modern' family was said to be based on an ideology that stressed the equality and individuality of family members, the achievement of personal happiness through emotionally-supportive family relationships and the right of the family to privacy. However, we have also seen that much of the historical and sociological research of the past fifteen years provides a somewhat different view of change in the family. Recent accounts emphasise continuity rather than change. They show that many elements of the 'modern' family – its nuclearity, its individualistic ideals and its emphasis on affective relationships – were present in the past. They suggest, further, that the modern family incorporates the patriarchal relations of the past and is neither as flexible in its division of labour nor as egalitarian as had once been supposed.

This 'revisionist' family sociology points to a remarkable continuity in family form and ideals. However, it would be impossible to argue that there have not also been important changes in family life over recent centuries. Among other things, we have, as the preceding pages indicate, experienced (i) a shift from a system of household-production based on familial relationships to a system of factory-production based on capitalistic principles and wage labour; (ii) the emergence of immensely powerful bureaucratically-organised public institutions with which the family must now coexist and interconnect; (iii) the development and use of effective methods of birth control; and (iv) declining mortality at young ages and consequently a decline in the prevalence of widowhood and of orphaned families.

———————————

When we examine the developments of the past twenty-five years, we again encounter contradictory tendencies: pressures for the preservation of traditional ways of ordering parental and sexual relationships as well as pressures for change.

We found in Chapter 7 that despite the development of powerful critiques of the conjugal family and of pressures for the legitimation of alternative ways of ordering sexual and parental relationships, the nuclear family remains the major locus of sexual relationships, and of child-rearing, and the major source of intimate relationships for the majority of people. Further, marriage and motherhood continue to be the primary focus of most women's lives and their occupational role the primary focus of men's lives. Moreover, there have been important recent reaffirmations of traditional family values. The development of strategies for resolving rather than ending unsatisfactory marriages are being urged on the basis of evidence of the lasting trauma of marital breakup. Beliefs in the importance of biological parenthood have been reaffirmed in legislation giving adopted children the right to know who their natural parents are. The value of stability in intimate relationships (including homosexual relationships) is beginning to be reasserted in part, it would seem, because of the anxieties which have been created by the rising incidence of sexually-transmitted diseases and by the outbreak of the potentially killing disease, AIDS (acquired immune deficiency syndrome). Furthermore, the numbers and proportions of the very old are increasing and this constitutes a mounting pressure for the reinforcement and extension of the family's caring role.

However, pressures for change are also strong and their impact has been considerable. The legitimation of divorce and of serial monogamy, the acceptance of unmarried cohabitation and parenthood, the greater visibility of same-sex pairings, and the re-creation of dual-worker families, with the greater involvement of married women – including mothers of very young children – in productive labour outside the home, all represent major breaks with conventional ways of ordering sexual and parental relationships. Even while this text was being drafted, many of these changes in family life were enhanced. For example, divorce law has been further liberalised. Under the Matrimonial and Family Proceedings Act, 1984, petitions for divorce may be presented after one year of marriage, instead of the previous minimum of three years. Further, 'neutral' divorce decrees which show only that a marriage has irretrievably broken down and has been dissolved, and not the 'facts' of breakdown, are being considered. To take another example, women's position in paid employment was strengthened by the introduction as from January 1984 of an amendment to the Equal Pay Act which enables individuals to claim equal pay for work of equal value.

The family of the 1980s is thus significantly different from the family of the 1950s, even though it remains nuclear in form, even though it is still seen as the basic unit of nurturant care, and even though the husband-father remains the family's primary breadwinner and the wife–mother continues to be identified with child-care and with other nurturant activities.

This suggests that the nuclear family is neither some fixed response to universal and fundamental biological, psychological and social needs (as some functionalist theories suggest), nor a way of living repressively reproduced by capitalist and/or patriarchal forms of social control (as some Marxist and feminist theories suggest). Rather, it would seem that its form and role at any particular moment in time are the outcome of the complex interplay of contradictory pressures for continuity and for change: of the ever-present need to provide for procreation and the care of children and other dependent persons; of the legacies of the past; of the tensions occasioned by current political, economic and ideological struggles between the classes and between the sexes; of prevailing religious, social science and other ideas about human needs and about the relationship between the biological and the social; and of the immanent search for a way out of the contradictions posed by our incompatible desires for freedom and order, for personal autonomy and support, for fulfilment of self and fulfilment of altruistic ideals.

Bibliography

Abercrombie, Nicholas; Hill, Stephen and Turner, Bryan S. (1984) *Dictionary of Sociology*, Harmondsworth, Penguin.

Abrams, Philip and McCulloch, Andrew (1976) *Communes, Sociology and Society*, Cambridge, Cambridge University Press.

Ainsworth, Mary D. S. (1965) 'Further Research into the Adverse Effects of Maternal Deprivation', in Bowlby, J., *Child Care and the Growth of Love*, 2nd ed., Harmondsworth, Penguin.

Ambrose, Peter; Harper, John and Pemberton, Richard (1983) *Surviving Divorce: Men Beyond Marriage*, London, Harvester Press.

Anderson, Michael (1971) *Family Structure in Nineteenth Century Lancashire*, Cambridge, Cambridge University Press.

Angell, Robert C. (1936) *The Family Encounters the Depression*, New York, Scribner.

Annual Abstract of Statistics (1984) Central Statistical Office, London, HMSO.

Archer, John and Lloyd, Barbara (1982) *Sex and Gender*, Harmondsworth, Penguin.

Ariès, Philippe (1962) *Centuries of Childhood*, New York, Random House.

Ball, D. W. (1974) 'The Family as a Sociological Problem', in Skolnick, A. and Skolnick, J. H. (eds) *Intimacy, Family and Society*, Boston, Little Brown.

Barnhart, Elizabeth (1975) 'Friends and Lovers in a Lesbian Counterculture Community', in Glazer-Malbin, N. (ed.) *Old Family, New Family*, New York, Van Nostrand.

Barrett, Michèle (1980) *Women's Oppression Today*, London, Verso.

Barrett, Michèle and McIntosh, Mary (1980) 'The Family Wage: Some Problems for Socialists and Feminists', *Capital and Class*, 11, 51–72.

Barrett, Michèle and McIntosh, Mary (1982) *The Anti-Social Family*, London, Verso.

Beechey, Veronica (1977) 'Some Notes on Female Wage Labour in Capitalist Production', *Capital and Class*, 3, 45–66.

Beechey, Veronica (1978) 'Women and Production: A Critical Analysis of Some Sociological Theories of Women's Work', in Kuhn, A. and Wolpe, A. *Feminism and Materialism*, London, Routledge & Kegan Paul.

Beechey, Veronica (1979) 'On Patriarchy', *Feminist Review*, 3.

Bell, Colin (1968) *Middle Class Families*, London, Routledge & Kegan Paul.

Bell, Norman W. and Vogel, Ezra F. (1968) 'Toward a Framework for Functional Analysis of Family Behaviour', in Bell, N. W. and Vogel, E. F. (eds), *A Modern Introduction to the Family*, revised ed., New York, Free Press.

211

Berger, Brigitte and Berger, Peter (1983) *The War over the Family*, London, Hutchinson.

Berger, Peter and Kellner, Hansfried (1964) 'Marriage and the Construction of Reality: an exercise in the microsociology of knowledge', *Diogenes*, 46, 1–23.

Bettelheim, Bruno (1969) *The Children of the Dream*, New York, Macmillan.

Blackburn, R. M. and Stewart, A. (1977) 'Women, Work and the Class Structure', *New Society*, 1 September, 436–7.

Bolewin (1982) 'Unmarried Cohabitation: A Marriage Form in a Changing Society', *Journal of Marriage and the Family*, 44, 763–73.

Bott, Elizabeth (1957) *Family and Social Network*, 1st ed., London, Tavistock.

Bowlby, John (1953) *Child Care and the Growth of Love*, Harmondsworth, Penguin.

Bowlby, John (1969) *Attachment and Loss, vol. I.*, London, Hogarth.

Briggs, Anna (1983) *Who Cares?*, Rochester, Kent, The Association of Carers.

Brown, Audrey and Kiernan, Kathleen (1981) 'Cohabitation in Great Britain: evidence from the General Household Survey', *Population Trends*, 25, 4–10.

Brownmiller, Susan (1976) *Against Our Will; Men, Women and Rape*, Harmondsworth, Penguin.

Burgess, Ernest W., Locke, Harvey, J. and Thomes, Mary M. (1963) *The Family, From Institution to Companionship*, 3rd ed., Cincinnati, American Book Co.

Burgoyne, Jacqueline and Clark, David (1982) 'From Father to Step-Father', in McKee, L. and O'Brien, M. (eds.), *The Father Figure*, London, Tavistock.

Campbell, Beatrix (1980) 'A Feminist Sexual Politics', *Feminist Review*, 5, 1–18.

Campbell, Beatrix (1983) 'Sex – a Family Affair', in Segal, L. (ed.), *What is To Be Done About the Family?* Harmondsworth, Penguin.

Caplow, Theodore (1954) *The Sociology of Work*, New York, McGraw-Hill.

Chappell, Helen (1982) 'The Family Life of the Unemployed', *New Society*, 14 October, 76–9.

Charvet, J. (1982) *Feminism*, London, Dent.

Cherlin, Andrew (1978) 'Remarriage as an Incomplete Institution', *American Journal of Sociology*, 84, 634–50.

Cherlin, Andrew (1981) *Marriage, Divorce, Remarriage*, Cambridge, Mass., Harvard University Press.

Chester, Robert (1971) 'Contemporary Trends in the Stability of English Marriage', *Journal of Biosocial Science*, 3, 389–402.

Chester, Robert (1972a) 'Current Incidence and Trends in Marital Breakdown', *Postgraduate Medical Journal*, 48, 529–41.

Chester, Robert (1972b) 'Divorce and Legal Aid: A False Hypothesis', *Sociology*, 6, 205–16.

Chester, Robert (ed.) (1977a) *Divorce in Europe*, Leiden, Martinus Nijhoff.

Chester, Robert (1977b) 'The One-Parent Family: Deviant or Variant?' in

Chester, R. and Peel, J. (eds), *Equalities and Inequalities in Family Life*, London, Academic Press.

Chodorow, Nancy (1978) *The Reproduction of Mothering*, Berkeley, L. A., University of California Press.

Clatworthy, Nancy (1975) 'Living Together' in Glazer-Malbin, N. (ed), *Old Family, New Family*, New York, Van Nostrand.

Cockburn, C. and Heclo, H. (1974) *Income Maintenance for One-Parent Families in Other Countries*, Appendix 3 of the Report of the Committee on One-Parent Families, Cmnd 5629, London, HMSO.

Cohen, Gaynor (1977) 'Absentee Husbands in Spiralist Families', *Journal of Marriage and the Family*, 39, 595–604.

Cole, Charles L. (1977) 'Cohabitation in Social Context', in Libby, R. W. and Whitehurst, R. N. (eds), *Marriage and Alternatives*, Illinois, Scott Foresman.

Committee on One Parent Families (1974) *Report*, 2 vols., Cmnd 5629 (The Finer Report), London, HMSO.

Corrigan, Paul and Leonard, Peter (1978) *Social Work Practice Under Capitalism*, London, Macmillan.

Coser, Rose L. and Rokoff, Gerald (1971) 'Women in the Occupational World: Social Disruption and Conflict', *Social Problems*, 18, 535–54.

Curtis, Bruce (1980) 'Capital, the State and the Origins of the Working-Class Household', in Fox, B. (ed.), *Hidden in the Household*, Ontario, The Women's Press.

Davies, Kathleen, M. (1981) 'Continuity and Change in Literary Advice on Marriage', in Outhwaite, R. B. (ed.), *Marriage and Society: Studies in the Social History of Marriage*, London, Europa Publications.

Delphy, C. (1977) *The Main Enemy*, London, Women's Research and Resources Centre.

Demographic Statistics (1980) Statistical Office of the European Communities, Luxembourg.

Demos, John (1970) *A Little Commonwealth: Family Life in Plymouth Colony*, New York, OUP.

Dennis, Norman; Henriques, Fernando, and Slaughter, Clifford (1956) *Coal Is Our Life*, 1st ed., London Eyre & Spottiswoode.

Dobash, R. Emerson and Dobash, Russell (1980) *Violence Against Wives*, London, Open Books.

Donzelot, Jacques (1980) *The Policing of Families*, London, Hutchinson.

Douglas, J.W.B. (1964) *The Home and the School*, London, McGibbon & Kee.

Dubin, R. (1956) 'Industrial Workers' Worlds, a Study of the "Central Life Interests" of Industrial Workers', *Social Problems*, 3, 131–141.

Edgell, Stephen (1980) *Middle-Class Couples*, London, Allen & Unwin.

Edgell, Stephen and Duke, Vic (1983) 'Gender and Social Policy: The Impact of the Public Expenditure Cuts and Reactions to Them', *Journal of Social Policy*, 12, 357–78.

Eekelaar, John (1984) *Family Law and Social Policy*, 2nd ed., London, Weidenfeld & Nicolson.

Eekelaar, John and Clive, Eric (1977) *Custody After Divorce*, Oxford, Centre for Socio-Legal Studies.

Ehrenreich, Barbara and English, Deirdre (1978) *For Her Own Good*, New York, Anchor Press/Doubleday.

Eiduson, Bernice T. and Alexander, Jannette W. (1978) 'The Role of Children in Alternative Family Styles', *Journal of Social Issues*, 34, 149–67.

Elliot, F. Robertson (1978) 'Occupational Commitments and Paternal Deprivation', *Child: Care, Health and Development*, 4, 305–15.

Elliot, F. Robertson (1979) 'Professional and Family Conflicts in Hospital Medicine', *Social Science and Medicine'*, 13A, 57–64.

Elliot, F. Robertson (1982) 'Men's Two Roles: The Dilemmas of the Middle-Class Husband', Unpublished Paper, Department of Applied Social Studies, Coventry (Lanchester) Polytechnic.

Engels, F. (1972) *The Origin of the Family, Private Property and the State* (first published 1884), London, Lawrence & Wishart.

Equal Opportunities Commission (1982) *Seventh Annual Report*, London, HMSO.

Equal Opportunities Commission (1983) *Eighth Annual Report*, London, HMSO.

Family Expenditure Survey (1983) Department of Employment, London, HMSO.

Feldberg, Roslyn and Kohen, Janet (1976) 'Family Life in an Anti-Family Setting: A Critique of Marriage and Divorce, *The Family Coordinator*, 25, 151–9.

Ferri, E. (1976) *Growing Up in a One-Parent Family: A Long-Term Study of Child Development*, Windsor, NFER.

Finch, Janet (1983) *Married to the Job: Wives' Incorporation in Men's Work*, London, Allen & Unwin.

Finch, Janet and Groves, Dulcie (eds) (1983) *Labour of Love: Women, Work and Caring*, London, Routledge & Kegan Paul.

Firestone, Shulamith (1970) *The Dialectic of Sex*, New York, Bantam Books.

Firth, Raymond; Hubert, Jane, and Forge, Anthony (1969) *Families and their Relatives*, London, Routledge & Kegan Paul.

Fletcher, Ronald (1973) *The Family and Marriage in Britain*, 3rd ed., Harmondsworth, Penguin.

Fox, Nathan (1977) 'Attachment of Kibbutz Infants to Mother and Metapelet', *Child Development*, 48, 1228–39.

Friedan, Betty (1982) *The Second Stage*, London, Joseph.

Friedl, E. (1975) *Women and Men: an Anthropologist's View*, New York, Holt, Rinehart & Winston.

Gardiner, Jean (1976) 'Political Economy of Domestic Labour in Capitalist Society', in Barker, D. L. and Allen, S. (eds), *Dependence and Exploitation in Work and Marriage*, London, Longman.

Gavron, Hannah (1966) *The Captive Wife*, London, Routledge & Kegan Paul.

General Household Survey (1982) Office of Population Censuses and Surveys, London, HMSO.

General Household Survey Monitor 84/1 (1984) Office of Population Censuses and Surveys, London, HMSO.

George, Margaret (1973) 'From "Goodwife" to "Mistress": The Transformation of the Female in Bourgeois Culture', *Science and Society*, 152–77.

George, Victor and Wilding, Paul (1972) *Motherless Families*, London, Routledge & Kegan Paul.

Gibson, Colin (1974) 'The Association Between Divorce and Social Class in England and Wales', *British Journal of Sociology*, 25, 79–93.

Glick, Paul C. and Spanier, Graham B. (1980) 'Married and Unmarried Cohabitation in the United States', *Journal of Marriage and the Family*, 42, 19–30.

Goldthorpe, John H.; Lockwood, David; Bechhofer, Frank and Platt, Jennifer (1969) *The Affluent Worker in the Class Structure*, Cambridge, Cambridge University Press.

Goldthorpe, John H. (1980) *Social Mobility and Class Structure in Modern Britain*, Oxford, Clarendon Press.

Golombok, Susan; Spencer, Ann, and Rutter, Michael (1983) 'Children in Lesbian and Single-Parent Households: Psychosexual and Psychiatric Appraisal', *Journal of Child Psychology and Psychiatry, 24, 551–72*.

Goode, William J. (1963) *World Revolution and Family Patterns*, New York, Free Press.

Goode, William J. (1966) 'Family Disorganisation', in Merton, R. and Nisbet, R. A. (eds), *Contemporary Social Problems*, New York, Harcourt, Brace & World.

Gordon, Michael (1972) *The Nuclear Family in Crisis: The Search for an Alternative*, New York, Harper and Row.

Gough, E. Kathleen (1968) 'Is the Family Universal? – The Nayar Case', in Bell, N. W. and Vogel, E. F. (eds), *A Modern Introduction to the Family*, revised ed., New York, Free Press.

Greenberg, Judith B. (1979) 'Single-Parenting and Intimacy', *Alternative Life Styles*, 2, 308–30.

Greer, G. (1971) *The Female Eunuch*, London, McGibbon & Kee.

Grieco, M. S. (1982) 'Family Structure and Industrial Employment: The Role of Information and Migration', *Journal of Marriage and the Family*, 44, 701–7.

Guy, C. (1983) *Asking About Marriage*, Rugby, National Marriage Guidance Council.

Hall, Catherine (1979) 'The Early Formation of Victorian Domestic Ideology', in Burman, S. (ed.), *Fit Work for Women*, London, Croom Helm.

Hall, Marny (1978) 'Lesbian Families: Cultural and Clinical Issues', *Social Work*, 23, 380–4.

Hamilton, Roberta (1978) *The Liberation of Women*, London, Allen & Unwin.

Harris, C. C. (1969) *The Family*, London, Allen & Unwin.

Harris, C. C. (1977) 'Changing Conceptions of the Relation Between Family and Societal Form in Western Society', in Scase, R. (ed.), *Industrial Society: Class, Cleavage and Control*, London, Allen & Unwin.

Harris, C. C. (1983) *The Family and Industrial Society*, London, Allen & Unwin.

Harris, Martyn (1984) 'How Unemployment Affects People', *New Society*, 19 January, 88–90.

Harrison, Rachel and Mort, Frank (1980) 'Patriarchal Aspects of Nineteenth-Century State Formation: Property Relations, Marriage and Divorce, and Sexuality', in Corrigan, P. (ed.), *Capitalism, State Formation and Marxist Theory*, London, Quartet Books.

Hart, Nicky (1976) *When Marriage Ends*, London, Tavistock.

Hartmann, Heidi (1976) 'The Historical Roots of Occupational Segregation: Capitalism, Patriarchy and Job Segregation by Sex', *Signs*, 1, 137–169.

Hartmann, Heidi (1981) 'The Unhappy Marriage of Marxism and Feminism: Towards a More Progressive Union', in Sargent, L. (ed.), *Women and Revolution*, London, Pluto Press.

Haskey, John (1982a) 'The Proportion of Marriages Ending in Divorce', *Population Trends*, 27, 4–8.

Haskey, John (1982b) 'Children of Divorcing Couples', *Population Trends*, 31, 20–6.

Haskey, John (1983) 'Marital Status Before Marriage and Age at Marriage: Their Influence on the Chance of Divorce', *Population Trends*, 32, 4–14.

Haskey, John (1984) 'Social Class and Socio-Economic Differentials in Divorce in England and Wales, *Population Studies*, 38, 419–38.

Henshel, Anne-Marie (1973) 'Swinging: A Study of Decision Making in Marriage', *American Journal of Sociology*, 78, 885–91.

Hetherington, E. M., Cox, M., and Cox, R. (1979) 'The Development of Children in Mother-Headed Families', in Reiss, D. and Hoffman, H. A., *The American Family*, New York, Plenum Press.

Himmelweit, Susan and Mohun, Simon (1977) 'Domestic Labour and Capital', *Cambridge Journal of Economics*, 1, 15–31.

Hipgrave, Tony (1982) 'Lone Fatherhood: a Problematic Status', in McKee, L. and O'Brien, M. (eds), *The Father Figure*, London, Tavistock.

Hirst, Paul (1981) 'The Genesis of the Social', *Politics and Power*, 3, 67–82.

Hotvedt, Mary E. and Mandel, Jane B. (1982) 'Children of Lesbian Mothers', In Paul, W., James, D. W., Gonsiorek, J. C., and Hotvedt, M. E. (eds), *Homosexuality; Social, Psychological and Biological Issues*, Beverly Hills, Sage Publications.

Houlbrooke, Ralph A. (1984) *The English Family 1450–1700*, London, Longman.

House of Commons (1982) *Weekly Hansard*, 18–24 June, Issue No. 1248 London, HMSO.

House of Commons (1984) *Weekly Hansard*, 6–9 November, Issue no. 1324, London, HMSO.

House of Commons (1984) *Weekly Information Bulletin*, 3 November, 44, London, HMSO.

Hubert, Jane (1965) 'Kinship and Geographical Mobility in a Sample from a London Middle-Class Area', *International Journal of Comparative Sociology*, 6, 61–80.

Humphries, Jane (1977) 'The Working Class Family, Women's Liberation and Class Struggle: The Case of Nineteenth Century British History', *The Review of Radical Political Economics*, 9, 25–41.

Hunt, Judith and Hunt, Alan (1974) 'Marxism and the Family', *Marxism Today*, 18, 59–61.

Ineichen, Bernard (1977) 'Youthful Marriage: The Vortex of Disadvantage', in Chester, R. and Peel, J. (eds), *Equalities and Inequalities in Family Life*, London, Academic Press.

Itzin, Catherine (ed.) (1980) *Splitting Up – Single-Parent Liberation*, London, Virago.

Jackson, Brian and Marsden, Dennis (1962) *Education and the Working Class*, London, Routledge & Kegan Paul.

Kanter, Rosabeth M.; Jaffe, Dennis and Weisberg, D. Kelly (1975) 'Coupling, Parenting and the Presence of Others: Intimate Relationships in Communal Households', *The Family Coordinator*, 24, 433–52.

Kanter, Rosabeth M. and Halter, M. (1976) 'De-housewifing Women, Domesticating Men: Changing Sex Roles in Urban Communes', in Heiss, J. (ed.), *Family Roles and Interaction*, Chicago, Rand McNally.

Kinsey, A. C., Pomeroy, W. B. and Martin, C. E. (1948) *Sexual Behaviour in the Human Male*, Philadelphia, Saunders.

Kinsey, A. C.; Pomeroy, W. B. and Martin C. E. (1953) *Sexual Behaviour in the Human Female*, Philadelphia, Saunders.

Kirkpatrick, Martha; Smith, Catherine, and Roy, Ron (1981) 'Lesbian Mothers and Their Children: A Comparative Survey', *American Journal of Orthopsychiatry*, 51, 545-51.

Kohlberg, Lawrence (1966) 'A Cognitive Developmental Analysis of Children's Sex Role Concepts and Attitudes', in Maccoby, E. (ed.), *The Development of Sex Differences*, Stanford, California, Stanford University Press.

Laing, R. D. (1971) *The Politics of The Family and Other Essays*, London, Tavistock.

Laing, R. D. and Esterson, A. (1970) *Sanity, Madness and the Family*, Harmondsworth, Penguin.

Laing, R. D.; Phillipson, H. and Lee, A. R. (1966) *Interpersonal Perception*, London, Tavistock.

Lancaster, Loraine (1958) 'Kinship in Anglo-Saxon Society – 1', *British Journal of Sociology*, 9, 230–50.

Land, Hilary (1980) 'The Family Wage', *Feminist Review*, 6, 55–77.

Lasch, Christopher (1977) *Haven in a Heartless World*, New York, Basic Books.

Laslett, Peter (1971) *The World We Have Lost*, 2nd ed., London, Methuen.

Laslett, Peter (1972) 'Mean Household Size in England Since the Sixteenth Century', in Laslett, P. and Wall, R. (eds), *Household and Family in Past Time*, Cambridge, Cambridge University Press.

Laslett, Peter (1977) *Family Life and Illicit Love in Earlier Generations*, Cambridge, Cambridge University Press.

Laslett, Peter (1983) 'Family and Household as Work Group and Kin

Group: Areas of Traditional Europe Compared', in Wall, R. (ed.), *Family Forms in Historic Europe*, Cambridge, Cambridge University Press.

Leach, E. R. (1967) *A Runaway World?*, London, BBC Publications.

Lee, Ron M. (1979) 'Communes as Alternative Families', M. Phil. Thesis, North East London Polytechnic.

Leete, Richard (1979) 'New Directions in Family Life', *Population Trends*, 15, 4–9.

Leete, Richard and Anthony, Susan (1979) 'Divorce and Remarriage: A Record Linkage Study', *Population Trends*, 16, 5–11.

Leonard, Diana (1980) *Sex and Generation*, London, Tavistock.

Le Play, Frederic (1935) *La Reforme Sociale*, Tours, 1887, 7th ed., Vol. 1, pp. 380–519, as interpreted and summarised by Zimmerman, C. C. and Frampton, M. E., *Family and Society*, Princeton, New Jersey, Van Nostrand.

Levitan, Sar A. and Belous, Richard S. (1981) *What's Happening to the American Family?*, Baltimore, Johns Hopkins University Press.

Lewin, Ellen and Lyons, Terrie A. (1982) 'Everything in Its Place: The Co-existence of Lesbianism and Motherhood', in Paul, W.; James, D. W.; Gonsiorek, J. C.; and Hotvedt, M. E. (eds.), *Homosexuality: Social, Psychological and Biological Issues*, Beverly Hills, Sage Publications.

Linton, Ralph (1949) 'The Natural History of the Family', in Anshen R. N. (ed.), *The Family: Its Function and Destiny*, New York, Harper & Row.

Litwak, Eugene (1960a) 'Occupational Mobility and Extended Family Cohesion', *American Sociological Review*, 25, 9–21.

Litwak, Eugene (1960b) 'Geographic Mobility and Extended Family Cohesion', *American Sociological Review*, 25, 385–94.

Litwak, Eugene (1965) 'Extended Kin Relations in an Industrial Democratic Society', in Shanas, E. and Streib, G. (eds), *Social Structure and the Family*, Englewood Cliffs, New Jersey, Prentice-Hall.

Lott, Bernice (1981) *Becoming a Woman*, Springfield, Illinois, Thomas.

Lowe, Nigel V. (1982) 'The Legal Status of Fathers: Past and Present', in McKee, L. and O'Brien M. (eds), *The Father Figure*, London, Tavistock.

Lupton, Tom and Wilson, C. Shirley (1959) 'The Social Background and Connections of "Top Decision Makers" ', *Manchester School of Economic and Social Studies*, 27, 30–51.

McCall, Michal M. (1966) 'Courtship as Social Exchange: Some Historical Comparisons', in Farber, B. (ed.), *Kinship and Family Organisation*, New York, Wiley.

McCulloch, Andrew (1982) 'Alternative Households', in Rapoport, R. N., Fogarty, M. P., and Rapoport, R. (eds), *Families in Britain*, London, Routledge & Kegan Paul.

Macdonald, Petrine and Mars, Gerald (1981) 'Informal Marriage', in Henry, S. (ed.), *Can I Have It In Cash?*, London, Astragal Books.

McDonough, Roisin and Harrison, Rachel (1978) 'Patriarchy and Relations of Production', in Kuhn, A. and Wolpe, A. (eds), *Feminism and Materialism*, London, Routledge & Kegan Paul.

Macfarlane, Alan (1978) *The Origins of English Individualism*, Oxford, Blackwell.

Macfarlane, Alan (1979) 'Review Essay: *The Family, Sex and Marriage in England 1500–1800* by Lawrence Stone', *History and Theory*, XVIII, 103–26.

McGregor, O. R. (1972) 'Equality, Sexual Values and Permissive Legislation: the English Experience', *Journal of Social Policy*, 1, 44–59.

Macintyre, Sally (1976) '"Who Wants Babies?" The Social Construction of "Instincts" ', in Barker, D. L. and Allen, S. (eds), *Sexual Divisions and Society: Process and Change*, London, Tavistock.

Macklin, Eleanor D. (1977) 'Heterosexual Cohabitation Among Unmarried College Students', in de Burger, J. (ed.), *Marriage Today*, Cambridge, Mass., Schenkman.

Macklin, Eleanor D. (1983) 'Nonmarital Heterosexual Cohabitation: An Overview', in Macklin, E. D. and Rubin, R. H. (ed.), Contemporary Families and Alternative Lifestyles, Beverly Hills, Sage Publications.

McNay, Marie and Pond, Chris (1980) *Low Pay and Family Poverty*, London, Study Commission on the Family.

Marsden, Dennis (1973) *Mothers Alone*, rev. ed., Harmondsworth, Penguin.

Marsden, Dennis (1982) *Workless*, 2nd ed. London, Croom Helm.

Martin, Jean and Roberts, Ceridwen (1984) *Women and Employment*, OPCS and DE, London, HMSO.

Mead, Margaret (1935) *Sex and Temperament in Three Primitive Societies*, New York, Morrow.

Mead, Margaret (1954) 'Some Theoretical Considerations on the Problem of Mother-Child Separation', *American Journal of Orthopsychiatry*, 24, 471–83.

Middleton, Chris (1974) 'Sexual Inequality and Stratification Theory', in Parkin, F. (ed.), *The Social Analysis of Class Structures*, London, Tavistock.

Middleton, Chris (1979) 'The Sexual Division of Labour in Feudal England', *New Left Review*, 113/114, 147–68.

Middleton, Chris (1983) 'Patriarchal Exploitation and the Rise of English Capitalism', in Gamarnikow, E., Morgan D. Purvis, J. and Taylorson, D. (eds), *Gender, Class and Work*, London, Heinemann.

Millett, Kate (1970) *Sexual Politics*, New York, Doubleday.

Mitchell, Juliet (1966) 'Women: The Longest Revolution', *New Left Review*, 40, 11–37.

Mitchell, Juliet, (1975) *Psychoanalysis and Feminism*, Harmondsworth, Penguin.

Mogey, John M. (1956) *Family and Neighbourhood*, Oxford, Oxford University Press.

Morgan, D. H. J. (1975) *Social Theory and the Family*, London, Routledge and Kegan Paul.

Morgan, D. H. J. (1979) 'New Directions in Family Research and Theory', *Sociological Review Monograph*, 28, 3–18.

Morgan, D. H. J. (1981) *Berger and Kellner's Construction of Marriage*, Occasional Paper No. 7, Department of Sociology, University of Manchester.

Mount, Ferdinand (1982) *The Subversive Family*, London, Cape.

Murdock, George P. (1968) 'The Universality of the Nuclear Family', in

Bell, N. W. and Vogel, E. F. (eds), *A Modern Introduction to the Family*, rev. ed., New York, Free Press.

National Child Development Study (1976) as reported on by Lambert, L. and Hart, S. in *New Society*, 8 July.

Nava, Mica (1983) 'From Utopian to Scientific Feminism? Early Feminist Critiques of the Family', in Segal, L. (ed.), *What Is To Be Done About the Family?*, Harmondsworth, Penguin.

Newson, John and Newson, Elizabeth (1963) *Patterns of Infant Care in an Urban Community*, London, Allen & Unwin.

North, Maurice (1972) *The Secular Priests*, London, Allen & Unwin.

Oakley, Ann (1974) *The Sociology of Housework*, London, Martin Robertson.

Oakley, Ann (1976) *Housewife*, Harmondsworth, Penguin.

Oakley, Ann (1981) *Subject Women*, Oxford, Martin Robertson.

Office of Population Censuses and Surveys (1984) *Monitor FM2 84/1, Divorces 1983*, London, HMSO.

Office of Population Censuses and Surveys (1984) *Series FM1, No. 8, 1981 Birth Statistics, England and Wales*, London, HMSO.

Office of Population Censuses and Surveys (1984) *Monitor FM1, 84/4, Live Births During 1983 by Mother's Age, Legitimacy and Birth Order*, London, HMSO.

Office of Population Censuses and Surveys (1984) *Census 1981: Household and Family Composition* CEN 81 HFC, London, HMSO.

Oliver, Dawn (1982) 'Why Do People Live Together?', *Journal of Social Welfare Law*, 209–22.

O'Neill, Nena and O'Neill, George (1973) *Open Marriage*, London, Owen.

Orthner, Dennis K., Brown, Terry and Ferguson, Dennis (1976) 'Single-Parent Fatherhood: An Emerging Family Life Style, *The Family Co-ordinator*, 25, 429–37.

Pahl, J. M. and Pahl, R. E. (1971) *Managers and Their Wives*, London, Allen Lane.

Parker, Diana (1983) 'The Cohabitant Father', *New Law Journal*, 6 May, 423–6.

Parsons, Talcott (1949) 'The Social Structure of the Family', in Anshen, R. N. (ed.), *The Family: Its Function and Destiny*, New York, Harper & Row.

Parsons, Talcott (1955) 'The American Family: Its Relations to Personality and to the Social Structure', in Parsons, T. and Bales, R. F., *Family, Socialisation and Interaction Process*, New York, Free Press.

Parsons, Talcott (1964) 'The Kinship System of the Contemporary United States' *and* 'Age and Sex in the Social Structure of the United States', in Parsons, T. *Essays in Sociological Theory*, rev. ed., New York, Free Press.

Parsons, Talcott (1971) 'The Normal American Family', in Adams, B. N. and Weirath, T., *Readings on the Sociology of the Family*, Chicago, Markham Publishing Co.

Peplau, Letitia A. and Amaro, Hortensia (1982) 'Understanding Lesbian Relationships' in Paul W.; James, D. W.; Gonsiorek, J. C.; and Hotvedt, M. E. (eds), *Homosexuality: Social, Psychological and Biological Issues*, Beverly Hills, Sage Publications.

Peterman, Dan J.; Ridley, Carl A. and Anderson, Scott M., (1974) 'A Comparison of Cohabiting and Noncohabiting College Students', *Journal of Marriage and the Family*, 36, 344–54.

Plummer, Kenneth (1975) *Sexual Stigma: an Interactionist Account*, London, Routledge & Kegan Paul.

Plummer, Kenneth (1978) 'Men in Love: Observations on Male Homosexual Couples', in Corbin, M. (ed.), *The Couple*, Harmondsworth, Penguin.

Plummer, Kenneth (1981) 'Homosexual Categories: Some Research Problems in the Labelling Perspective of Homosexuality' in Plummer, K. (ed.), *The Making of the Modern Homosexual*, London, Hutchinson.

Pollock, Linda (1983) *Forgotten Children: Parent–Child Relations from 1500 to 1900*, Cambridge, Cambridge University Press.

Ponse, Barbara (1978) *Identities in the Lesbian World: The Social Construction of Self*, Westport, Connecticut, Greenwood.

Popay, Jennie; Rimmer, Lesley and Rossiter, Chris (1983) *One Parent Families*, London, Study Commission on the Family.

Population Trends (Winter, 1984) 38, Editorial: A Review of 1983.

Poulter, Sebastian (1982) 'Child Custody – Recent Developments', *Family Law*, 12, 5–12.

Rapoport, Rhona and Rapoport, Robert N. (1976) *Dual-Career Families Re-examined*, London, Martin Robertson.

Rich, Adrienne (1980) 'Compulsory Heterosexuality and Lesbian Existence', *Signs*, 631–60.

Richards, M.P.M. (1982) 'Post-divorce Arrangements for Children: A Psychological Perspective', *Journal of Social Welfare Law*, 133–51.

Richards, M.P.M. and Dyson, M. (1982) 'Separation, Divorce and The Development of Children: A Review', *Childcare and Development Group*, University of Cambridge.

Rigby, Andrew (1974) *Alternative Realities*, London, Routledge & Kegan Paul.

Roberts, Elizabeth (1984) *A Woman's Place*, Oxford, Blackwell.

Robertson, Norma C. (1974) 'The Relationship Between Marital Status and the Risk of Psychiatric Referral', *British Journal of Psychiatry*, 124, 191–202.

Rosser, C. and Harris, C. C. (1965) *The Family and Social Change*, London, Routledge & Kegan Paul.

Rossi, Alice S. (1977) 'A Biosocial Perspective on Parenting', *Daedalus*, 106(2), 1–31.

Royal Commission on the Distribution of Income and Wealth (1978) *Report No. 6, Lower Incomes*, Cmnd. 7175, London, HMSO.

Royal Commission on Marriage and Divorce, (1956) *Report 1951–5*, Cmd. 9678, London, HMSO.

Rushton, Peter (1979) 'Marxism, Domestic Labour and the Capitalist Economy', *Sociological Review Monograph*, 28, 32–48.

Rutter, Michael (1981) *Maternal Deprivation Reassessed*, 2nd ed., Harmondsworth, Penguin.

Sachs, Albie and Wilson, Jean Hoff (1978) *Sexism and the Law*, London, Martin Robertson.

Sacks, Karen (1974) 'Engels Revisited: Women, the Organisation of Production and Private Property', in Rosaldo, M. and Lamphere, L.

(eds), *Women, Culture and Society*, Stanford, Stanford University Press.

Sanday, Peggy Reeves (1981) *Female Power and Male Dominance*, Cambridge, Cambridge University Press.

Sarsby, Jacqueline (1983) *Romantic Love and Society: Its Place in the Modern World*, Harmondsworth, Penguin.

Sayers, Janet (1982) *Biological Politics*, London, Tavistock.

Schaffer, H. Rudolph and Emerson, Peggy E. (1964) 'The Development of Social Attachments in Infancy', *Monographs of the Society for Research in Child Development*, 29 (3).

Seccombe, Wally (1974) 'The Housewife and Her Labour Under Capitalism', *New Left Review*, 83, 3–24.

Segal, Lynne (1983) ' "Smash the Family", Recalling the 1960s', in Segal, L. (ed.), *What Is To Be Done About the Family?*, Harmondsworth, Penguin.

Shimmin, Sylvia; McNally, Joyce; Liff, Sonia (1981) 'Pressures on Women Engaged in Factory Work', *Employment Gazette*, 89, 344–9.

Skolnick, Arlene (1978) *The Intimate Environment: Exploring Marriage and the Family*, Boston, Little, Brown.

Smart, Carol (1984) *The Ties That Bind*, London, Routledge & Kegan Paul.

Smart, Carol and Smart, Barry (1978) 'Accounting for Rape: Reality and Myth in Press Reporting', in Smart, C. and Smart, B. (eds), *Women, Sexuality and Social Control*, London, Routledge & Kegan Paul.

Smith, Dorothy (1975) 'Women, the Family and Corporate Capitalism', *Berkeley Journal of Sociology*, 20, 55–90.

Smith, Peter K. (1980) 'Shared Care of Young Children: Alternative Models to Monotropism', *Merrill-Palmer Quarterly*, 26, 371–89.

Social Trends (1984) Central Statistical Office, London, HMSO.

Spanier, Graham B. (1983) 'Married and Unmarried Cohabitation in the United States: 1980', *Journal of Marriage and the Family*, 45, 277–88.

Spender, Dale (1985) 'In the View of Others', *The Times Higher Education Supplement*, 1 February.

Spiro, Melford E. (1968) 'Is the Family Universal? The Israeli Case', in Bell, N. W. and Vogel, E. F. (eds), *A Modern Introduction to the Family*, rev. ed., New York, Free Press.

Stacey, Margaret and Price, Marion (1981) *Women, Power and Politics*, London, Tavistock.

Stafford, Rebecca, Backman, Elaine and Dibona, Pamela (1977) 'The Division of Labour Among Cohabiting and Married Couples', *Journal of Marriage and the Family*, 39, 43–57.

Steady, Filomena C. (ed.), (1981) *The Black Woman Cross-Culturally*, Cambridge, Mass., Schenkman Publishing Co.

Stone, Lawrence (1977) *The Family, Sex and Marriage in England 1500–1800*, London, Weidenfield & Nicolson.

Sussman, Marvin B. and Burchinal, Lee (1969) 'Kin Family Network: Unheralded Structure in Current Conceptualisations of Family Functioning', in Edwards, J. N. (ed.), *The Family and Change*, New York, Knopf.

Tanner, Donna M. (1978) *The Lesbian Couple*, Lexington, Mass., Lexington Books.

Thorne, Barrie (1982) 'Feminist Rethinking of the Family', in Thorne B. and Yalom, M. (eds), *Rethinking the Family*, New York, Longman.

Thornes, Barbara and Collard, Jean (1979) *Who Divorces?*, London, Routledge & Kegan Paul.

Tiger, Lionel and Fox, Robin (1971) *The Imperial Animal*, New York, Holt, Rinehart & Winston.

Titmuss, Richard M. (1963) 'The Position of Women', in Titmuss, R. M., *Essays on 'The Welfare State'*, 2nd ed., London, Unwin.

Wainwright, Hilary (1978) 'Women and the Division of Labour', in Abrams, P. (ed.), *Work, Urbanism and Inequality*, London, Weidenfeld & Nicholson.

Walby, Sylvia (1983) 'Patriarchal Structures; the Case of Unemployment', in Gamarnikow, E.; Morgan, D.; Purvis, J. and Taylorson, D., *Gender, Class and Work*, London, Heinemann.

Walker, Kenneth N. and Messinger, Lillian (1979) 'Remarriage After Divorce: Dissolution and Reconstruction of Family Boundaries', *Family Process*, 18, 185–92.

Wallerstein, Judith S. and Kelly, Joan B. (1980) *Surviving the Breakup: How Children and Parents Cope with Divorce*, London, Grant McIntyre.

Watson, W. (1964) 'Social Mobility and Social Class in Industrial Communities', in Gluckman, M. (ed), *Closed Systems and Open Minds*, Edinburgh, Oliver & Boyd.

Werner, Barry (1982) 'Recent Trends in Illegitimate Births and Extra-Marital Conceptions', *Population Trends*, 30, 9–15.

Willmott, Peter and Young, Michael (1960) *Family and Class in a London Suburb*, London, Routledge & Kegan Paul.

Wilson, Elizabeth (1977) *Women and the Welfare State*, London, Tavistock.

Worsley, Peter (1977) *Introducing Sociology*, 2nd ed., Harmondsworth, Penguin.

Wortis, Rochelle P. (1974) 'The Acceptance of the Concept of the Maternal Role by Behavioural Scientists: Its Effects on Women', in Skolnick, A. and Skolnick, J. H. (eds), *Intimacy, Family and Society*, Boston, Little, Brown.

Wrightson, Keith (1981) 'Household and Kinship in Sixteenth-Century England', *History Workshop Journal*, 12, 151–8.

Young, Michael and Willmott, Peter (1957) *Family and Kinship in East London*, London, Routledge & Kegan Paul.

Young, Michael and Willmott, Peter (1973) *The Symmetrical Family*, London, Routledge & Kegan Paul.

Zaretsky, Eli (1976) *Capitalism, the Family, and Personal Life*, London, Pluto Press.

Zaretsky, Eli (1982) 'The Place of the Family in the Origins of the Welfare State', in Thorne, B. and Yalom, M. (eds), *Rethinking the Family*, New York, Longman.

Zweig, Ferdinand (1961) *The Worker in an Affluent Society*, London, Heinemann.

Author Index

Subject Index